e

of a YouTube

Zacharanda

For anyone who has ever lent me any money

"Why did I come to Miami? I came here because I wanted to be here for history. The trouble is, the readers of the Birmingham Mail are gunna get my version of history, and I'm just a little bit pissed."

Adam Smith, aka Steve Zacharanda, November 5, 2008

Going Places - Eventually

Manchester Airport international departures lounge was deserted. I breathed a sigh of relief. 'Great, no queues,' I thought. The middle-aged receptionist at the American Airlines counter looked bored. I could help her with that. "Hi. Do you know when the flight to Miami is boarding?" She looked at me as if I was mad.

"Miami? Have you got the right time? There are no afternoon flights to America from this airport, so either you've missed it or it's tomorrow morning. Let's have a look at your ticket, love." I pulled a screwed up e-mail confirmation out of my pocket and handed it to her. She looked at it. Looked at it again. Then looked at me, at the ticket, and then at me again: "Wrong airport, love."

"What do you mean, wrong airport?" I replied as a sick feeling rose from my stomach into my throat. "You're out by about 2,000 miles, this flight is booked from Manchester, New England, not England," she said with an amused smile. I couldn't help but yelp "for fuck's sake," as I completed a kind of deflated, backwards pirouette. I was going to apologise for my bad language but I had more important things to worry about. She added: "Perhaps you didn't look properly when you booked online. I'm sorry, there's nothing I can do. Can you leave the desk please?"
Then with no sympathy or trace of human feeling she did an about turn and walked into the back office.

How could I have been so stupid? Booking the wrong bloody Manchester. What an idiot. Everyone I knew would think I was the biggest fool to walk the earth; I thought the dream was over. Barack Obama would have to become the 44th President of the United States of America without my help.

I sat down and thought about how I'd got into this situation. *Helping Obama become the first Afro-Caribbean President of America was my dream, my obsession. I'd seen his electrifying speech in 2004 after the Democrats lost to George Bush and followed his progress ever since. After reading his autobiography Notes from my Father I became mesmerised at the thought of him mounting a successful campaign - if he won it would be without doubt one of the biggest historical moments of my lifetime.*

I was delighted when he announced his candidacy in 2007, and over the next year stories about his campaign grew and grew in the British media. One night when I was drunk on a bus in Smethwick, reading one of many articles on his campaign, I had a brilliant idea. Why don't I go over and volunteer for him? The more I thought about it, the more it made sense. I knew it would be a generation defining moment and I wanted to be part of it. Britain's biggest political moment happened when I was 21 and I totally missed it, as I was mostly stoned for Blair's 1997 landslide. This time I was determined to have a front row to history.

All of this was before Obama had even beaten Hilary Clinton in the Primaries, of course. I knew that it'd be hard to save the money up to go to America as well, as I'd never saved up any respectable amount of money in my life. However, like many people from Perry Barr I was more engaged in this American election than any British one. Having grown up in inner city Birmingham I've always reviled racism, so when I saw Obama's unbelievable speech on race I became even more determined to volunteer for him.

I told everyone I was going over to help, to put pressure on myself and prevent me from doing the sensible thing and staying at home. I booked the time off work months before, and even the prospect of redundancy from The Birmingham Mail didn't deter me from preparing to spend a load of cash during three weeks in America. No faceless, corporate decision would stop me having a life-changing experience!

More importantly, I was 'dialled in' with the Obama campaign and had been for nearly eight months. I'd given a Goggle-eye (my ill-fated lads magazine that folded after one edition) 'You're Officially Fit' card to Erika Dunlap, Miss America 2004, during a press trip to Nashville in December 2007. Less than two months later I received an e-mail from her asking if I'd show her around London. My first feeling was elation, but this was soon replaced by terror. How could a penniless hack like me entertain an international A-grade lady like her?

Nonetheless, the big day arrived and I borrowed £150 off a mate - thanks Doug – and blagged two gold tourist cards from the London Tourist Board, saying I was doing a travel feature for the Birmingham Mail ('How many London Tourist Attractions can two Brummies see within 48 Hours?'). After jumping on the train to London I decided to phone the MP Tom Watson, an old mate of mine, from the station:
"Alright Tom, I need a favour."
"Money?"
"Nah, I'm meeting Miss America 2004 and wondered if you could take us round the Commons?"
"Ok, when? What date? I'll put it in the diary."
"In about half an hour"

"Fucking hell Adam, you do realise I'm a Cabinet minister and running the country?!"
"Go on mate, you know you want to."

I asked her to pretend she was on a mercy mission to talk about women's rights in Afghanistan and the great man got her and a friend VIP access to the House of Commons, to the Cabinet Office and even a lift in a ministerial car. We ended up drinking champagne in Soho, an interesting contrast with the holes in my shoes and the shrapnel in my pocket. Meanwhile Tom had spent much of the day telling the two American beauties what a sharp political mind I had.

It's probably safe to say that Miss America had an amazing time in London. Sadly I never got a chance to try it on with her, but maybe that was just as well. It turned out she was happily married, as was her mate, but I was just happy I'd done a good turn for a fellow traveller – despite loads of texts from friends asking 'Have you got the ride yet?'. In a beautiful twist of karma, however, one of her best friends from Florida - Nate Jenkins - was a big cheese in Obama's campaign. And after Miss America explained that I was a political player with a bit of clout in Westminster, we corresponded on Facebook and I sent him a CV. He told me to keep an eye on the Florida election races and promised to get me 'dialled in' to the campaign when I made it over…

A month before polling day I had no money and had all but given up on my dream. That was, until the bank forced my hand by giving me 24 hours notice that my £500 overdraft would be withdrawn. Naturally I hotfooted down to HSBC, withdraw everything I could, and booked my flight.

Then, whilst admonishing myself in a deserted international departures lounge, pulling at my hair and looking deranged, I remembered I hadn't booked the ticket online. I'd walked across the road from the bank to the Going Places travel agency in Sutton Coldfield and paid cash. The nice but dim assistant looked through several flights to Miami and was amazed to find a flight from Manchester for £250. I remember being surprised by how cheap it was - everywhere else I'd tried was over £500 - and so I handed over the cash there and then.

That meant it couldn't have been my fault, it had to be Going Places'. My spirits rose.
I looked for their sign in the airport, but to no avail, so I sat down and gave it some thought. I realised I had to get them to give me a replacement flight, and for no extra cost. I had less than £5 credit on my pay-as-you-go mobile so I couldn't afford to spend ages on hold on a customer services line. Luckily I had my works laptop with me and managed to track down a cheap landline to

phone. I wanted to get through to Sutton Coldfield office. I wanted to speak to the idiot who had got me into this trouble.

Needless to say that was impossible and I had a nervous five minutes wasting credit on hold on a national Going Places number. I explained the situation to a woman in a call centre and she promised to get someone to phone me back. All I could do is sit and wait it out; after counting my money three times, I decided not to buy a coffee.
Stuck for something to do, I phoned my friend Bod. Hearing him laugh down the phone made me feel a lot better. In fact, I wouldn't even had have made it to Manchester without Bod. He'd lent me £100 and dropped me at New Street train station earlier that day.

Matthew Boddington, old friend, Birmingham.
When the phone rang I knew it would be Adam asking for money. He wanted £100 to go to America with. When I asked him how much he'd raised himself he said £100. I said: "You'll have £200 when I give you my £100?" He hesitated and said, nope, he'd only have £100. My £100. I thought he was fucking nuts to go to America with £100 but he seemed desperate so I gave it to him. I dropped him off at New Street and he ran into the station and waved me goodbye. I had to beep him to remind him he'd left his piece of shit suitcase in my car.

Facebook status: Steve Zacharanda is sitting in the airport seeing the funny side of how going places booked him a flight from the wrong MANCHESTER!! He is about to get EVIL!!

After ten minutes the phone rang. I was calm; I knew I couldn't blow my top because I'd worked in a call centre myself and knew how to speak to people bored out of their brains. I decided to go for the confused and worried customer approach, but I had an ace up my sleeve: my profession.

"Is that Adam? I'm from Going Places. What's the problem?"
"Oh thank God you've phoned, I'm worried sick! I've just been told I'm 2,000 miles away from the correct airport because your operative booked me a flight from the wrong place. Your employee booked me to fly from Manchester, New England, not our England, the England where I'm standing now. I think it's only fair to lay my cards on the table – I'm a travel journalist for the Birmingham Mail, in fact if you look at today's paper I've just done a big piece on Toronto. I also work for the Sutton News and have friends at the Sutton Observer and if I don't get a flight to America I'll be writing lots and lots of stories about how rubbish Going Places is, and in a credit crunch I'm sure that is the last thing you need."

There was silence.

"Ahh, I see. OK. I will get back to you, Mr Smith."

Twenty minutes later he was back on the phone.

"I'm so sorry about this Mr Smith, it appears there was a mistake with the booking of your flight. We've got you on a flight to Miami via Philadelphia from Manchester tomorrow morning. If you stay at a hotel we'll repay you."

"Brilliant, but I don't have any money for a hotel," I replied.

"What about a Visa card?" he said, the first of about 100 occasions on which I would hear this over the next three weeks.

"That boat, I'm afraid, sailed in the 1990s. Is the flight first class because of all the trouble I've been put through?" I asked. It was worth a try.

"Err… no Mr Smith, there's no chance of that. Look on the bright side; you got a flight cheaper to Miami than anyone else this year! Have a good a trip".

The funny thing was, I could never have afforded to go to Miami if that lovely woman in Sutton Coldfield hadn't ballsed the booking up. If she'd said £500 I'd never have been able to afford it. I laughed to myself - someone up there was looking after me, and Mr Obama would be getting the Perry Barr cavalry after all.

Then I did a quick inventory. I had about £60 in cash. There was no way I was going back to Birmingham and I had nowhere to stay. It was Tuesday, and there was no prospect of any cash until payday on Friday. Even then I didn't have a cash card to withdraw anything with, so it would be a nervous visit to a foreign HSBC…

Facebook status: Steve Zacharanda knows the best threats are said politely, and is flying out tomorrow, £250 did seem too good to be true :)

I phoned Graham, a former flat mate and great friend dating back 20 years, who lives in Manchester. Hearing him call me a twat and then laughing at me made me feel better. Then it dawned on him. "Hold on, you're not staying at my place!"

"Go on, I can't afford to get back to Birmingham and come back again," I pleaded.

"You'll mess my place up and leave socks everywhere - I lived with you before, you smelly bastard - and you owe me £25."

Sensing an opportunity, I said: "Brilliant, want to make it £50? I'll give it you back on Friday."

"No chance. Absolutely no chance, and anyway you'll be in America on Friday you lying twat, but make your way to Manchester Piccadilly and I'll meet you there," he said, putting the phone down before I could say thank you.

I found a pub, drank some Strongbow, waited for Graham and then drank some more Strongbow. He came in for one pint which turned in to seven and then a few more back at his house. Thankfully in my stupor I remembered to phone the hotel in America my dad had booked for five days after a begging phone call the night before. I explained I wouldn't be there for the first night but would still need it reserved for the next few days.

I was woken up at 7am by Graham's fat rabbit running around the cage. I looked in my pocket and I had £30 - I'd spent half my budget in the pub. Graham told me I'd be OK on the bus to Manchester airport because I had hours to spare, but after freezing my arse off in Eccles I decided to get a cab. I made it to the airport with minutes to spare.

By the skin of my unbrushed teeth

Facebook status: Steve Zacharanda had a great night with his old mate in m'chestah and has a cheeky old skool house cd to listen to on the way to Miami!!

"Where do I have to board?" I asked the pretty mixed-race woman at the American Airlines desk.

A security guard said: "Over here sir, just some security first". My passport was taken from me and I was left on my own.

I looked at the officials and they were clearly discussing me. Then one came over. "Who booked your ticket sir?" he said.

My heart sank. I explained in detail what had happened, but had a nagging thought in the back of my mind. I didn't have a journalist visa for America and even though I was going on holiday it could present massive problems. However, my confused idiot routine worked and they said I was good to go. I went outside and had my last cigarette for what would be over 10 hours.

Whilst I waited to be called for boarding I considered phoning Mr Mensa, my landlord, to tell him he wouldn't be getting his rent for the month because I was trying to change the world. Shamefully, I didn't have the balls and didn't make the call; I knew *that* decision would come back and haunt me. Instead I phoned my girlfriend Nicole, told her that I loved her with all my heart, and boarded the plane. I looked in my pocket. I had £22.

I slept most the way from Manchester to Philadelphia. My hair looked like a loose afro and I smelt rather bad. I got off the plane knowing the next ten minutes would decide whether the dream of helping Obama win would become reality. The last time I entered America, immigration at Chicago airport subjected me to a full search, almost making me miss my connecting flight to Nashville. I was on a press trip and the immigration officer advised me to get a US journalist visa for the next time I came back, or I wouldn't get in. Needless to say I never got round to paying the £90 fee and taking the trip to the American embassy in London.

However, going to Miami was always going to be a holiday. I wondered if journalists could just go on holiday, or are they somehow always working? Considering I'd be leaving my job in two weeks anyway, the optimist in me thought I'd sail through.

With each step closer to the immigration desk I became weaker and weaker. "What is the purpose of your visit to America Sir?" the Latin immigration officer asked sternly.

"I've come to see some friends in Miami and enjoy the sun," I replied with a carefree smile.

"How much money have you got sir?" the immigration officer asked, wrongfooting me totally.
My response was more a nervous stutter than a reply.
"Err, £22 Sterling"
"What credit cards do you have sir?"
"Credit cards?"
"Debit cards?"
"Nope, none of those. I don't really trust myself with credit - neither lender nor borrower be! I'm getting a money transfer on Friday."
I didn't want to say wages were going in because it could trigger the whole job situation and admitting being a journalist was the last thing I wanted to do.
He gave me back my passport. Unstamped. "There is a problem, go to the end of the room to the immigration office," the officer said without looking up.

I felt sick. I knew I'd be in trouble now. What would happen if they wouldn't let me in? I had £22 and no phone credit. Everyone was right, it was madness to go abroad with no money. How much of a dickhead would I look not even getting in the country because I couldn't be bothered to pay for a visa? I got my case and wandered in to the immigration office. I watched as a Manchester student was grilled for not having a visa and accused of trying to work in America illegally. I walked to the desk and bile rose to the back of my throat. I opened my mouth but nothing came out. The perfectly groomed officer just stared at me. I managed to rasp: "I've been told to come here, mate." He pointed at the seat and that was it.

My mind was racing. My story did sound totally daft - I was on my own, with no money, and I didn't even know the rules about helping out politically in America.
Did I need a visa to do volunteer work? I knew if I played the Obama card all it would take would be for a McCain fanatic to be in charge of my fate and I'd be stuck in an airport without a flight. I decided to appeal to the immigration officer's romantic side; I was coming to America to get a girl back. My ex. The One. Yes, that should just about do it.

After 45 minutes stewing I was called up to the desk.
"Why are you going to Miami?" the same immigration officer asked.
"I'm going on my holidays, my missus, err I mean my ex missus, is in Miami. Well, I hope she will become my missus again," I said.
"But why are you going now?"
"Because I've lost my job and thought it was the perfect time. I need to get her back, I've been going out of my mind since we split up."

"You are a journalist, are you not?"

I felt weak, sick.
"Yes. No...err, yes. Erm, well, I've lost my job - the credit crunch has hit British papers, me and 65 others were sacked from the Birmingham Mail, so I'm not a journalist anymore."
His poker face betrayed no thoughts, but his eyes felt like they were boring into my very soul.
"So you are not here to do any work for your paper? Because that would be illegal," he said.
"Nope, I write about dogs up trees and wedding anniversaries in North Birmingham. The Mail isn't like a national paper, it just does what's going on in Birmingham. I just want to meet my missus. Ex-missus."

There was a brief pause.
"How much money do you have?"
"£22"
"And you have no credit cards?"
"Nope"
"So you're trying to tell me that you're coming to America with £22 and no credit cards. Are you totally mad, or are you mentally ill?" he said with no trace of irony.
"What about if something goes wrong, what will you do?"
I pulled my HSBC chequebook out and told him I'd be visiting the global bank on Friday. 'Right, here goes' I thought. I was getting more confident now.
"I'm just in love mate. Perhaps it is a form of mental illness, all I know is if I don't get into America, my missus, my ex-missus, won't believe me, she'll think I didn't want her back. I'm getting a bank transfer on Friday. I will have money then."

His silence was doing nothing to help me out. 'Probably time to stop talking', I thought, as he looked through paperwork, looked at my passport, looked at the computer, shook his head then disappeared in to the back of the office.
Five minutes later he came back and said: "Go and take your case to that table over there and wait for my colleague." I dragged my case to the desk. Another officer came over. Again, he was immaculately turned out, and he looked more senior than the others.

There was no 'Hello', 'How do you do?', no pleasantries. Just straight to the point.
"So you're coming here to work as a journalist without a journalist visa."
Fuck.
"No, I'm not coming to work as a journalist. I am here to get my missus – err, I mean ex missus - back. I took voluntary redundancy as a journalist, and

everyone who knows me knows I am leaving the job I love. Not to get in to your country for being a journalist when I've just taken redundancy will be a real kick in the teeth."

He unzipped my case and threw it open. We both looked at the contents and then in perfect symmetry recoiled backwards, overcome with the smell. I'd just thrown everything into a case from my bedsit when I packed. Nothing was folded and a packet of biscuits had broken open and covered everything in crumbs. There were a few rogue pairs of dirty socks which stunk. The officer put his rubber gloves on before picking up a piece of clothing.
"Do you normally travel like this sir?"
"No," I replied. "This was a bit of last minute decision. I got a cheap flight and decided to come and find my missus. Ex-missus. I'm not being funny mate, but does it look like I'm coming here on business? No journalist would travel on assignment like this."

He looked at the case and then at me and then back at the case again. His face said it all. He looked constantly as if he was smelling shit.
"You are extremely unorganised" he said to himself as much as to me. "Why did your girlfriend split up with you?"
This was getting surreal, but I thought I'd bite. "She said she couldn't live with me because I was smelly, unhygienic and like a child".
He just looked at me. He said nothing. For the next 10 minutes he fished pieces of paper out of the case, including Birmingham City Council meeting minutes, crumpled bookies coupons and other assorted rubbish I'd never seen before.

Then he picked up an Obama badge.
"Obama, are you a fan?" he said with absolute contempt.
"Err…my dad gave me the badge for good luck."
He sent me back to the desk. The original officer looked at me with even more disdain, if that was possible.
"Good luck"
"Have you let me in?"
"Yeah, you can go now. Enjoy your trip to the United States sir, I suggest you get a credit card for your next visit."
He stamped my passport. I was in. I felt ten feet tall. I was back in the USA, and it was one of the best moments of my life. I'd gone from sheer terror to priceless elation within a single hour – an hour that had cost me several months' worth of sweat and tears.

Back in the USA

Thursday, October 24

Facebook status: Steve Zacharanda is BACK IN THE USA! Two hours being searched and questioned after 'there is a problem sir, go to immigration'.

I changed my £22 into dollars, bought a packet of cigarettes and wandered out of the airport for a wonderful, life affirming fag. It took an hour to get back in after all the checks, after which I I unpacked my laptop to listen Aston Villa play Ajax in the Europa League. I bought a beer and nursed it; the flight to Miami wasn't for another hour. I looked at my money. I had $30, and I was desperately hungry. I looked on the internet for the price of a bus ticket from Miami airport to my hotel. It was $45. Bugger, I didn't even have enough money to get out of the airport.

It was about 3pm and I'd be arriving in Miami about 10pm. I logged into Facebook desperately hoping to see one name under the 'Online Friends' section: Samantha Lawton. Sam's an amazing woman and, some time after sharing a very enjoyable fling with me at journalism college, she'd landed the job as Caribbean correspondent for Splash News, based in Miami.

Her name popped up. I instant messaged her with: 'THEY LET ME IN!". She asked when the flight got to Miami and agreed to pick me up. I thanked her profusely, in the knowledge that I could at last buy some food. I got a beer, burger and a few magazines. I had $10 left. Job done, result.

And the Villa won.

Facebook status: Steve Zacharanda is BACK in the USA, and the 1st thing he did after getting through immigration hell was listen to the Villa win in Philly airport!! go on the lads!!

I slept all the way to Miami and looked like a disorientated tramp when I got to Miami International. I washed and wandered around the airport before I saw Sam, and I honestly don't think I'll ever be as happy to see a friendly face again. Looking every inch the Miami woman she now was, Sam gave me the first beaming smile I'd gotten since arriving in America hours before. We hugged. I smelt her hair and goose pimples ran up my neck. I felt on top of the world.

During the long drive to Miami Sam kept saying "$10?! You're unbelievable!", and also "You've come to Miami with $10, what would have you done if I wasn't here?". It was obviously the time to ask if I could borrow some money until Friday, and my angel from Stoke agreed. A little later we found the shit hotel I was staying in and after an argument about my lack of a credit card to pay for a deposit (this time I said I'd lost my wallet) I threw my stuff on the room's floor and we hit the bars of Miami South Beach. It was a great night, made all the sweeter because of all the shit I'd gone through to get there. We downed drinks, we laughed and danced the night away; it was pure bliss. I couldn't have wished for a better first night in America. The adventure had begun.

Samantha Lawton, journalist, Miami

An instant message came through from Adam asking if I could pick him up from Miami airport because he only had $10. I thought he was joking until he asked to borrow some money a few hours after. He looked like he'd been dragged through a hedge backwards when I picked him up. I've no idea what he would have done if I hadn't happened to live in his choice of holiday destination and hadn't been on Facebook that day. Anyway, we hit the bars of South Beach straight away. I woke up the next day with a bad head, an aching back because we'd fallen over trying to do the Lambada, and I'd lost my credit card. "Adam's in Miami," I thought.

Landing on my feet

Facebook status: **Steve Zacharanda** is Tony Montana, with a bad head after a simply wonderful first night in Miami, might put off that whole 'workin for Obama thing' till Monday!

Friday morning was spent in the Miami South Beach branch of HSBC. I managed to transfer all my wages into a different account so direct debits would not swallow any up. In the end, it took me four hours to get $400 - but at last I had money. I spent the weekend sleeping, watching endless hours of election coverage, buying a cheap phone, drinking, being shown Miami by Sam, writing copy, and getting all my clothes clean:

Facebook status Friday: Steve Zacharanda ate the finest foods, drank the finest wines with the finest of company, but has a bad arm cos he keeps on pinching himself.....

Facebook status Saturday AM: **Steve Zacharanda** paddled in the Caribbean sea after a wonderful night in which he was given an idea which he is literally going to broadcast to the world!

Facebook status Saturday PM: Steve Zacharanda is working hard whilst watching Saturday Night Live, and realises it's not gonna be all fine food, fine wine, fine company and paddling!

Facebook status Sunday AM: **Steve Zacharanda** is in his hotel's courtyard listening to the footie and working at a Miami pace.

Facebook status Sunday PM: Steve Zacharanda has got a bit of a tan without trying and has been told it hasn't even got hot yet! Off for a Sunday roast now! Don't even get them at home :)

Facebook status Sunday PM: **Steve Zacharanda** enjoyed the bangers and mash washed down with a bit of bow, spending the night watching NFL and baseball whilst writing copy.

Monday, October 27

Facebook status: <u>**Steve Zacharanda**</u> is going to the Miami Obama campaign offices suited and booted.

Monday morning I put on my suit (well it was my mate Mark's actually) and flattened my crumpled CV. The Obama website told me the nearest office was in Little Havana in Miami, by the famous Orange Bowl. Three hours later I was totally lost in the middle of downtown, sweating profusely and searching desperately for the right bus. I finally found one and the driver told me it would be 45 minutes to my destination. My heart sank. I didn't fancy a two hour journey to work every day.
About ten minutes into the journey, however, I got a rather important phone call.

(Now, this is why I love Americans. I'd met a journalist called Tonya Pendleton on a Toronto press trip a few months before, and I emailed her the day before I flew out to say I was coming over to the U.S. She then took it upon herself to write a lovely email to all of her Florida travel contacts asking them to help me.)

The lady on the line was from The Miami Tourist Convention, and she was a member of Jewish Women for Obama: Susie Sponder, one of Tonya's contacts. A wonderful person, in many respects the perfect PR woman - someone who bent over backwards to ensure this journalist was looked after. And someone I let down very, very badly. But more of that later.

The New York-tinged accent shouted down the phone, as the signal was breaking up. "Little Havana? No no no, you're going totally the wrong place for the Obama campaign, there's no point going over there if you can't speak Spanish. Come and see me at my office on Brickell and we'll have a chat about how we can help you."
Like I'd just hopped onto the 51 bus in Birmingham, I jumped off immediately, thinking I could catch one going the other way to downtown Miami. The sun was scorching. I felt so uncomfortable sweating in a suit, and my CV was now dying a death in my breast pocket. Worse still, the road was deserted. In fact most of the houses were boarded up. I looked closely and almost all of them had repossession notices in the garden. This was the sub-prime mortgage crisis made flesh, shops and houses falling apart in front of my eyes. It was also deadly quiet…but I knew I was being watched.

There's an old Handsworth saying – well, my mate's brother-in-law Kane coined it when he was in Brownsville in New York - about being in a foreign area. Refusing to take his chains off and believe he would ever be mugged, Kane said: "Ghetto mans knows Ghetto mans", meaning no matter where you are in the world if you act hard there is a good chance you will be left alone. I looked at myself in a window. I looked like a human sprinkler. I'd sweated so much my trousers had ridden up to shin length, so my shoes looked as if they'd had an argument with my trousers they were that far apart. I smelt bad too.

A black man in a hoodie, riding a BMX which looked too small for him, circled me.
He did an impressive skid to stop in front of me, which he seemed way too pleased with considering he had to be nearly 40-years-old.
"Yo, you got a spare cigarette?" he said.
He was in luck. I had a full box of Marlboro Lights on me.
"Yeah course mate, ee' are," I said. His eyes went straight to my pocket as I brought out my pack.
"Any idea how I how get back to downtown Miami mate, I'm lost?"
His stony face broke out in to a goofy smile and he roared with laughter.
"You ain't no policeman," he said whilst sparking up my fag.
"Fucking hell mate, how bad are the policemen in Miami if they look like this when they're undercover?" I joked.
"What kind of accent is that?
"Birmingham, England mate. I'm here to help Barack Obama but I've got lost."

He looked me up and down then asked for another cigarette, despite still smoking the one I'd just given him.
"You got money for a taxi?" he said seriously.
"I've got about $10 on me," I replied, thinking I was clever by lying.
"Find a taxi and get out of here, this ain't no place for anyone from the UK. It doesn't matter who is President, look at this place, no-one gives a shit about places like this."
His hopelessness and the boarded up houses said it all really; I was somewhere that nobody wanted to be. I thanked him, gave him three more cigarettes, stopped looking for a bus stop and started looking for a taxi.

Twenty nervous but fascinating minutes later, after getting some great quotes from various passersby (all of whom scrounged cigarettes from me too) for a future Obama article, I finally saw a taxi and headed to Brickell Avenue. I had a good wash and went to the Miami Tourist Convention, gazing down on the city from the 50th floor reception. I was transfixed - it really is an amazing cityscape. Suzie came and showed me to her cramped office; she'd heard of the Birmingham Mail, and I showed her my travel press cuttings, which I carried around with me everywhere to prove I was a bona fide travel journalist. I knew the game by now.

We had lunch at Le Pistine and she promised to send out an 'email blast' to all her contacts to see if anyone could give me a place to stay. I had digs at the concrete floored Argentinean hostel for the next three days so the race was on to find me a place. It looked liked I would be living the high life at some stage of this holiday.
Suzie was a single mother, about 40-years-old, really great company and it was a welcome change eating fine food in a fine restaurant. After lunch she gave me instructions to my nearest Obama office and and told me to ask for Nate Sherwood. I finally got there two hours later after getting lost, rapidly realising that America is no place without a car.

The North Beach Barack Obama Presidential Campaign office was a nondescript place. I had to ask the security guard to get taken to the right floor, where a fifty-ish lady manned the reception. I'm not sure if I expected a fanfare when I said: "I'm Adam and I've come from Birmingham to help with Obama, when can I get started?", but she looked at me as if I was mad. "Well what are you doing in this office? Who told you to come here? Wait there."

The place was a hive of activity, and no-one was in a suit, and I bet no-one had bought a CV either. Most of the people looked under thirty and from what I could tell were mostly white middle class. No-one could find Nate either. I got passed around a few other volunteers who didn't really know what to do with me except make me fill out a few forms.
After sitting around for about half an hour I remembered Matt Damon was doing an Obama procession in South Beach in about half an hour and I didn't fancy putting in a shift in a suit, and smelling - I didn't want to get the 'smelly limey' tag just yet (and after all, I was on holiday). I made a sharp exit, explaining I'd phone Nate tomorrow to find the South Beach office, which seemed like it might be walking distance from my hotel. By the time I got to the Town Hall I'd missed Matt Damon, who everyone said was great and had posed for photos with anyone who asked. It seemed everyone had been rewarded for helping Obama, except me, but then I hadn't helped out much. I'd spent most of my first day wandering around lost, which didn't do for much for the cause. On the upside, I had had a wonderful lunch.

Monday night Facebook status: Steve Zacharanda is drinking a pint of Strongbow in an Irish pub contemplating to see Pharrell Williams after missing Matt Damon through getting lost in the ghetto....

Facebook status: Steve Zacharanda popped back to the hotel to drop his laptop off before going the Pharrell Obama concert, it's time to drop the A-bomb on a Miami dancefloor

Getting started - finally

Tuesday, October 28

I woke up on Tuesday morning with a raging headache and a mouth like a Ghurkha's jockstrap. I looked at the clock. It was 10am. I cursed the Argentineans outside my room that had woken me up. Memories of the night before started to flood back to me. I'd barged to the front of a massive queue and convinced the bouncer, manager and event coordinator at a Pharrell Williams Obama concert that I was a reporter for the Birmingham (Alabama) Mail. I'd gone in on my own, thinking I wouldn't have the chance to see Mr Williams at this proximity again and that I could chat to some like-minded Obama fans. I mean, could you imagine a decent hip-hop concert in England before a General Election? This was democracy at its wonderful best. People who wouldn't have done a thing in previous elections flocked out because of one man: Barack Obama.

I had money and you could smoke inside the club so it wasn't long before I got chatting to an entertaining chap called David Mayer and his female friend. We sneaked in to the VIP section, swapping stories, drinking loads and occasionally roaring with laughter. We were sitting next to Fat Joe, so I decided in my drunken state that the huge Latin star would be fascinated that I was his fan club secretary in Birmingham. In one move his burly security team managed to throw me back exactly where I was sitting before I stood up.

(Pharrell never turned up. Well, it wasn't really his fault, because I later found out he didn't know anything about the event. I vaguely remembered arguing with the manager, saying it was a rip off and that I wanted my money back. I also remembered him telling me I didn't pay anything to get in and to fuck off.)

After losing myself in this reverie for a bit, I snapped back to reality. I opened my emails and there was an invite, which I'd accepted in my drunken stupor, to lunch with a PR agent in Miami at noon. I threw some clothes on, collected my crumpled press cuttings, and jumped in a taxi because I was running late. Being driven across the causeway from South Beach to Miami I was awestruck by the giant ocean cruise ships lined up one after another like buses.

When I got to to the restaurant in Mary Brickell Village a beautiful PR called Destiny was waiting for me. We had a great lunch and she was fascinating company as well as great to look at. The Village is as close as Florida can be to California and Destiny explained all her colleagues were allowed to take their dogs into work.
How can you not love America?

After a while I excused myself and went to the toilet, at which point I noticed a woman go into a cubicle and turn to lock the see-through door. I was amazed that the toilet doors automatically frosted from top to bottom when they were locked. I found a free cubicle, locked the door and sat down for a well deserved shit; as I waited to drop the kids off at the pool I couldn't help but think it was nice to have a dump in such a classy toilet. I was also intrigued by the way that, despite the frosted glass, you could still see outside.

A short time later an impeccably dressed fifty-something blonde lady who oozed style and sophistication appeared in front of the toilet door. The split second when I realised she could see me, because of the look of contorted horror on her face, seemed to last an eternity. I'd obviously not got the hang of locking the see through toilet doors. She let out a scream and dropped her bag. I was now in a quandary, because I was still in mid-shit and this train wasn't stopping for nobody.

My instant reaction was to leap forward and lock the door but I realised if I did I'd leave a trail of shit on the marble floor that would put this attractive Milf, or Grilf, off her food for the day. Instead I did an apologetic wave, put my head in my hands and strained like a motherfucker. When I finished I sprang up to lock the door and fell flat on my face because I hadn't pulled my trousers up. I looked up through the glass and was mighty relieved the lady was nowhere to be seen and there wasn't a crowd looking at my hairy arse sticking up in the air. I locked the door properly and it frosted instantly. I cleaned myself up with what remaining dignity I had left, threw my boxer shorts in the bin and reminded myself to buy a new pair.

I walked back in to the restaurant with my head down and went straight to my table praying the Milf, or Grilf, wasn't a friend of Destiny.
"Are you alright?" Destiny asked.
Had she been told? I gambled that she hadn't and it was a general question because of how long I'd been - and I could hardly say: "Christ bab, some bint has just seen me on the shitter," could I?
I just smiled and said: "Wow, those toilet doors are crazy aren't they?"
"Yeah, they are way out, they're the only ones in Miami".
Thank God for that, I thought, I won't be coming here again. We finished up with her saying that she'd send out an email blast to her clients to see if anyone could help me find a hotel or nice free meal.

It was Tuesday afternoon, and a week after I'd left Birmingham I hadn't lifted a finger to help bend the arc of history with Barack Obama. I got back to South Beach and headed to the Obama office, just off the world famous Ocean Drive. The playing was over. I was ready to change the world; the cavalry had arrived.

The South Beach Miami Obama office was adorned with posters and t-shirts. The shop front could hardly have been smaller, but inside was packed. I walked up the small flight of stairs and took a deep breath; I couldn't be bothered to make a speech about where I'd come from and why I was here, I'd keep it simple. There were about 15 people in an office that shouldn't really hold three. There was a mass of laptops, tangled up wires, a TV in the corner tuned into MSBC and stacks of pens and paper on the tables. Giant Stars and Stripes flags hung on the wall and each desk had miniature flags surrounded by mobile phones. Then I noticed the food:
pizzas, cake, Chinese, more cake, and huge bowls of salad, bread, packets of Pringles, bottles of Root beer, half eaten sandwiches and other stuff I'd never seen or heard of. There were two rows of tables, one with all the computers and food on and the other piled high with every type of Obama t-shirt available. All of them had great slogans like 'Europeans for Obama' 'Jews for Obama' 'Afro-Caribbean's for Obama' 'Latinos for Obama' and 'Dog lovers for Obama'.

Two twenty-somethings, both wearing white t-shirts and black baseball caps, looked like they were in charge and were surrounded by mounds of papers and reports.
"Alright mate, I'm here to volunteer for the campaign, is there anything I can do?" I said.
"Hi, thanks for helping, my name's Mark and this is Kale and we're in charge of volunteers," he said in a laid back Californian accent.
He gave me a phone and a massive list of names with addresses and numbers.
Each had several abbreviations next to them like NC, PB, NA and others, all denoting whether they had been phoned before or were up for coming to help.
"Phone these people and ask if they can spare any time to volunteer for the campaign."
He explained the abbreviations and gave me a rough script to stick to. Brilliant, I thought, let's get on with this.

My heart skipped a beat when the first person's phone started to ring.
"Hi, my name is Adam and I'm phoning from the South Beach Miami Barack Obama office. We were wondering whether you could give some time to change the world and get our man elected. It could be an hour or a day, and we will be very grateful for whatever time you could give up."
There was a long silence and then a high pitched nasal voice came on the line.
"WHHHHHHAAAAAAT?" came the reply.
"Hi, my name is Adam and I'm phoning from the South Beach Miami Barack Obama office and we were wondering whether you could give some time to change the world and get our man elected," I repeated.
"WHHHHHHAAAAAATT? What language are you speaking? I can't understand a word you're saying."
I took a deep breath and repeated my first line but a little slower.

The nasal voice came back on the line: "I don't know what you're talking about, goodbye."

Chastened, I tried not to let my disappointment show to those around me, but they all seemed pre-occupied anyway. 'Errm, I'll put 'phone back' next to that name'.

Now it was onto the next one.

"He-lo, my name is A-dam, and I am phoning from the South Beach Miami Barack O-bama o-ffice. Is there any chance you could give up your time to volunteer for the campaign this weekend, we need all the help we can get." There was silence on the end of the line but it sounded like the person was in a car.

Then a woman shouted down the phone: "Qué estás hablando de loco? Sólo hablan español pueden hablar español a alguien que me pueda hablar español? You no speaka Spanish?" she barked.

"Wait there. bab," I said in a panic, "Does anyone speak Spanish in here? This woman can only speak Spanish."

An elderly West Indian lady with a kind face took the phone off me, as she spoke fluent Spanish. She nailed the deal, getting the woman to volunteer at the weekend as well. The lady explained to me that a lot of Spanish speakers would crop up and to hand the phone to her every time.

She was lovely and I later found out she had worked every election for the Democrats since the 1960s. She had grown up witnessing lynching in her town in Alabama and was now working towards getting a black man elected to the White House. Her story was awe-inspiring and made me even prouder to be on the campaign. I told her I couldn't speak Spanish but that I'd still been asked to go to the Little Havana office, and a cool looking Moroccan dude with an Ireland cap on took his head out of his laptop.

"Yeah man, I did the same, the Democrat website said it was the closest office to South Beach and it took hours to get there. You're lucky you didn't reach there, I had an awful day because I can't speak Spanish and I was in a call centre all day," he said in a vaguely European accent.

He stretched out a hand and said with a smile that illuminated his whole face: "Hi, I'm Karim." He and I would have many an adventure before our time was out in Miami.

His story about Little Havana put me at ease because I hadn't been a total idiot getting lost going there. I grew in confidence and attacked the phones with fervour. I love speaking to Americans, and I learnt to speak slower and slower so I would stop being asked if I was Australian. After an hour I was in my element with my feet up, phoning people for Obama. I asked a woman if she would help Obama after giving her the usual spiel.

"I'd love to but, you know what, I just have not got the time, he's going win anyway," she said quite rudely.

I thought I'd try and use my charm to talk her round.

"Look love, if everyone thinks Obama is going to win and doesn't do anything to help or doesn't make the effort to vote then he is going to lose. And how are you going to feel then? How is America going to feel then? How will the world look at America then? It will look like you couldn't be bothered to make history. I can't even vote and I've come to help. I'm from Birmingham in England and I jumped on a plane last week, I haven't paid my rent so I could come over here, I had to phone the Mrs to tell her I loved her at the airport and I don't even know where I'm going to be staying when my hotel runs out tomorrow night. But you know what, when my grandchildren ask me what I did in the most important election of my lifetime, I will be able to say I did everything I could. So please just an hour to say that you made history."

Now I'd love to say she heard my emotional plea and hotfooted it down to the office and signed up. But she said: "You're crazy, don't phone this number again, and what business of yours is our election?" The words 'Because we have to deal with the shit that your insane presidents do to the world' were on the tip of my tongue, but instead I said thanks and hung up, grunting 'stupid bitch' under my breath. I looked up and all eyes were on me.

Mark was first to speak.
"Was that true? Have you come from England to help?"
"Yes"
"I wondered what accent that was. Cool, man. Awesome. And you haven't paid your bills so you could help? Welcome aboard," he said.
Then everyone came over and shook my hand, it felt wonderful. It appeared that I wasn't the only out of towner either. Mark and Kale had come from California to Miami six weeks before, leaving their lives on hold to help Obama without being paid. I was honoured to be in their presence. Karim, meanwhile, was Belgian but lived in London and had flown in a few days before. Despite having Cuba and Morocco on his passport he'd sailed through immigration.

In fact the only local in the office at that time was Ericka. The mother of the office, she was a sixties hippy with civil rights and anti-Vietnam protests under her belt, and a truly lovely woman who must have heard all manner of crude and inane conversations from her younger colleagues during the campaign. She was in charge of the t-shirt empire - she'd order new ones every day and look after the cash box.
As the election got closer and closer Obama t-shirts became a fashion must and Ericka was there to provide every combination of slogans and colours. There was even a 'Hilary for Supreme Court' t-shirt for sale, not that it was a big seller.

The sheer amount of people who came in the office was an eye-opener. Every few minutes a head would pop up the stairs and ask a few questions along the lines of 'Is this the Obama office?', as if they were blind. We also got "Can I get a t-shirt?" or "Can I have some posters/banners?" or quite often "How can I help?" The more nonsensical enquiries led the team to either stifling laughter or breaking into fits of giggles as the confused visitor disappeared down the stairs."Do you sell cigarettes?" "Are these t-shirts, like, you know, being given away? "Do you have any alcohol?" "Do you know when Obama is coming to this office?" were among some questions I heard.

The office opened from 10am until 10pm. It was small, cramped, often too hot, the electric went off a few times, and it was a miracle the mass of tangled wires on the floor hadn't caused a fire - but it was without doubt one of the most wonderful places in the world. Despite the whiskey in the toilet and the beers under the tables people were doing a fantastic job in their own time as well. A lot of the credit has to go to the wonderfully laid back way the office was run by childhood friends Kale and Mark.
At the end of my first day I felt like a king when they both smiled and said in unison: "Welcome to the team, Dude."

Facebook status Steve Zacharanda phoned loads of Americans at work, went out with a good lookin media type who can take her dog to work, had an embarrassing incident with a c-thru bog door.

My first day at work had been cut short by a phone call from Destiny. There was a drinks soiree for journalists at The Tides Hotel, one of Miami's famous resorts, on Ocean Drive. She asked me if I'd like to come along, and frankly I thought it would be rude not to, especially as I had an eye on blagging a few nights at the hotel. I only had two days left in my hostel so I was getting desperate for a free night somewhere. I went back to it and had to argue with another load of Argentineans to get an iron. My clothing options were limited. I went with my brown trousers that I'd worn every working day for the last three months and my black 'Michael Douglas' v-neck top.

The Tides looked beautiful as the sea air blew over Ocean Drive and into the Art Deco lobby. I followed the signs to the Coral Bar for the drinks reception. The bar was a small oak panelled room with tall gold tables, a reverse mirror with sea creatures inside it and a stone bar. There were already about ten people there and it seemed half full. Within a moment of stepping through the doors I was greeted by Destiny, who explained it was a press get together to show off the hotel's recent refurb. "This is one of the World's best rum bars, please go ahead and try for yourself," were some of the most welcome words spoken during the entire holiday.

Rum and Coke has always been my drink – I love a good dark rum – so I was like a fat bloke let loose in a pork pie factory on Easter Monday, after giving up meat for lent.

When I woke up the next day a haze of rum hovered three inches from my face. I learnt a lot about rum that night, so it was a shame I drank so much of it I forgot the lot. I turned out my pockets and found a business card that intrigued me:
'Donamarie Baptiste – Mount Gay Rum Caribbean Saleswoman'. I remembered her straight away, she was six foot tall and that didn't include her perfect afro. What a human being. She had her shit together. I guess she must have been in her forties but she looked early thirties, tops. She'd been perfectly dressed in chiffon and had one of the best jobs on the planet. We'd chatted, exchanged cards, then she'd said she was a clubber and if I needed anyone to go partying with to give her a call. She radiated energy and probably had a few free bottles of rum up her sleeve.

To complement this, when I turned my phone on a reminder flashed up. I assumed I'd left it the night before in my drunken stupor, and it said 'Miami Herald's Freddie Gonzalez has invited you to a party at the Versace Mansion!' I thought to myself 'Wow – I must have been on form last night'. My first day working for Obama had been spectacular, I'd worked hard and partied harder; luckily for me, that was how it would be until I got on my flight home.

Within Touching Distance

I was told to wait for someone called Caesar at the South Beach Miami Music School. I sat on the wall watching the world go by waiting for him, my ride to the Bank Atlantic Centre. After spending hours lost in various places in Miami I had learnt that 'getting the ride' was all important if I was to get anywhere on time. I was also delighted because I was going to see Barack Obama.

Obama was speaking in Orlando with Bill Clinton and I was all set to go on a two day expedition to Mickey's home town before discovering he was coming to Miami.
Obama was holding a rally which would be included in his unprecedented half an hour advert on all the major networks that night. It was going to be a historic event and I wanted to be part of it.

Obama was due to be on stage at 8pm and six hours before hand Caesar arrived.
He was 30 minutes late but I never ever criticise anyone for being late, because I've spent a lifetime doing it. He was 24-years-old and drove a Honda as messy as my suitcase. I instantly liked him. What I love about Americans is that they all have a story to tell, and Caesar had a great one.

He grew up in Puerto Rico (well, somewhere Latin and very poor anyway) and as a way out he left his family as a teenager and came to live with his uncle and his wife in America. However, the two subsequently split up, up leaving him in danger of being sent home to a life of poverty. In the end, Caesar's uncle's ex-wife saved the day. Her name was Suzie Sponder.

Caesar, despite his laid back demeanour and messy car, was one of Miami's best Hip-Hop video cameramen. He had worked with Florida's biggest music stars including Rick 'The Boss' Ross, and we had a fascinating chat about the world he worked in. As well as working with music stars he'd met Barack Obama, because a few months before his company had been hired to film an Obama advert.
"We had all our phones taken off us and told to turn up at a certain time, then Barack Obama walked in. Yeah man, he was pretty cool, I liked him, man," said Caesar in his chilled out way. I shook the hand that had shaken Obama's hand, but that was as close as I was to get to the new President of the United States.

It was sunny as we drove across Miami to pick Suzie up, who lived in a really cool house with her daughter. She had contacts in the Democratic Party and reckoned we would have tickets waiting for us at the box office. We jumped in her 4x4, which was filled with Obama stickers, flags and posters and headed out to the Bank Atlantic Centre. It turned out to be miles away; although it was classed as Miami but seemed like nearly 20 miles away from South Beach. The traffic got slower as we approached the giant indoor stadium until it was pretty much a crawl. We could see the car parks and they were already full.

It was four hours before Obama was supposed to get on stage and the traffic was bumper to bumper, with all eyes on the policeman letting people in to the car park. It would be touch and go whether we would be allowed in because it was nearly full. I got out of the car and wandered up to the policeman to find out what the situation was. He was a tubby white guy with a bright brown moustache.
"Alright mate, we are ten cars back are we going to get in?" I said.
"Sir, I cannot say that you will or you won't. But it is one in one out at the moment, you can see how many problems we have at this time."
One in one out? I swore quietly to myself. I thought I'd heard the end of that phrase when I stopped going to nightclubs without a spot on the guest list. This was like getting into the Dome in Birmingham circa 1995, not seeing a historical political moment.

As far as I could see there were cars in every direction and the noise of people beeping their horns was becoming deafening, which was pissing this cop off. I smiled at him and said 'good luck' just before someone tried to drive across the road into the car park. The cop exploded with rage and screamed at the impatient Obama fan to turn around or he would stop anyone else coming in. He said it so loud everyone in the cars around him heard and started booing and hissing the driver until he had to leave entirely. We were the very last car they let in and we cheered wildly as we sailed through.

We drove into the car park and were stunned into silence as there were tens of thousands of people in line already. We were about half a mile away from the stadium but the queues snaked around far as the eye could see. This was mind blowing, but inspiring as well. The majority of people waiting were black, but there were all ages and all colours patiently waiting to see their hero. All these families were there just to see a politician, and for the vast majority I spoke to it was the first time had ever engaged in any type of politics.

Suzie had VIP tickets so we had to go to the box office. This meant putting our heads down and walking past the queue. I've always enjoyed jumping queues and this one was no different. The atmosphere was like a carnival, with countless children singing and dancing while they waited. When we got to the box office there was a small queue and the Democratic staff behind the desk were rushed off their feet. The contact we were waiting on didn't have his phone and his list wasn't ready so we were told to wait. One after another people came to the counter demanding their tickets. There were some wonderful 'Don't you know who I am?' moments and a lot of skincrawlingly badly dealt with people. No-one wanted to be told that they had to go to the back of the queue, which by this time must have been over 30,000 people long, so there were tears, arguments, lots of shouting and then heartbreak as it slowly dawned on more people that they wouldn't get into the Barack Obama show.

We were told we were going to get white wristbands, but they had no white wristbands and we'd have to wait until they got some. Which was barmy - why not give us something else instead?

There was nothing we could do though. We held back, every so often popping our head over the counter to ask whether our white wristbands had been delivered or if our contact had been found. We watched as people were given red wristbands, which in the pecking order of wristband were not as good as white ones, as we had to wait. After nearly an hour, with the VIP section swelled by red wristband people, the atmosphere was becoming electric as the anticipation grew. Then the stressed out blonde woman behind the counter called us. She said she wanted us to get in to the stadium so she'd give us red wristbands now, instead of waiting for the mysterious white wristbands that would never come. All three of us hugged each other and jumped up and down with excitement. We were pointed to the VIP queue, which was no longer than 200 people. Our wristbands would get us just yards from where Joe Biden and Barack Obama would speak.

Everyone in our queue was connected with the party and seemed to be the chairman of this or the organiser of that for the last 10 or 20 years. All were fuming about the organisation and were complaining about how they should have got more tickets. "We've been waiting for this moment to see Obama and so have all our volunteers back in Miami and we are the only ones who have got wristbands," an overweight Latino woman moaned. We'd been outside for over two hours now and waited in the VIP line for another hour, inching closer to the double doors and what looked like a full body search.

I looked at the giant queue and was delighted to be in the VIP line. Then I saw the fathers who had bought their children to see the future President and felt sad that the majority wouldn't have a treasured memory, just a lifetime fear of queuing. I was an imposter who had landed on his feet whilst real Americans, whose lives the election would influence far more than mine, wouldn't get to see him. Then a tall Obama worker approached me and my guilt vanished as soon as I took my eye off the miserable father and son waiting in the long line. "Let me look at your t-shirt," the Obama worker said. I turned to face him. "John Taylor Hospice? That's fine, I was checking to see if you have any offensive slogans because you'll be behind Mr Obama and could be in shot." Thank God I hadn't wore my 'One Man's Maverick Is Another Man's Silly Cunt' t-shirt. All those people back home who said in jest: 'I bet I'll see you'll next to

Obama on TV, if anybody could it'd be you," would be in hysterics when they watched News at Ten.

This was going out on every network during a historic political broadcast in the middle of the biggest election in a generation. And I was going to be yards from him. I phoned my dad and my mate Stuart to tell them to watch out for me. I suppose that jinxed me.

There was a noise from the massive line running parallel to ours. Suddenly hundreds of people started to run towards the turnstiles and the main entrance. The scream went up: 'OBAMA!' Then thousands of people started running towards where he was walking into the building. No-one in the VIP line moved. We had the golden ticket, a mere glimpse of Obama wouldn't compare to being on the goggle-box.

I could see the commotion but not the man himself. The massive queue was all over the place. There was no order and the inexperienced stewards, who normally marshalled baby boomers going to see the Eagles, didn't have a clue. I looked behind me and the VIP queue, which before the mad rush to see the Black Beatle was only about twenty people, was now about 20,000. When the other queue broke rank the people behind had seen another one and joined it. Our VIP queue was now about as VIP as a Two 4 One pub in Coventry. I was about 50 people from the door, but the queue wasn't getting shorter and it was becoming dusk.

There was a strange atmosphere as thousands of people suddenly clicked that they weren't going to see Barack Obama and they had just wasted five hours of their life. I still held out hope, but it was fading quickly. The VIP doors were now the main focus of the entire crowd instead and not the rest of the entrances which were suddenly closed.

Barack Obama and Joe Biden, who I also was looking forward to seeing speak, were in the building and I was still outside. People were now barging to the front and were demanding to get in. For a second I felt like saying 'Hey, I'm a VIP' but I stopped myself. The crowd would hardly part like the red sea and say 'We've got an Australian who needs to get in, let him pass." I have pushed in enough queues, blagged enough bouncers and sneaked in enough back doors in my time not to be precious about queue-jumpers.

A voice came over the tannoy: "Please be calm." I looked behind me and there was a sea of faces far into the distance. All of them pissed off. Suddenly the line was a distant memory and I was in the middle of a throng thousands deep. Then one of the funniest, most irresponsible and dangerous things I've ever witnessed happened. Adjacent to the entrance doors was an emergency exit with flights of stairs behind it. Behind the glass doors a teenager in a fast food outlet uniform sauntered up them. I spotted him early, thought 'Lucky bastard' and watched his face as he peered out a thousands of faces looking back at him. "Open the door," someone shouted.

I felt my body tense. This could be my only chance to see Obama, and I presumed that he'd open the door so that if he did I'd have a decent chance of getting in. When Oasis played Maine Road I'd bought a ticket for the first concert but couldn't remember a thing, so I went down the next night and decided to try and 'do the doors'. I ended up following the moodiest scallies I saw and ran in with them after they broke down an emergency exit. It was one of the best nights of my life. If it took bending the rules in order to be part of history then so be it. I hadn't come this far to miss out on Barack Obama because the wrong bloody colour wristbands had got lost.

Again came the shout: "Open the door!" The kid looked about 16-years-old, was afro-Caribbean and wore his cap at an angle with a burger in his hand. He smiled and pretended to open the door, and let out a wonderful giggle. He went to walk up the stairs, turned his head and must have thought those two wonderful words 'Fuck it'. He grinned and nonchalantly pushed the emergency exit door open.
Now, this was an act that could technically have led to the death of hundreds of people, but there was something wonderful about that moment. He broke the rules, he did something he shouldn't have and then he revelled in the brief limelight. However, the look on his face when the shriek went up as the door opened and thousands of crazed Obama fans stampeded was priceless. He was shit scared.

It was every man, woman, pensioner, child and teenager for themselves in a mad dash for the door. All I can say is animal instinct took over as I leapt towards it. I was about five metres away and about ten people had already got in and were jumping around in ecstasy. I managed to get a hand on the frame of the door and watched as an old woman elbowed a man in the guts to pass him. A woman let out a scream that was so full of pain it chilled me to the bone. I looked down to my right and saw a pushchair on the floor that people were jumping on and across to the door. I turned my head and there looked like thousands of people behind me. I was hanging on the frame for dear life, pushing people aside to get closer to the opening.

In one move I jumped on someone's thigh as leverage and spiralled through the door. My adrenaline was pumping and when I landed on the floor inside I felt a surge of relief, not for being in the venue at last but because I was out of the crush. I ran up the stairs, gathered myself and couldn't believe my luck. I'd got inside, through sheer bloody mindedness and without a thought for my own safety, or (I'm embarrassed to say) anyone else's. There were about 20 of us on the stairs and we all hugged each other and looked out as people were fighting to get inside the door, before some bright spark opened another one and people poured in. We ran excitedly up the stairs feeling on top of the world. I tried to get my camera out to record what I was witnessing but it wasn't working. We kept on running until we got to the top and there was a door into the auditorium. Needless to say it was locked. I'd risked life and limb for a locked door!

There was nowhere to go but back down the stairs. I looked down the gap between the flights and there looked like thousands of people rushing up the stairs, with the sound of shouting and feet pounding concrete everywhere. I immediately thought of the Hillsborough disaster, as it was a confined space with thousands of people pouring into the stairwell. I assumed if I made the wrong decisions in the next five minutes I could be dead. Now, looking back I must admit I was a bit of a prat because it's harder to get crushed to death going upwards than it is going down, but the danger seemed real enough.

Screams filled the stairwell as people were meeting others coming down. I was shouting 'It's locked, we can't get in', but no-one was listening. I battled down a few flights of stairs and noticed a ledge above me and figured if I could jump up on to that then I wouldn't be killed. I jumped on the hand rail and was ready to try and leap up on to the ledge when I noticed a flash of brown on my right hand side. It was the police, with batons.

I've never been so happy to be attacked by a baton wielding police officer in all my life. The police rushed down the stairs screaming and swinging, pushing people back. Everyone did an about turn and ran down the stairs, me included. I got my phone out and thought I'd do some mini-videos. I looked through the glass doors as I was escorted out and saw Caesar. He jumped up and waved at me, mouthing 'Well done' for getting in. I started videoing myself and doing a piece to camera but was thrown out by security as I was doing so.

When I got outside I linked up with Caesar and Suzie and then got interviewed by a Miami TV station. I spoke slowly and peppered it with quotes like 'I could have been killed' and 'I'm just glad to be alive'. We walked back to the car, but the disappointment about missing Obama had been forgotten because the adrenaline was still pumping. Fighting my way into that open emergency exit was like football violence, raving and sex all rolled in to one and as I'm no good at the previous three it was one hell of a life experience to say the least.

On the front line

The phone rang in the Miami South Beach Obama office - the ring tone was the familiar Ode to Joy, which seemed to be continuously playing - and Mark answered.

"Yep...Ok...great...yeah we're off Ocean Drive...really? Ok, well we're open from 10am to 10pm."

Mark put the phone down and uttered the immortal words:

"He's the Jewish Elvis."

My ears perked up: "He's the what?"

Mark answered like he'd had a conversation with a Jewish Elvis a thousand times before. "Yeah, he said he was in New York and wanted to fly down and help out, then said he was the Jewish Elvis."

Now, God love Barack Obama, and I really do hope he makes the world a better place, but campaigning with The Jewish Elvis is my kind of politics. The first time I met the Kosher King (real name Willard Morgan) was the day I returned safe and sound from the Obama rally. I knocked on the office door to find out where Mark and Kale had gone for a beer and he opened it. I gasped; perhaps because I was worse for wear, I thought it was Dustin Hoffman.

Willard had been the rally and had had more luck than me. He told me that Mark and Kale had gone off to a sports bar, so still dazed I joined them to watch their basketball team The Oakland Warriors lose. "I've just seen a Dustin Hoffman lookalike at the office," I told the pair. "Nah, that must have been Jelvis," they replied.

I should have known, he had a certain star quality.

The next day, after spending three hours in HSBC begging some idiot in their Indian call centre for my money to be transferred, I went to work determined to help Barack Obama get elected. After eating some humongous beef sandwiches, dropped off at the office for the troops, I hit the phones. My success rate was not as I'd hoped, mainly due to those answering the phones not understanding a word I said, but I carried on regardless. However, this would be the day I would get my first taste of campaigning on the front line.

Again Beethoven's ditty went off, and Mark picked up first. He asked: "Is there anyone free to go to the polls? We're outnumbered." Before his question had even finished I'd volunteered. After all, I wasn't setting the world alight on the phones. In Florida voting had started two weeks before the vote, because of the controversy over voter exclusion in the past, and the interest was so high people were queuing for hours to cast their vote. To give Obama supporters, who were more likely not used to voting, encouragement we needed volunteers at the polls to prevent harassment from Republicans.

Mark explained that the Republicans pay people to stand outside the polls all day waving placards and shouting slogans, whereas the Democrats don't. Florida's role in the disputed 2000 election was never far from the mind of any Democratic volunteer because of all the dirty tricks, the disenfranchisement of poor blacks and voter intimidation that lead to Gore losing the state. No-one wanted a repeat of that monumental injustice, and everyone was doing everything in their power to stop that happening again, be it the hundreds of lawyers who flew to Florida from across America to act as witnesses at polls or volunteers like me who just wanted to help.

When I arrived, there were hundreds of people snaking around the building waiting to take part in the biggest election in a generation and the average wait was well over an hour. Mark said: "Go and find Ophelia - you can't miss her. She'll tell you what to do, and don't take no shit. Thanks for helping, buddy."

In front of the town hall there were six or seven Republicans and other groups I didn't recognise shouting slogans and waving placards. There was only one visible Democrat, a light skinned black lady in her fifties who wore her hair in pigtails, and she was delighted when I introduced myself. "I'm Adam, what can I do to help?" She said with a smile: "Wow, what an accent. I'm Ophelia, and we're being outnumbered." We walked over to what looked like a changing area for political activists, a walled flowerbed filled with countless placards with different slogans, bags full of badges and different flags. She dug out a big 'Obama – Biden' sign, handed it to me and told me to stand on the corner of the intersection outside the town hall.

"Is that it?" I asked. "Yeah, at the moment that's all you need to do. It's all about visibility, it'll be a great help and it will stop them lot getting fresh," she said, pointing to the Republicans. She whispered in a conspiratorial way: "They get dropped off and picked up by the same guy in an unmarked SUV every day. They're paid, so watch them like a hawk, they'll try anything. They aren't supposed to have that flag on that lawn, but they're being allowed to. I've already complained about it to the electing officer." No political paraphernalia was allowed on the town hall grounds and even some voters with Obama t-shirts were being turned back, so the McCain flag stuck in the front lawn pissed Ophelia off. She smiled at me and said: "Here's some water. It's going to be hot."

I walked to the corner of the intersection and held up my 'Obama – Biden' placard. No longer than 10 seconds later there was a chorus of boos and hisses. I span round and for the first time took a long look at the three Republicans standing about 10 yards from me. They were a funny looking bunch. A man and a woman in their sixties and what must have been their special needs son. He looked about thirty but his mom and had dressed him up as a teenager and though handicapped was singing his heart out for McCain: "MA-CAIN, MA-CAIN, MA-CAIN HE SO GOOD".

They all had McCain placards and wore so many pin badges they would have fetched a pretty sum at a scrap dealer. The father had a Cuban hat and the mother a Cuban t-shirt. I was shocked at the booing and hissing but I wasn't going to let anyone know they'd got to me, so I gave them a big smile and said: "Hello. Nice day for it." They bit, the special needs son frothed at the mouth and shouted something which I couldn't understand, the dad whistled and the mother shouted "traitor."

I was over the moon. This was proper front line campaigning.

Before I could shout something back a car drove past me, honked and the driver gave me the thumbs up. I waved back. He got a load of abuse ten yards up the road from the Republicans. For the next few hours we tried to get people to beep us, and Americans being Americans, there was lots of beeping. When you're on strike, campaigning or protesting and someone beeps at you, though a small gesture, it means a lot and that's why I always beep strikers. The difference between me and the world's weirdest political dynasty was that if someone beeped them I didn't boo and hiss - I'd just smile.

I comforted myself that I was a good representative of the Obama campaign: young, enthusiastic, happy go lucky and giving my time for free whilst the Republicans were old, a bit weird, being paid and had a nasty streak. It was about five beeps to one in favour of me and people were hanging out of their cars cheering for Obama. Old, young, black, white, gay and straight, the diverse nature of his supporters was an inspiration. The only people jeering me were all over 40-years-old and white or Cuban. Then a middle-aged woman with thin lips drove past in a Buick and yelled 'Baby killer!' at me.

The three Republicans cheered and shouted 'Baby killer' at me too. I suppose I should have been shocked, hurt or otherwise upset, but I was delighted. This was the campaign experience I wanted. I wasn't going to be abusive but I enjoy the wind up, and they were fair game. It was a license to be offensive for the right reasons, and there was no way I'd lose my temper - everything I said and did would have a smile attached. That's why I put two fingers up and mouthed: "Two babies! I've paid for two abortions, just couldn't afford any kids. Easy peasy." Then I mimed giving birth and kicking a baby across the road - ensuring only those three saw me. It seemed a quite funny at the time. I'd just like to point I've never got anyone pregnant, let alone paid for an abortion, but I just wanted to wind the bad guys up. And it worked.

The woman came running over, her face contorted with anger, and started shouting that I would go to hell and all Obama fans were 'baby killers'. I thanked her for praying for me and but told her that a woman's body was hers to do with it how she pleased. I added: "How can an atheist woman be denied an abortion because someone who believes in a God passes a law? It's bonkers bab." This very reasonable argument was greeted with one of the strangest insults I've ever been treated to. "You scum, Cuba hater, you hate Cuba, you scum!" By this time the special needs son was covered in dribble and shouting 'Kennedy, Kennedy!' and the dad was calling me 'Kennedy scum' too

How do you reply to that? I start a nice debate about abortion, then I'm compared to the iconic JFK. What would the next insult be? That I sing like Elvis Presley or play guitar like Hendrix? Something clicked and my mouth was off. "How the fuck can you blame me for the Bay of Pigs? I wasn't even born then and I could hardly help out from England, could I?" They all crossed themselves at the same time when I said the word 'fuck' and spat on the floor when I said Castro wasn't all bad.

The worst thing about it all was that the special needs son was now covered in spit, sweating buckets and looking on the verge of tears. In the last ten years I've done fundraising for disabled groups, set up Sutton and Erdington Disabled Against Charges (SEDAC) and worked with Sandwell and Dudley Vulnerable Against Cuts (SADVAC) and carried out investigative journalism on behalf of the disabled in Birmingham. That's why it made me sick that this poor sod had been dressed up like a neo-con mascot, indoctrinated with generational hate and forced to stand in the boiling heat for hours on end for cash.

I was getting angry at the parents because of their poor son but kept my cool and said: "Look, piss off over your side of the grass and leave me alone. Oh, and Obama is going to win." They hissed and retreated.

The whole Cuba thing had got me thinking and I was glad I was pretty up to speed on the different political battles in Florida. This is when I realised that Ophelia and I were really outnumbered. Because though there were only six or seven overt McCain supporters there were other groups campaigning on right wing issues or for local Republican candidates. One strange looking and extremely vocal bunch were campaigning against an amendment in the Florida constitution to allow same sex marriage in the state. I tried to work out exactly what I was for and what I was against in case I got in a debate at the polls. Saying I'm an Obama fan just wouldn't cut it.

So I had a chat with Ophelia.
"Right, obviously I'm a pro-Obama Democrat, I'm pro-gay without being gay so that means I'm pro-amendment 10. I believe in a woman's right to abort a child but do I really have to say pro-abortion - it's not as if I'm going to go round demanding more abortions is it? Pro-life sounds better, doesn't it? They won the PR battle on that one."

Ophelia laughed: "Baby, you're pro-choice."

"Ok, what about Cuba? I've got a bit of sneaking admiration for Fidel Castro but obviously don't agree with repression, but think its two faced for America to deal with China and not Cuba when there are massive human rights issues."

She laughed: "In Miami, just keep any thoughts about Cuba to yourself baby."

I replied: "And am I also supposed to be supporting (Democrat) Raul Martinez in the Florida race, the bloke who's on that advert every night beating someone up?"

Ophelia laughed again and rolled her eyes about the advert, but said: "It's a dirty fight that one, but yes you are for him, and you're for Tapia, right?"

I said: "Tapas! Yep I'm starving." Unfortunately it wasn't lunch - Tapia was a Latino lady standing in the local elections.

I chatted more to Ophelia. She'd been suspended from her job as a waitress because an argument with a colleague about Obama. Being suspended, however, had given her time to volunteer for the campaign and she was happy with the outcome. So for two weeks she turned up every day at the town hall to hold up her placards and encourage people to vote. Ophelia had been the target of some abuse but she was determined to do her bit to help Obama win. And that's what I loved about the Obama campaign. So many people just decided to help out and picked a job that suited them and got a lot of satisfaction from trying to change the world.

Ben was another volunteer who made a difference. He was a cool dude in his late thirties who'd seen Ophelia outnumbered and when he'd cast his ballot asked if she needed help. He phoned his wife to explain he'd be late, then spent the next five hours doing a visibility shift, and was back again the next day with his wife in tow.

When I asked why he was helping he gave a great answer: "I want to be able to sleep at night. I mean if McCain wins and I did nothing to help Obama then I couldn't forgive myself, the last eight years have been a disaster." I told him about the 'baby killer' row and he laughed and said he'd been called 'nigger-lover' twice the day before.

It got me thinking about what I'd say if someone called me a nigger-lover. Being a fan of the tan I've been it called a few times before, so I was looking forward to being ultra-offensive to some racist twat. I got my chance a few days later. I'd had it shouted at me from people in a car but that's no fun because you can't look in to the whites of their eyes and give them grief back. An unpleasant man, white and aged about fifty in brown trousers and a beige t-shirt came wandering towards me while I was on my corner. I offered him an Obama badge. He didn't say a thing, just looked me up and down.

I was wearing my yellow Obama t-shirt with Caribbean flags on it, which must have been like a red rag to a bull. He was about five yards from me and in a low voice so no-one else could hear him - probably because 20 yards away there was the ballot queue with a hell of a lot of black faces in it - said: "You make me sick, you fucking nigger-lover." Quick as a flash I smiled and replied: "You're right mate, I am a nigger-lover. My missus is black and I love her. (Which was true)
"And you know what? We're a hell of a lot closer since she got over her third abortion, we couldn't afford a new TV if we had kids." (That was untrue)

His face was a picture after the first line but the second one brought an absolute look of disgust and he let out a gasp. He was losing his temper and not very originally he called me a 'nigger-lovin' baby-killer'. Now I was ad-libbing, unlike the first line which I had ready when Ben told me he'd been insulted in racial terms. I'm fairly quick-witted, but sometimes surprise myself what comes out my mouth when under pressure.

In a Brummie accent I asked: "So you wouldn't let Beyonce or Naomi Campbell suck your cock?" Not bad eh? Then I followed it up with: "So you're gay then right? I should have known wearing them trousers, have you come to back the same sex marriage amendment? Good on you, I'm not gay but what two men in a locked room do with two erections is no business of mine. But I'll let you know when I have got some black-heads on my bum need squeezing."

Which I figured was about as offensive as you can get to a highly strung racist homophobic anti-abortion fundamentalist Christian with bad dress sense. His face screamed hatred and he was bigger than me, so I instinctively stepped back as I figured he was about to 'get physical'. As I retreated I used my wits and the oldest trick in the book. I pointed behind him and said 'Police'.

There were a few officers around, not taking any notice, but I'd sensed my opportunity. I didn't want to get into a fight because as a foreigner I'd probably be nicked, so I learned forward and said: "Fuck off or I'll tell the police you called me a nigger-lover." He stopped in his tracks and said something like 'I'll see you around', then stormed off. It was a sweet moment. Using playground tactics from Perry Barr I beat an American arsehole all ends up.

Yep, as you may have guessed I was the annoying kid at school who'd keep on teasing someone until they grabbed me, at which point I'd beg for forgiveness or feign an asthma attack. Then when they let me go and I was out of reach I'd start all over again. Anyway, hopefully he went home and told his wife, if he had one, that "I met this nigger-loving, homo-loving, baby-killing Australian Barack Obama fan today who accused me of being a fag, then tried to get me arrested. This country is going down the pan."

It was great fun at the polls. It was tiring and sometimes a bit boring standing on an intersection but I loved it because it felt I was making a difference. Lots of people came over for a badge after casting their vote and I had fascinating conversations with Americans fresh from the ballot box. The biggest enemy of politics is apathy and it was so refreshing hearing people over the moon because they had been given the chance to take part in democracy. It was as if so many people didn't believe they would get the chance to vote because of political corruption. Amazing, really, considering America is a superpower and not a banana republic. I particularly loved chatting to black voters who had given up on their country after being denied the vote in previous elections but had proudly voted. Although I wasn't working as a journalist I still noted down interesting stuff because I was still sending copy back to Birmingham most nights.

At the end of my first day something weird happened. The Republican family packed up their McCain signs, calmly walked past me and, nice as pie, all said: "Goodbye, have a nice day, see you tomorrow." I was flabbergasted, and even more so the next day when they all said "Hello" when they saw me walk to my corner, but as soon as I picked up my Obama sign started booing and hissing. I don't know why but it all seemed to make sense, like two boxers beating the hell out of one another then embracing after the bell.

When I think back of campaigning for Obama those days outside the Miami Town Hall were some of the happiest, whether it was seeing Ophelia scold the Republican family for taking her water or when she pulled the disabled son out of the road then shouted 'Don't call me a baby killer again, I've just saved your son!". So many wonderful memories - it was political campaigning, but not as we know it! If I thought all that was strange, though, nothing could have prepared me for the call: "Are you guys still outnumbered? Jelvis is coming down with 20 dudes from Denmark."

I was the only Brummie in the Miami Obama campaign and that made me proud. In fact I've yet to hear of another one even now, anywhere in America, but I've no doubt there would have been some crazy ex-pat Brummie helping out somewhere.

I love educating people about Birmingham, whether it's telling them the city has more trees than Paris and more canals than Venice or that Brummies are up there with the Greeks, Persians and the Romans because the industrial revolution started in Brum. We changed the world. But anyway I was the only Brit I'd met on the campaign at that time; I'd heard there was a delegation from the Labour Party knocking about but I had no desire to meet any fellow Brits, as I see them every day of my normal life. Karim was the only Belgian I met. There were other European students who passed through the campaign, but when Jelvis turned up at the polls with a minibus full of strapping Danish Obama volunteers my jaw dropped to the floor. I mean individuals like myself, from all over America and abroad, were common enough but a job lot of Scandinavians? Madness.

All of them were beautiful looking in that clean way people from that part of the world are; both the men and the women seemed over six foot, all with blonde hair, blue eyes, and carefree smiles and seeming to be in their early 20s. They looked like they'd just walked out of a Gap advert. The Obama campaign was certainly winning the beauty contest anyway. The strange Republican supporters' faces were priceless when they saw the Danes picking up Obama gear - they were dumbstruck. Jelvis, who was in his civvies, waved goodbye, winked and said: "About 20 of them have turned up to help in North Beach. I heard you guys needed to help so I thought I'd drop some down. Have fun!"

The Danes bounded over and told Ophelia and I they were here to help. Ophelia was like the cat that got the cream. She chatted to three of them and before long she was in a deep conversation about the Miami Beach Town Hall Republican flag conspiracy.
Meanwhile I spoke to the other two.
"What do we have to do?" said a Claudia Schiffer lookalike wearing shorts and a khaki top, standing next to what looked like her identical male twin.
Scratching my head, trying to look cool in a European way but realising my trainers were falling apart and reeking in a way only tropical heat sweating feet can, I picked some posters up and said: "Hold these and just stand around, it's all about the visibility bab."
"Wow, are you Australian?" she said.
"No, I am a fellow European. I'm English, from the city of Birmingham," I replied.
"Awesome," they both replied.
We had a nice chat. It appeared there were about 25 of them and they were in Miami anyway on some trip or another and wanted to help out and be part of history. They were so optimistic and enthusiastic.

The Danish were set for day in a non-descript office so were delighted the call came to help out at the front line. I don't think they believed me when I told them about the nigger-loving and baby-killing jibes; they seemed so innocent so I didn't tell them about me miming drop kicking babies. I didn't want them to think I was weird.

Needless to say they were getting a hell of lot of honks and beeps. Ophelia was over the moon, she just kept on coming over and hugging me and counting all of us and saying we'd outnumbered the McCain supporters, the other Republicans and the anti-gay protestors put together. Standing on my corner I had time to think, something I never really get chance to do at home.

My journalist radar was twitching. I was thinking about what I could write about the campaign.

Facebook status: **Steve Zacharanda** was getting called a baby killer by McCain supporters then the Danish turned up with the Jewish Elvis and everything was fine...

Letters from America

The morning I met the Scandinavians I checked my email and there was an email from my boss back home:

Hi Adam,

Pass on my regards to Mr Obama.
I'm afraid I can't get anyone to do your weekend duty. I thought you had sorted this.
I'm afraid I will have to ask you to come back for Saturday and Sunday.
We'll leave you a list of weekend jobs.

Many thanks,
Andy

I read it again and again. I even thought, 'Shit, how am I going to get home for the weekend shift?' Then I laughed out loud. I cursed myself for not getting someone to cover my weekend; it had crossed my mind briefly before leaving for Miami but as it was a bit of a spur of the moment decision, and I didn't really believe I'd make it there anyway, it was just one of the many practicalities that were left in England when I jumped on the plane.

I read the email again and chuckled. Andy and I had a long history and this was just another chapter. He was the toughest boss I had ever encountered in my career, but he was fair. He gave me the two best lines anyone had ever said to me in a workplace:
- "You gave me the best interview I have ever seen in journalism. Now you've got the job I feel violently mugged."
- After turning up to some editorial meeting two hours late: "I wish to God I had never laid eyes on you. I have the horrible feeling that I will go down as the idiot who hired Adam Smith."

The last thing he said to me before I left for America, besides saying Barack Obama must be in trouble if he needed my help, was: "I just hope you won't cause an international incident when you're in Miami."

If truth be known I would have ran through walls for him, though. If there was a job no one else would do, I would always give up my own time to help him out. He cared about the Mail and every local newspaper in the country would be in trouble if there were not people like him.

Gurdip Thandi, former colleague

I opened my inbox and got an email from Andy saying Adam was in Miami and had a weekend to do, and that he was 'unlikely to return' for the shift.
I think there probably was a collective sigh in the newsroom when they opened that email because it was no surprise Adam would have forgotten.

I'm not sure who did the shift that I forgot but I would like to take the opportunity to thank them now. Anyway, the crux of the matter was that Miami was a holiday. Simple as that. However, as a journalist I would have been mad not to want to cover such a pivotal election; however, as I wasn't getting paid for it I was going to cover it on my own terms.

When I was at the Great Barr Observer, thanks to two wonderful bosses called Sam Holliday and Gary Phelps, I was given a month off to travel the length of New York state with the Rotary Club, talking about Birmingham and visiting newspapers as I went. The papers I had visited all printed 'An Englishman in New York' piece and their editors seemed to enjoy them. My own stable of papers at CIN had published 'Adam's Big Apple', a letter from America every week, which readers liked. I knew there was no chance the Mail would give me the freedom to do that. To tell you the truth I think they took all my Obama talk with a pinch of salt and didn't think I'd end up getting out there, and I can't blame them. Nonetheless I kept the news desk up to speed with my delays in getting into America, but received no reply. For the first week I sent stories religiously and I was proud of them. Then I found out they were not all being published, although something had been published because everyone on Facebook making fun of my cowboy hat picture.

I was also trying to set a blog up but whoever was dealing with that seemed to be dragging their feet. I sent my copy to colleagues who I respect and they couldn't understand why it wasn't being printed, but I was on holiday so that wasn't my concern, despite being a little narked. I mainly sent pieces back because I knew that for the people from the areas I grew up in or around, namely Perry Barr and Handsworth, the American election was big news and people were engaged. They wanted to read about the election in the Mail. In the end, though, I just gave up, as I wasn't about to bust my balls and end up with nothing in print to show for it.

That's why as the holiday progressed I became more and more detached from my news desk. I'd taken redundancy anyway and my stuff wasn't getting published so I threw myself into my work with the Obama campaign. Tony Larner at the Sunday Mercury (now doing a fine job on the Birmingham Mail) was great, though, and asked if I could send a feature. I was delighted when it went in word for word in the Mercury. Here it is:

Adam Smith
In Miami

A terrified mother's scream filled the air as the manic crowd trampled over her baby's pushchair to catch a glimpse of Barack Obama. It was every man, woman, pensioner and child for themselves as they fought each other to get in to an opened emergency exit of Miami's Bank Atlantic centre. The exhilaration I felt when I got into the venue was simply breathtaking and everyone was hugging and cheering as we dashed up the stairs. But when we got to the top the doors were locked and if the police had not had intervened there was a real chance we would have been crushed to death by the oncoming thousands.

All this just to get in to a political meeting. Over thirty thousand people had queued for five hours and more to see the remarkable Democratic presidential candidate speak.
But only 19,000 people could get in to see the televised speech which was broadcast on all the major networks in a bid to win the most important American election in a generation. The majority of people at the rally had never been to a political event in their lives but Barack has caught the imagination of so many parts of American society.

Former President Bill Clinton summed it up standing next to Barack Obama at a 40,000 strong rally a few hours later in Orlando.
He said: "Look around you, have you ever seen such a diverse crowd in one place, there is every type of American here, even old grey haired men like me.
"This campaign is bringing Americans together like no campaign ever before and it is wonderful to see all ages and all races together fighting for change in this great country."

In the Miami South Beach office weary Californian Mark is coordinating jobs for the volunteers. These can include phoning voters, offering lifts to vote, selling t-shirts and tracing Obama pictures on to pumpkins. Also holding signs at polling stations just yards from McCain supporters where volunteers run the risk of either being hugged to death or having 'babykiller and niggerlover' screamed at them.
Mark said: "It is crazy out here on South Beach, 25 Danish students just turned up to help with a Jewish Elvis Impersonator who wears a jump suit with St David stars on it.
"So many people want to help and give their time to ensure Barack Obama wins, the next few days are just going to be unbelievable, and we are seeing history unfold in front of our eyes."
In swing states like Florida, where there are 200,000 volunteers, it is impossible to get away from the election with a constant stream of adverts on

television, radio and the internet. There are new polls everyday which range from predicting an Obama landslide to a difference of three per cent to the Democrats. There is even a nationwide coffee cup poll run by 7-11 shops where customers can buy either McCain or Obama coffee cups, the Democratic candidate is winning that one 60 per cent to 40 per cent.

The significance of this election is hammered home every day to American voters.
There could be the first mixed race president just fifty years after the civil rights movement, the first woman vice president and the banning of abortion, the future of the economy, the composition of the supreme court and the Iraq war are all in the balance. The eyes of America are on Florida after the recount fiasco of 2000 which handed the presidency to George Bush. Voters are already queuing for up to five hours to vote early in Florida and all everything points to a massive turnout on Tuesday which will severely test the official electoral apparatus.

There have already been several stories about voter suppression with poorer areas having out of date equipment and African-American voters being asked to bring social security records in order to vote. And everyone is talking about the election.
The fat Latino man next to me at a Miami barbers lay impassively as the Cuban barber shaved a perfect goatee beard. The customer in the scruffy Miami barber shop never said a word but it took five minutes for me to read all his tattoos.
My barber never stopped talking.

He and his colleague could have been chatting about the election none stop but I wouldn't have known because they were speaking continuously in Spanish.
The Cuban flags, Latino Playboy magazines and the comedy cigars are a familiar sight in Miami due to its massive Cuban population.
Juan, my barber, who was from Panama, piped up in English as soon as the election was mentioned by another goatee bearded customer, Mike.
He said: "I like McCain, he is a good man, he fought for his country and is a true hero, but I just cannot understand why he picked that crazy lady Palin when he is that old, she is mad and could be President."

The phrase 'one heartbeat from the presidency' is one that is repeated every day in America and Vice President hopeful Sarah Palin is never far from conversations about the election. The remarkable mother of five from Alaska whose lack of world knowledge was shown up in a series of legendary national interviews is currently the butt of a massively popular parody on Saturday Night Live. She even appeared on the show along the actress that plays her,

Tina Fey, last week.

On the more liberal East and West coasts of America, which includes Miami, New York, Boston, Los Angeles and San Francisco she is a figure of fun. Hustler's Larry Flint has even released a pornographic film called 'Who's Nailin Palin'.

However, in states like Kentucky, Tennessee, Iowa and Montana further in to the country her bible based politics are a massive hit with more rural and small town voters.

Her rallies attract tens of thousands of fanatical Republican supporters, as she is much more popular than John McCain in her party, and she is a consummate communicator that millions of voters can relate to. She wants to scrap legal abortions, opposes abortions of pregnancies conceived through rape and incest and in Alaska demanded Creationism be taught in schools. Her selection was a massive boost to the McCain campaign but as the weeks have gone by the Democrats have hammered home the 'one heartbeat' argument and now polls are showing she is not gaining the female voters who wanted Hilary Clinton as president.

And in the big cities it is the anti-abortion stance is often her undoing. Daniella King, a 32-year-old living in Miami's South Beach, said: "It is just madness to think that abortion could be made illegal. It would be a backward step for America and would be unworkable and would see a return to back street abortions that my parents told me about."
She added: "I understand the pro-life argument but to ban abortions to women raped and victims of incest to me is very offensive."

But whatever happens in the election, America will not lose its love - hate fascination with Sarah Palin. The consensus in the barber shop, as with most voters I have spoken to in Miami, is that Obama will win by a landslide but life in decadent Latino Miami could not be further than rural America where the electoral landscape is radically different. Despite Obama's growing poll lead the nagging worry for Democrats is that the Palin inspired Republicans will get organised and get their voters out in massive numbers on polling day. Whereas the Democrats are relying on poorer and younger voters to get out and vote, both groups have let them down in the past. Whoever wins, it is sure to be a close shave.

Well, history has since shown that it wasn't a close shave at all, but in the campaign no-one dared speak of a landslide and no-one dared speak of defeat. Though Miami was safely for Obama, the rest of Florida was not, so a volunteer in Miami was working just as hard as elsewhere in the state because every single voted counted. Another example of how I left my journalist hat at home was the chance I had to write a story that could have gone national in America.

Standing on my corner watching the Danish volunteers got me thinking. The fact the Miami South Beach office had an International Brigade (I made the name up as a jokey nod to the Spanish Civil War and my Communist Grandad) would have been a great story for the Miami papers and could easily have been picked up by the national networks. However, Fox News would have an absolute field day with the fact that foreigners were helping Barack Obama. So I left it, even though I knew it would have been great for my CV.

There were a few reasons, one of which was that I never got round to doing it, but the main sticking point was that I would have hated going into the office I loved and pissed off people I liked and respected for damaging the cause.

Alexander the Great

Money was getting tight. I was still getting $400 every four or five days from the bank, even though it did take hours each time phoning all manner of shit HSBC call centres. I also had no idea how much was left because of the exchange rate. It was like Russian Roulette every time I went to the bank. I should have just transferred all my money into Sam's account, as that would have solved so many problems.

I knew I didn't have enough money for any more hotels after my wages ran out. What was weird is that my wages lasted longer in Miami than in Birmingham - but then again I had cancelled all my direct debits and dodged my rent.

I had opted to stay a few more nights at my concrete floored Argentinean paradise, and I was getting desperate for free accommodation. Then I got an email I'd been waiting for from the Miami Tourist Board. A hotel had responded to the E-blast. The Alexander Hotel, North Beach, which was about a twenty minute walk from where I was staying, had said I could stay for three nights. Perfect. I went to the bank and got $400 out of the bank as I knew I needed cash for a deposit for the room.

I checked out of my place and was hit with a massive phone bill. About $70 I think. I'd committed the cardinal sin. I'd used the hotel room phone to ring home. The amount of times I've done the same thing made me even more annoyed. Then again the phone call was to HSBC to cancel my direct debits (I'd quickly learned I could phone for free at the bank) and to my girlfriend who'd I'd left home. I wanted to do a bunk but the hotel reception had my passport, so I paid the bill, bid my farewell to the Argentineans, jumped into a cab and headed to the Alexander.

We drove up Collins Avenue for about a mile, then around a corner where I was greeted with the sight of about six hotels, all looked if they were built in the sixties or seventies, in a row. It was like something in the Costa del Sol. I couldn't help but laugh when the cab pulled into a giant 1970s pink multi-story hotel: The Alexander Hotel. An elderly gentleman in a bell boy uniform immediately took hold of my battered case, said hello and opened the door in to the lobby. The lobby was gigantic and my eyes tried to take in all the oak wood, gold knobs and claret carpets.

I was impressed and amused at the décor, and I certainly wasn't about to complain as it was free. Then my stomach turned. I realised this could be a tricky situation because I had no credit card - I bet Alan Wicker never had that problem. I collected myself, straightened my back and confidently strode to the reception leaving my battered case with the bell boy so as not to ruin my image.

"Can I help you?" said the formidable looking middle aged black receptionist. I spoke slowly and in my best accent. "Hello, my name is Adam Smith, I am here to write a travel feature about this hotel, the Miami Tourist Board should have reserved my room." I knew what was coming next.
"Can I have your credit card please?" she said.
"I haven't got one." I said simply.
She looked at me as though I'd just asked if I could take a young child up to my room and butcher them to death.
"You haven't got a credit card Sir? How so?"
I said: "I just haven't got one for this trip I'm afraid. Why, it isn't going to be problem is it?" I asked as if I was shocked by her shock, before adding "It's no problem in Europe; I thought the customer was always right in America."
She disappeared somewhere before coming back and saying I'd have to pay a cash deposit. I pulled out sweat stained, creased up bank notes and gave them to her.

I felt relieved to get my keys. I got the lift to my floor and wandered up and down corridors before finally finding my room. Well I say room - it was a three room hotel suite. Everything was in beige and other shades of brown. All it needed was a space hopper in the corner and I would have thought I'd stepped back in to 1976. I ran and jumped on the bed with delight. It even had a kitchen. OK, the lights didn't work, but it was still a kitchen. I put some tunes on the radio, cracked open a beer, sat on the balcony, had a fag and felt like a king. And then chuckled about where I was going that night. The Versace Mansion.

Who to take though? A small part of me wanted to take Donamarie Baptiste, the stunningly beautiful rum saleswoman, who'd said to give her a ring to party. A ticket to the Versace Mansion would have been an incentive to listen to me talk shite all night. But, no, there was only one person to take. Sam, from Stoke, who lives in Miami, who'd saved me from walking 20 miles to South Beach on the first night, and who had lent me money. She also happens to be pretty stunning, intelligent, funny and can dance. I phoned her up.
"Alright Sam, Adam here. I've got an invite to a party at the Versace mansion tomorrow night. Wanna come?

She laughed: "I've lived here for nearly a year and I've never got in for a party. You're here for five minutes and blag yourself straight in, typical!"
It turned out she could make it anyway. As I sat on the balcony of my free 1970s heaven I realised it could be a great night, and that finally it was time to hit the clubs of Miami.

Facebook status: Steve Zacharanda is in a 1970s beige and brown heaven in his freebie hotel for three nights, off to the Versace mansion masquerade ball tonight!

I ironed my old work trousers, put my trusty v-neck top on, did a bit of that grooming stuff, jumped in a cab and picked Sam up. She looked a million dollars. We walked up to the Versace gates on Ocean Drive, resisted the touristy temptation to have a photo where the great man had been murdered, and spoke to the tuxedo wearing gentleman with the clipboard.
"Mr Adam Smith, plus one." I said.
He looked down the list of names and found my name. Relief swept over me.
"Welcome Mr Smith, have a great night."

We strolled through the front door into the mansion. The first courtyard looked like a restaurant and every diner looked like a film star. We were shown through to the steps of another courtyard where we were greeted by a great looking Latino lady who told us to 'pick a mask', and stepped down into the central courtyard. There were mosaics on the floor, a giant swimming pool that all manner of celebrities must have taken a naked dip in, beautifully ornate statues, palm trees, jacuzzis and most importantly – a free bar. It was wonderful to think that I, a Brummie hack, was standing where Princess Diana, Naomi Campbell and Kate Moss partied and frolicked the night away.

The crowd was wonderfully cool, less false and plastic than California, more laid back than New York and ten times less pretentious than Birmingham. There was a great mix of white, black and Latin revellers all enjoying the beautiful summer's night.
Call me arrogant but Sam and I didn't look out of place among the Miami set, although I doubt anyone else was hiding holes in their shoes. There were games to play, cocktail stands, people in fancy dress and, of course, decks spinning house music.

We met Freddie, who was basking in the achievement of organising a great event, and dressed as a pimp. We met other journalists and we drank more free cocktails, and then some more. Everyone I spoke to was interested that I'd come to Miami to volunteer for Obama. I tried to convince all of them to volunteer. To some people it was the promise to be part of history; however, to others it was the promise of 25 Danish birds to chat up.

After the party finished we headed to one of Miami's most famous clubs, Set. The free bar was a distant memory as it was about $30 a drink, but I had cash. It was full of beautiful people, everyone dancing with one another, revellers dancing on tables and funny scenes cropping up at any given time. There's something wonderful about a great night in a club, especially when you're with a beautiful woman, and this was one of them.

The night ended with the Sam and I rambling rubbish at Jerry's diner. Thank God I had a missus because I might have made a very crass pass, but instead I just fell asleep in my cheeseburger. I didn't think a night like that could be beaten in Miami but I was wrong. I hadn't bargained on Halloween.

Muppets for Obama

Friday, October 31

Facebook status: Steve Zacharanda had an unforgettable Miami night at the Versace masquerade ball, dropped the A-bomb on the dance floor of a perfect club then fell asleep in a cheeseburger :)

I woke up with a raging hangover, but I was all the better for waking up in the Alexander. The bed felt wonderful compared to the friend's houses, airports, planes and rock hard hostel beds I'd kipped on over the previous week or so. I even went for a big breakfast at the hotel's giant restaurant despite not being able to get it free.

I had a stroll down Lincoln Road and thought it was weird as there were queues outside fancy dress shops. Being still hung over my brain didn't compute why there were so many people queuing for costumes on a Friday afternoon. I popped into a phone shop for some credit and waited behind two cops. The older white one was taking the piss out of a younger Hispanic policeman. He was saying: "Do you mean you've never heard of the official You Tube Sensation cop of South Beach?" The other cop bit: "Ok, ok I'm an official YouTube Sensation baby, 20,000 hits in a week, fighting crime my way." I thought: 'Blimey 20,000 hits in a week? I wonder what he did to get that', but I also loved the importance he put on being 'an official YouTube Sensation'. They disappeared before I had the chance to ask them what he had done to become a minor South Beach celebrity.

I caught sight of myself in a shop front and looked at my trainers. They were now literally falling apart and stunk. I ambled into Foot Locker and was greeted immediately by a pretty young afro-Caribbean attendant.

"Hello sir, everyone at Foot Locker is a VIP. How can I help you?" she said.

"I need a new pair of trainers, I'll just have a look around thank you" I said.

"Wow, you're English, I luuurve your accent. Please let me help you. What do you want them for, playing soccer, running, basketball or gym work?" she said with an endearing smile.

"Erm, just to walk around in." Not a word of a lie there.

"You're so funny! Well I think you better buy some Converse, an American Icon and they're 100 years old this year."

I was bowled over by her optimistic charm, and she had short hair and a smile that lit up her face. Needless to say I bought some Converse, and at £25 they were a bargain.

She commented on my Obama badge and asked where she could get one. I explained I was a volunteer, which as usual went down well, and went in to my spiel asking if she had voted yet. She hadn't but by the time I'd finished with her she'd agreed to volunteer and vote.

"Err soz bab, is there any chance you can lace them up for me," I asked as she was about to put the Converse in the box.

"I'm not supposed to do that for you Sir, but as you've come all this way to help Obama I will. How do you want them laced?"

It appears there are about 10 ways to lace up your Converse, each having a different meaning.

"Give me the Ghetto way please bab!"

"Ghetto!" she let out a raucous laugh.

"Yeah, I'm from Perry Barr, proper Ghetto, I needs to represent when I get back."

She laughed but my English charm was undone within seconds. I put the Ghetto laced Converse on and put my battered trainers in the new box.

"Can I bag them up for you?" she said.

"No, you can keep them, put them in the bin or give them to charity."

I handed her the box. She opened it and recoiled with the putrid smell of feet that had walked miles in sweltering heat. Her face was one of disgust when she held the box away from her and ran off in to the back shrieking.

She returned a little more composed. "You English are crazy, you're not supposed to buy sneakers and leave them in the shop for charity. No-one would ever wear them again! It's a good job you're an Obama guy". Then she smiled.

"Soz bab, what more can I say? I sweat for Obama and a better America!"

Thankfully she laughed and gave me a hug. My work there was done – I'd part exchanged my trainers and recruited another volunteer for the cause. I looked in the mirror and felt better. There's nothing like a new pair of trainers to boost the confidence. I decided to stop off at an Irish pub to get a 'hair of the dog' pint of Strongbow, as it was one of the only places I could get my favourite pint, and finally got to the office about 3pm.

In the office a new dude seemed to be giving orders. His name was Eric. He'd come from Canada and was an election veteran. He was in his late 20s, didn't have much hair and wore a baseball cap. He seemed pretty intense and had the wild look of a zealot in his eye. He gave me a list of numbers and told me to start phoning them. I had to find out whether people had voted and if they hadn't did they need a lift to the polls.

My success rate was better because I'd got used to speaking slowly after a week or so in America. Loads of people said they had voted and were proud to say they'd cast their vote for Obama. As usual one prat had got through the countless phone lists without a 'don't phone' put next to his name.

A deep voice came booming across the phone after my preamble. "What have you got to do with our election Limey? Are you a socialist like everyone else in Europe? Obama is a socialist."

No-one was listening so I took the phone outside for chat with this obnoxious fool. I said: "I'm from England, mate, and we have to put up with dickheads like George Bush. Our troops have had to die because of the bullshit wars your idiotic presidents get us in to, and if you know anything about economics then you must realise that in the last few months George Bush is a socialist. How more socialist can nationalising the banks be? You're paying taxes to help pay for bankers' wages, and no I'm not a socialist. I'm a communist."

'That should wind him up', I thought. Silence. Then he said: "You red bastard. I'm not voting for anyone" and with that he slammed the phone down. 'Great', I thought, if someone like that isn't going to bother to vote McCain then Obama must stand a good chance.

After another one of my calls had finished I heard someone laughing behind me. I turned around and saw a lean six foot guy with a strawberry blond haircut and matching beard. His features were like that of a chiselled film star, like a taller young Robert Redford, and he had ice-blue eyes which sparkled with life. With a big grin he said: "Ahhh it's the famous South Beach Broooomie on the phones, Aww-rite mayteee, I'm from Eng-er-land don't you know."

The whole office laughed. I thought it sounded like an Aussie accent; no-one I'd encountered could pull off a Brummie one. I suppose me and my fellow Brummies habit of saying 'Alright mate' to people must be where the frequent Aussie mix ups came about. However, I was flattered that my reputation had gone further than the South Beach office. "I'm Nate, Nate Sherwood" he said, and stuck out his hand.

After weeks of being sent around the houses I had finally met the famous Nate Sherwood and he lived up to expectations. Everyone spoke highly of him and not just because he was the boss. He spoke in a lilting Colorado accent, and it didn't surprise me that he was also a bit of singer songwriter in his spare time. This dude had depth.

Word has it Nate changed when he went to training for Obama supervisors a few months before. He, like everyone who went on the camp, came back with a streak of determination to get Obama elected and to get the job done. Had they been told the modern world as we knew it was up for grabs in this election?

Nate was Kale and Mark's immediate boss and was answerable for the South Beach operation. He had a wonderful manner about him and unlike other election bosses understood that a lot of people in his command were volunteers and not there to be screamed and shouted at. He was a top class political organiser. Whenever I quoted him in articles or on the radio it would always be with the moniker 'the sharpest political operator on the East Coast', and to me he always will be.

He disappeared as quickly as he arrived and people seemed to melt away as the evening approached. Unlike most days, the office was pretty empty by 8pm. Volunteers were making their excuses and heading off to get ready for Halloween. It started to dawn on me that Halloween was a pretty big deal in South Beach

Mark and Kale were having nips of whisky. Then they said they were off to get changed. They came back dressed in black t-shirts, black caps and jeans whilst all a chunter about not having earpieces. They settled down after agreeing to use their hands free sets.

"Who are you supposed to be?" I asked.

"Security" they both replied.

"For who?"

"Jelvis, of course. He's on his way. We're hitting the South Beach with him tonight."

My stomach turned with excitement. A night out with Jelvis was imminent.

"Have you got your costume ready?" Kale asked.

"I haven't got one," I said gloomily.

"It's Halloween, you're going to have to wear something if you come out with us. What about the Fancy Dress shop?"

I explained there was a queue at 3pm so it would be murder now.

I was wearing jeans and a t-shirt from Asda which had a massive picture of Animal from the Muppets on the front. I looked around the office and saw loads of Obama signs and had an idea.

"I'm going to rig up a Muppets for Obama sign!" I said in an eureka moment.

They looked at me as if I was mad, but I took an 'Obama – Biden' lawn sign and scrawled 'MUPPETS FOR' over the top of it on both sides, and stuck Obama badges in the eyes of Animal. Hey presto, I had a costume! Why shouldn't there be a Muppets for Obama? There were badges and t-shirts for Cat Lovers for Obama, Dog Lovers for Obama, Gays for Obama, Europeans for Obama, Jewish Women for Obama, Latinos for Obama, Cubans for

Obama, Christians for Obama, Costa Ricans for Obama and a plethora of other weird groups for Obama.

Muppets, being a universally recognised brand, seemed a great idea. I would be spreading the word whilst celebrating Halloween – perfect! The door opened and in walked Jelvis, resplendent in his Star of David jumpsuit complete with gold sunglasses and gold shoes. He looked the part and within seconds his arm was waving around doing the windmill on his guitar. To the tune of Blue Suede Shoes he was singing: "Keep keep, keep my blue State blue." The Jewish Elvis was bastardising the King's work to urge voters to keep Florida Democratic. "Muppets for Obama, brilliant!" Jelvis said.

He explained in detail to Kale and Mark how they should undertake their security duties, asking them to take over if anyone wanted a photo with him. "It's going to be crazy out there guys. If you've never seen Halloween in South Beach, prepare to be amazed".

We bought various bottles of whisky and rum and put them in coke bottles because it's against the law to drink alcohol on the street in South Beach. There must have been over 30,000 people crammed in to one little district and everyone seemed to be in fancy dress. Young, old, middle aged, black, white, Latin, gay, straight, ugly and beautiful - everyone was represented.

It was better to be drunk than sober because it was so surreal. When a drunk Fred Flinstone comes up demanding to know whether Obama would lift the blockade of Cuba if he got elected and whether he would have ordered the Bay of Pigs if he was in Kennedy's shoes, it's better to be pissed. Why anyone would value the political opinion of a bleary eyed Brummie with a Muppets for Obama sign is beyond me, but I duly explained that he would probably lift the blockade and that I wouldn't want to second guess Obama under the duress of time travel. I was getting loads of whistles and loads of "Go Obama" as I wondered through the crowd, so I came up with the Muppets song 'Mamanamana, Ba-rack O-bama'.

The costumes were amazing and very intricate, and fancy dress seemed to give hundreds of women the license to wear next to nothing, but the female costume choice of the night was Sarah Palin. There were fat, thin, ugly and pretty Sarah Palins, all in power suits and glasses. Alas, none of whom were as sexy as the bird in the porno 'Who's Nailin' Palin?'. They all made a beeline for me and asked to have photos taken with me and my Obama sign. There were a smattering of Obamas and a few John McCains too.

The crowds parted like the Red Sea when we walked through with people breaking out in spontaneous applause and begging for photos. It was like being with royalty, but then again Elvis is as close as anyone has come to it in America. Kale and Mark played their part to perfection working in tandem, talking into their microphones and not smiling once to any of his fans. Willard, a great character (one of the greatest I've ever met anyway) was a New Yorker and ran a hotel in Greenwich Village but also went all over the world as Jelvis. He took his art seriously and as a sideline he was a big cheese in the world of ukuleles. He also loved Barack Obama.

Someone would shout "Give us a song, Elvis!" and I would act as his MC: "He's not Elvis, he is THE Kosher King, he is the Jewish Elvis, pray silence for Jelvis," then he'd launch in to 'Keep my Blue State Blue', ending it with "Vote Obama".

He had a whole set of songs in fact, happily playing requests, some with Jewish phrases inserted in them and some without. We were campaigning for Obama on our own terms and ensuring we left people with a smile on their faces - but, and this is why I empathise with some celebrities, it was hard work. It took about ten minutes to walk for about ten metres, so after shaking hundreds of hands and taking countless photos we thought 'Fuck it, let's go for a beer'.

We found a pool hall and sat down exhausted. Sam, who'd dressed up as Amy Winehouse, joined us. Kale and Mark couldn't understand a word she said in her Stoke accent, but it was good to be out of the crush. There was a bloke dressed up as the Joker next to us as. He was falling all over the place, but he ended up singing a duet with Jelvis, which has to be one of the most bizarre things I've ever seen. Jelvis was shattered; if I'd have taken a picture of him slumped on a couch staring melancholicly into the middle distance I'm sure it would have been an award winner. It's hard being a star.

I was in my element chatting with Kale, Mark and Jelvis and getting a real feel for the campaign. The next day was going to be monumental because a deluge of keen volunteers were going to descend on the South Beach Office and Kale and Mark would have to marshal the troops along with the new, super keen Eric. After midnight we decided to brave the crowds again and do our thing. Jelvis had been revived by some hard liquor and we stepped in to the breach.

Within two hours the place had gone crazy and everyone seemed to be pie-eyed and in the full throes of hedonistic abandon. People were cavorting half naked in the street, climbing on the roofs of cars, swinging from lampposts and kissing everything that stood still long enough. Women were baring their breasts at the drop of a hat. It was a single man's paradise, but Mark and I were taken, so we had great fun watching Kale give it his all.

The streets were packed, however, most of our time was spent waiting for a space to walk forward Jelvis decided he'd had enough and wanted to go to a hotel bar away from Lincoln Road. We got there and he was treated like a hero by the barmen. He did a turn for a few drinks and we sat outside in the beer garden on loungers, merrily drinking our rums and thinking that we might be the luckiest Obama volunteers in America. Mark and Kale regaled us with horror stories of volunteering in Las Vegas in the 2004 election in 100 degrees.

As I stumbled to the toilet a little later in the evening one guest took a dislike to me, though. He looked like a bodybuilder, was covered in tattoos and had what looked like a high class prostitute on his arm. He shouted at me as I staggered past "Obama scum, Obama scum!" and then did the international sign of cutting my throat. I was stunned.

To be honest, he shit me up. I wish I could have said something clever, but instead I said in a tiny voice: "Mate, I'm a Muppet. Stop bullying a Muppet." His bird laughed but he just growled. It amazed me how much hatred there was from certain sections of society for Obama. Whether it was inbred Cuban Democratic resentment, or the bile of white racists, there really was a minority who hated everything he stood for and couldn't bear the prospect of having Obama as their President - and I was in South Beach, which is about as liberal as it gets. I reckon I'd have been strung up if I'd taken a flight to Kentucky and paraded around in a Muppets for Obama costume.

After we'd finished up in the hotel bar we headed back, coincidentally bumping into the YouTube Sensation cop who I claimed to have seen on the internet. He and his mates wouldn't let us go until Jelvis performed. When they were satisfied we headed to Jerry's Diner, the iconic South Beach restaurant where I'd fallen asleep in a cheeseburger. Mark got his camera out and before I know it Jelvis walked in bold as brass and got ready to perform.

I did the MC bit, getting the bemused diners ready for the best Jelvis in the world, and he did an unbelievable rendition of Blue State Blue. Halfway through a fat woman sitting with her mom and eating a supersize dinner shouted: "You make me sick, Elvis would have voted McCaaaain." Jelvis just winked at her, bent his knees, did a bit of a flourish and carried on as I doubled up with laughter. Mark was recording it and Kale was doing his security bit. As soon as he finished there was a massive round of applause. Unforgivably I was laughing that much I didn't shout "Jelvis has left the building!" as he exited.

It was about 2am and all the phone networks had gone down because so many people were trying to phone one another in such a dense area. Jelvis had decided to retire to his penthouse, but only after giving another crowd a quick turn. I lost Kale and Mark and staggered back to The Alexander about 4am, knackered but content.

In trouble with the law...

Saturday, November 1

Facebook status: Steve Zacharanda wore a Muppets for Obama outfit (manamana Barack Obama) with the king of kosha J-elvis and a pre-addiction Amy Winehouse lookalike, every little helps, OBAMA!

It was bedlam when I got to the office about 11am. There were queues of excited people popping their Obama volunteering cherry. I pushed my way into the office as it was standing room only. Mark and Kale looked like they were moving in slow motion in a world rushing around them. My hangover was bad but I was glad I didn't feel as bad as they looked. Eric was in his element giving new volunteers motivational speeches and sending groups off in teams with lists of doors to knock.

My phone went and I stepped outside. "Hello, is that Adam? I've been told to phone you because you have a spare room." I'd forgot I'd put my name down because I had a spare room at my hotel and thought I might as well do my bit for the campaign and let someone use the spare bed. I replied: "Yeah mate, I'm at The Alexander Hotel." When he started talking again I realised the bloke behind me was saying the exact same sentence and I turned around. Staring at each other talking into our mobiles we realised we were on the phone to each other.

We laughed and hugged each other. "I'm Mark, can I stay with you?"

"Of course," I said without thinking.

He was in his thirties and had a complexion like he was maybe half Mexican, but there was a hint of an Army look too. He was wearing a Nike t-shirt, jeans and shoes and had very short hair. He was a big guy with a bull neck. He had flown from California and had nowhere to stay, so I rooted around my pockets and discovered I had two hotel room keys. I gave him one, told him the room number and that he was free to come and go as he pleased.

He had hired a car and was there to give people lifts to the polls. We shook hands and as he turned to walk up the stairs, I noticed the hair on his neck was perfectly cut in to a square. Now call me a natural neck snob but I should have known this bloke would have been trouble from that moment; however, I chose to ignore my instincts, especially as I couldn't very well just ask for the key back.

Any worries I had then were forgotten when I saw the smiling faces of Caesar and Suzie. They had come over to help out at South Beach and we formed a team and went in to the office to get our orders. We were given a massive list of addresses in South Beach and told to find each one and enquire whether the people there had voted for Obama yet, and, if not, whether they'd like a lift to the polling station.

The weather was baking hot, I was wearing my shorts and Yellow Obama t-shirt and we got started in the midday sun; as I feared a chafing situation I hummed the song 'Mad dogs and Englishmen go out in the midday sun'. The three of us found ourselves about a mile from the office in a tree lined avenue with condos and houses on either side. Each street on our list had about 10 addresses so we started door knocking.

I loved it. So many people were positive about Obama, with only a handful of negatives as usual, but on the whole most of the addresses were vacant or the person we were looking for had moved on. Everyone we passed in the street was offered an Obama badge and asked if they had voted. It was great connecting with everyday Americans going about their business. We had leaflets which gave people directions to the polling stations which we hung on door knobs. What was a bit off-putting was some of the addresses had already had door leaflets on them.

Nonetheless we carried on regardless, dodging dogs and irate neighbours. We were given some duff addresses, with one place in particular looking like a gang headquarters in The Shield. The house had about six rooms at the front, with bare-chested, tattooed dudes hanging out of each window, and about five standing out the front, all of whom looked to be Haitian. It was certainly the address on my list but somehow I didn't think a Miss Stevens lived there.

"Hello, does a Miss Stevens live here?" I asked the dudes patrolling the gate.

They all laughed as if I'd just said the punch line to the funniest joke on earth.

"Naaah man, just men live here man," said a guy whose jeans were so low they looked like they were about to fall down at any second.

I said: "Ok, well I'm here on behalf of Barack Obama, can we count on your vote on Tuesday?"

He shouted something in Haitian to his gallery of idiots hanging out of every window like a gangster version of Celebrity Squares. They all howled with laughter and started cat calling me and shouting OB-AM-A OB-AM-A, but they weren't intimidating and I laughed with them, even though it looked like they were in a halfway house after just being released from prison.

It turned out I wasn't far wrong. The topless baggy-trousered gate keeper studied me for a bit then gave me a thoughtful look.

He said: "Yaw homes, you not from America are you?"

"Nope" I said. "England."

"Well, can criminals in England vote?" he replied.

"Of course they can, as long as they're not in prison" I said.

"Well, in Florida, if you've been found guilty of a felony you can't vote in elections, so that's why everyone is laughing at you," he said.

I had an idea. I should ask these dudes to volunteer, because even if they couldn't vote they could still help out. Just before I could ask Caesar and Suzie came up, looked at me as if I was stark raving mad and told me to hurry up.

Almost all of the addresses we were given were in apartment complexes so naturally we went in and knocked doors. All of them had some sign or another saying permission was needed to enter. I had a few people say I shouldn't be in their complex but most were fine. After all this is America, the self- styled beacon of free speech and democracy.

After about two hours of zigzagging across South Beach looking for 'super super Sporadics' (that's what it said on our sheet) we noticed there were about 30 addresses in one tower block. We ambled over to it, with me just glad we'd be in somewhere with air conditioning for a while and Caesar and Suzie trying to get the intercoms working, buzzing each address.

I noticed a couple exit the front door and I dashed up and kept it open. "Come on, we're in!" We sneaked past the reception and into the lift, and dutifully went through our list knocking on every door we had to. It was a nondescript building with massive corridors with doors either side. When there was a Jewish sign Suzie would do the bidding, and when a Latino answered Caesar would launch with the spiel. Anybody else I would start the conversation.

A quaint old English saying is 'nowt as queer as folk' and seeing people in their houses lets you into a strange world of the owners making, although as usual at least half the people we were looking for had moved on. Worse than that though, we were apparently making a lot of noise, maybe because of the echo in the corridors.

Now I'm not sure which of the residents complained. Perhaps it was the bodybuilder and his stunning half naked girlfriend who we interrupted having what must have been vigorous sex, or maybe the old Jewish man who told us no-one had knocked his door for five years. It could have been the fifty-something bald guy who answered the door in just a towel with a look of immense paranoia as we pretended we hadn't seen a naked teenage boy darting across the room behind him. Then again it might have been the white, forty-something bloke with the wild hair who opened his door in just his pyjama bottoms with a look of pure hatred that can only be created by waking someone up from a deep sleep. His house stunk and there was rubbish strewn across the floor, something else we had to pretend we hadn't seen. The look of total disgust when we asked him if he had voted and the venom he slammed the door in our faces with might be the giveaway that he was the complainant. Then again I bet he just went back to sleep.

Perhaps it was the young couple in the lift who asked us how we got in to the building, or it might have been the middle aged woman who told us Obama was going to ruin the country, that we were trespassing on private land and that she would complain.

Well, whoever it was they got us in trouble with the law. As the three of us were on one of our last addresses I noticed a flash of black in the corner of my eye. I looked down the corridor and sure enough two cops were making their way towards us. I alerted the other two. Caesar looked pretty pensive when he saw the cops. I couldn't believe it, I mean surely the building had security so there was no need for the police? Whatever the situation a cop with a gun is a different proposition than some pint-sized little Hitler with a notebook in Birmingham.

The lead cop was about 50-years-old and immaculately turned out. He was Latin and had the perfect arrogant cop face complete with the suspicious sneer. As he approached he puffed up his chest and there was an air of violence about him. He was flanked by a younger black female officer with a kinder face but who still looked as if she could give a decent left hook.

"Hello officers," I said.

There were no niceties from the servants of the state.

"You are breaking the law. Are you aware you are breaking the law? You are trespassing on private land, you could even be described as soliciting or burglarizing this property, we have had a lot of complaints about your behaviour in this building. What are you doing here?" the male cop barked with contempt.

Al three of us said at the same time: "We are campaigning for Obama."

Wrong answer.

"And that gives you right to break the law, you guys make me sick."

I was getting angry at the power crazed bully and his last sentence crossed the line because he was getting personal. He was obviously a McCain fan, but I noticed the black cop's lips betrayed the tiniest of smiles. "You have to leave the building now, and we are going to escort you out. Let's go, you have had you're fun," he said.

We waited in silence for the lift and I could feel his hatred for us as he was running his hand up and down the handle of his baton.Without thinking I said:

"Sorry about this, we didn't realise we were doing anything wrong. Please accept our apologies."

The cop started on a rant about breaking into apartment blocks and all the laws we had broken when he stopped, and looked at me.

"Hold on, you're not American" he said, looking like he'd just done a stellar bit of Sherlock Holmes style deduction.

"Nope, English." I replied.

"And you are campaigning in an American election. Do you have citizenship?"

I was trying to keep calm about the situation because it was so bizarre, and I felt a little sick because I had no idea about any of the laws of the country I was standing in.

"I am on holiday and am helping out Obama. There are loads of people from across the world helping out."

As we walked out the lift the cops forced us in to the lobby and out of the door before stopping on the steps.

"Can you read? Did you not see this sign saying permission is needed before entry?"

We all did our best hangdog impression, apologised and walked down the steps and off to freedom.

"Where do you think you are going? I haven't finished with you."

He made us stand up against the wall and started asking Caesar and Suzie loads of questions about the details and the black cop started to chat to me. Within seconds I knew she was an Obama fan, as she started asking where the office was and I got the impression it wasn't to complain but so she could go down and get some t-shirts and badges.

Then idiot cop started back on me about being an illegal alien disturbing an American election. I tried to just give him one word answers because I knew anything I said would be twisted, but I was a bit scared because he reckoned he needed to get in touch with his station to find out whether I was breaking the law. The last thing I wanted was to spend any time in a cell. I protested about America being a democracy and built on immigration. Then Suzie said something and he barked: "Do you think I need you guys fucking around in this street? Do you not think I could be doing better fucking things?!"

Shocked at his language, and how he must have some serious anger management issues, I interrupted and said: "Hold on mate. There's no need to swear. We're sorry for entering the building, but we were only following orders (white lie), but we'll go back and tell our bosses to remove the building from the list."

We showed him the list. He now looked as if he was going to kick the shit out of me and had his hand on his baton. I was glad there were witnesses about as my plan was to do my old trick and have an asthma attack when I hit the ground. Who knows, I might have been able to sue him. Thankfully the black cop interjected and told us and him to calm down. He instantly did, taking step back and talking into his radio. I thought 'Here goes, time to be arrested', which to tell you the truth I was starting to think would be a fascinating experience and a great anecdote about life on the campaign trail. I've never been arrested in England so how weird would it be to be nicked in America on behalf of Obama. I'd become a martyr to the cause!

"Yeah, we have a problem with three individuals campaigning for Obama. I want to put an alert out." He described us to a tee, saying I was overweight, and then said: "If they are seen in this neighbourhood again at anytime today I want them arrested."

He turned to us and said: "You guys are lucky you have not been taken down the station, but I'm giving you one chance to leave. If you get seen anywhere in this neighbourhood campaigning you will be arrested, and you, Englishman, will be in a whole heap of trouble."

He stormed off and the black cop, mouthed silently: "Did you say the Obama office was on Ocean Drive?" We all smiled and whispered yes.

Suzie was fuming for being sworn at, I was relieved not to have been beaten and shot to death and Caesar was cool as a cucumber.

"That cop doesn't like me Suzie, he always gives me shit" said Caesar calmly.

"What! You know him?" Suzie and I said at the same time.

"Yeah, he knows me from the Hip Hop videos. He's one of the cops who the producers hire to be private security because they can carry their guns off duty. He got humiliated by one of the rappers, and I was there, and he's given me shit ever since" he said matter of factly.

"But he didn't give you any shit, he gave it to me and Suzie!" I replied.

"Yeah I know, just trying to prove a point."

We all laughed out loud and then made our way back to the office and Suzie phoned Nate.

"Yeah, sorry we have to come back, Adam, Caesar and I have nearly just been arrested by the cops and we've been excluded from the neighbourhood."

Nate was probably knee deep in campaign stuff and this was the last thing he needed but he took it in good humour and must have asked what we were doing to get in trouble.

"We went in to an apartment block to knock doors which it appears is illegal."

When I got back to the office Kale and Mark gave me a cheer. "Nothing ever goes simply where you are concerned," they said. The office was alive with our antics and we had a debate about entering apartment blocks without permission. I said we should carry on regardless, if we asked we'd nearly always be refused permission. Nate was unsure of the laws surrounding political campaigning and made some phone calls to his bosses asking the question.

Whatever the legal ins and outs I wasn't going to go out in to the streets again that day. I was sure the legions of rather well off volunteers who had come to help for one day could go and knock doors, so I ate some more food, which alarmingly was lower than at any time in the campaign because of all these one day wonders. I couldn't even find enough space in the office to go on Facebook.

I was starting to think I was a bit useless as a volunteer. I was pretty shit on the phones because no-one could understand me, if sent anywhere I usually got lost and my door knocking methods nearly got me arrested. I'd never made it in to the office for 9am due to being lost, spending hours in the bank, being hungover, writing articles or trying to blag free hotel rooms. For me Karim was a great example of an Obama volunteer. He'd come with his Mac and sat all day doggedly entering data into the Democrat party computer programme.

It started playing on my mind, especially as the election was now just days away. I didn't want to leave Miami with any regrets that I hadn't pulled my weight. I spoke to Mark about how I felt and asked how I could improve my effectiveness for the campaign. He gave me a curious smile, lifted his cap above his eye line and said: "Dude, you've come all the way from England to volunteer for Obama, whatever you do is good enough. Stop worrying about it. You've provided a lot of laughs in this office, so be cool, you've just got to play to your strengths."

He gave me confidence and I started to think about what I'd enjoyed the most during the campaign. It was probably being on the front line with Ophelia and talking to people in the street, and making people laugh via Muppets for Obama the night before. I knew I'd had success recruiting volunteers when I spoke to them face to face, whether it was on duty or off duty, and what was great about the campaign under Mark, Kale and Nate was that they would let people play to their strengths. I thought I'd do what suited me best – getting out there, speaking to as many people as I could and convincing them to vote for Obama.

Me and my mate Barry

I sat with my feet up in the office wondering what to do next. What could I do? How could I get the message across in the best way possible, in a way that played to my strengths? I looked at the cardboard cut-out Obama in the office and remembered taking pictures of Jelvis the night before. I had an idea. I shouted across the office to Mark and Kale: "Can I borrow the office Obama for a few minutes?

I could have asked them if I could piss in their secret bottle of whiskey and they would have said yes. They were getting bombarded by all manner of questions from the new volunteers. I picked up Barry Obama and walked out of the office. My original idea was Sing-a-long Obama where I would stand behind the cut out and belt out hits and ask passers-by to join in. But, alas, I couldn't get the office Karaoke machine working.

I had a cigarette outside with Barry, and within five minutes three people came up and asked for a photo with 'Mr Obama'. I took their cameras and snapped 'the next President of America'. I asked everyone who had their photo taken if they had voted and if not, why not? It dawned on me that the cardboard cut-out Obama was the perfect foil to engage with voters and to find out whether they had cast their vote.

Caesar came around the corner, and I explained my idea to him. As we were banned from the residential streets in South Beach it seemed logical to take Barry down to Lincoln Road and set up stall giving badges out and letting people take snaps with him. Caesar loved the idea and said he had a proper camera in the car and he'd take the photos, within five minutes was planning a Hip-Hop montage video. He called Suzie, who was picking her daughter up, and she agreed to meet us.

We stocked up on sticky Obama badges and leaflets and headed to Lincoln Road, which has been described as 'the Fifth Avenue of the South'. We found a great place outside the Lincoln Theatre and set up. The theatre was a little gem, built in 1936, and its history reads like a who's who of Hollywood stars; it was *the* place for a film premier in Miami until it closed as a cinema in the early 1980s. It was now home to the New World Symphony orchestra.

Suzie and her daughter turned up. She was adorable, a blond ten year old with a cheeky smile and the cutest American accent possible. We all looked at each other and wondered what to do next.

Barry had a handle on the back and he was the same height as me. I strode in to the centre of the pavement trying to think of something clever to say, but the voice of an angel beat me to it. My 10-year-old new best mate bellowed: "Come and get your picture with the next President of America!" Everyone turned around and looked at us. We all broke down in laughter, then set about spreading the gospel according to Barry.

A smart looking black family strolled past and one of their children ran up to me and Barry. The mother and father both gave us a wonderful smile and asked us if they could take a photo with Barry. I crouched down and hid behind Barry so it looked from the front as if he was free-standing. The mother, father, daughter and son all hugged Barry like he was a long lost friend. Caesar took a photo with their camera and then his own. As soon as they finished they asked for badges and we in turn asked them if they had voted.

They all left happier after they had seen us. Barry was becoming a star. It took us about five minutes to start getting smoother and ensuring there was never any silence coming from our little camp. Suzie's daughter was great and we all egged each other on. Whether it was 'Don't forget to vote for me this Tuesday!' or 'Have a photo taken with the next President!' or 'Get your Obama badges, get a perfect Facebook profile picture, baby!' they all worked.

Within ten minutes we were having people running up to us and asking us for photos. The sheer joy that Barry gave people was unbelievable, and this is a cardboard cut-out of a politician we're talking about. Imagine walking around with a cut-out of David Cameron in Birmingham. I doubt there'd be crowds flocking to have their photo taken with it. It'd probably be covered in phlegm within the hour.

In the week before the election the enthusiasm Obama generated was astonishing and infectious. We had women sidling over demanding photos and sizing him up to see if they made a nice couple. We had Hispanic and black gangbangers speaking in hip hop language queuing up behind old white ladies to get their photo taken with Barry. We had bald, tongue-pierced gay men having photos taken with their hands on his crotch. We had people putting their hats on him or wrapping their scarves around him.

Caesar regaled everyone with the story that we were putting together a video 'Barack Obama's South Beach Day Out', and of course people lapped it up. Everyone wants to be famous in Miami. They all had their photos taken and as everyone has a phone with a camera we took one with theirs too. Then we asked all of them if they'd voted. Worryingly, more and more people seemed to think it was a foregone conclusion he was going to win.

Each time I had to explain if everyone thought he was going to win he was bound to lose, before slapping a guilt trip on them. "How are you going to feel on Wednesday morning if John McCain wins and you didn't even bother to vote?" It worked every time, and over the course of a few hours we must have chatted to hundreds of people so we were really doing our bit.

When the theatre opened it got really bizarre. They had someone on the street who was trying to get people to see the performance inside. He was about six foot three, was dressed as an American Gothic style farmer and had a massive booming voice. The theatre was showing a 20 minute performance by students trying their hand at classical music.

Our angelic helper made the first move and it worked a treat. I mean how can you be annoyed at a 10-year-old picture perfect girl in an Obama t-shirt? The huge theatre MC must have thought 'If you can't beat 'em, join 'em'. "Come and see the stupendous, wonderful, tear jerking, heart wrenching performance at The Theatre, and why not have your photo taken with Barack Obama as well. Yes, that's right, Barack Obama loves our theatre!" he shouted.

We all laughed and then took it in turns MC-ing and as the sun went down the clubbers started to come out and it became funnier. I had another idea. I got a cigarette and tried to stick it to Barry's mouth. I thought his habit was well known and would cause a laugh or two. However, Suzie saw what I was up to and admonished me because she thought a smoking Barry would not help the cause.

Just to see the look on people's faces was wonderful, seeing someone walk past and pester either their parent or partner to come back and have a photo taken. Sometimes the wait would be about 10 minutes after people had all the different poses taken. We had about three people asking if we were charging for photos, and the funny thing was that if we'd said yes they probably would have paid.

It wouldn't have been a proper day campaigning for Obama without a nasty side though. I was doing my thing with Barry when I noticed a white bloke in his fifties. He was wearing shorts, a t-shirt and a red cap. He had thin lips, mean eyes and above his nose a muscle didn't move. He also had one hell of a belly. He walked past us, stood on the corner and then walked back again and stood about 10 yards away from us like a statue. He waited until there was a lull of people. I'm glad our little girl was out of the way before he opened his mean minded mouth.

"Ay you," came the low sinister voice.

I turned around to look him in the eyes, and as if he was a movie Mafia boss ordering a hit on a rival, he said: "You won't be laughing when he's shot. Which he will be if he wins."

Caesar's jaw dropped like a stone and his Suzie's face flashed with horror.

I shouted straight back: "Well come and get a photo then sir, it'll be worth even more! Come on, have a photo, I know you want to. Ebony and ivory and all that."

His face was a picture of disgust and he scurried off around the corner.

"I cannot believe that man just said that," said Suzie.

"I can't believe you didn't react in an angry way. You just carried on as if he hadn't said that he wanted Barry dead," said Caesar.

"Ahh fuck him, never let people like that know that they've rattled you in any way. You've just got to rise above it."

Though no-one would ever talk about it, Obama being assassinated was the elephant in the room throughout the campaign. I said it once to Suzie and she was so shocked I thought I would never mention it again, but I guarantee everyone had thought about it at some stage or another.

I wasn't surprised I'd heard it but Caesar and his auntie were properly shocked and every so often would just think aloud: "I just cannot believe that man said that." However, if we'd pitched up in some Hicksville in the Bible Belt then I bet we'd have heard a lot more threats and nasty remarks, but we luckily we were in South Beach. Lincoln Road had to be one of the best streets in America to take Barry because of the party animals that inhabit South Beach and the diverse range of characters walking up and down every day.

It was tiring, it's not easy speaking to so many people and trying to be funny all of the time. I was now communicating better because I was speaking slower and I was filtering out the English words that Americans do not understand like 'fortnight', 'pissed', 'trainers', 'irony' and 'twat'.

I wish I could have taped all the comments me and Barry received because they were priceless, although the pictures probably tell the best story. The wide spectrum of support for Obama made for a perfect political campaign, and I was happy to bask in the glow of my mate Barry. I admit I loved talking about my personal journey to support Obama because of how interested people were about it. I must have gone through the tale thousands of times and by the end of the holiday I had it down to tee, like a well-oiled stand up routine. What was particularly satisfying is that through my story and my belief in Obama I know I got lots of people to seriously think about taking the time to vote for him.

If they walked off and did nothing, then that's their business, but getting them thinking was good enough for me. Due to my snaffling up of any information about the election I knew the issues pretty well as well. Health reform was always a great winner because I could throw the NHS in anyone's face. Sometimes it takes a stranger to tell someone in their own home what is wrong with their situation. Of course George Bush was a winner, as were the Wall Street bankers who he'd let off the leash then bailed out with taxpayers' cash, and the Iraq war deception. Sarah Palin was a gimme, obviously.

After a few hours we were all fading, especially our ten year old heroine. Caesar and I took Barry back to the office and all the talk was about the party that night. The Democrats had hired a bowling alley in Miami and every volunteer was invited. We thought it would be rude not to go so we were all set to party the night away in the early hours. Then Caesar received a phone call from Suzie.

"Hey Adam, how do you fancy being a steward at the Jay Z/Puff Daddy/ Mary J Blige concert in Miami tomorrow?"

"Yeah baby! Let's do it!" I said without thinking.

When the details emerged it sounded hard work. We'd be showing people to their seats and if there were going to be shitloads of people turning up we'd have to tell most of them that they couldn't get in. More ominously, it was an early start, as we had to be on the other side of Miami by 9am.

Facebook status:Steve Zacharanda nearly got arrested for soliciting, took a cardboard Obama out in Miami and got 200 people to have their photo taken with it, shake, rattle and shalom baby.

The bowling alley was packed. Jelvis was in his civvies. Mark, Kale, Nate, Karim, Claire, square neck Mark and others I recognised were there. We mistakenly thought there might be free drinks, but alas the hundreds of millions raised by the campaign had to be spent on advertising and not beers for the people who gave their time to get Obama elected. I waited 20 minutes for a drink but it was great to meet so many people letting their hair down after a tough week on the campaign trail.

"Oh my gawd, are you the English phone guy in the South Beach office? Wow, I wanted to meet you, I'm from the North Beach office," a pretty looking twenty-something woman said in the highest pitched voice I had ever heard.

I couldn't work out if it was a compliment, but she was the second person after Nate who had made a remark about my phone manner.

"Yep, that's me. Have I got a bit of a reputation then?" I asked, not really wanting to know the answer.

Her screech pierced the air. "Yeah, you came from England with no money leaving your girlfriend back home to come out and help Obama, and you're always repeating yourself on the phone because no-one can understand you and you always seem to go off script if they annoy you! And you nearly got arrested today for breaking into an apartment block."

I suppose there could have been a worse, or at least less accurate, description. Being with everyone from the South Beach office in a social situation was great, as I could hear about people's lives outside the campaign. Nate proved to be as popular as I'd thought. Sometimes he seemed to have people queuing up to speak to him, and he certainly had a female fan club because if you looked around him there'd be either a middle age woman wishing he was her son or a younger girl wishing he was her beau. He had star quality. When he spoke people listened, and even I shut up, but he wasn't arrogant and had a generous spirit. He never hogged the limelight, which he easily could have.

In the smoking area Caesar, Mark and I had a drunken conversation about Obama being assassinated. The consensus was that America would be destroyed because the rioting that would follow would be unprecedented. Race relations would be damaged forever and it would take generations to heal. With answers like that I'm not surprised the subject that was taboo, but the fact that pricks like the fella in the red cap entertained the idea showed that those men in the dark suits, sunglasses and earpieces would need to be on the top of their game for as long as he was in the White House.

P Diddy and Co – I'll be Missing You

Sunday, November 2

Facebook status: Steve Zacharanda is off to volunteer at the Jay Z, P Diddy and Mary J Blige rally with his new mate Caesar, (get your Sunday Mercury folks)

Unbeknownst to me by the time I'd woken up the next day the clocks had gone back an hour. I didn't realise for two days that I was an hour ahead of everyone else, but as I was about an hour late all of the time no-one else noticed either.

I woke up in the Alexander Hotel about 8am and rang Caesar. There was no answer which is no surprise because it was really 7am. About 9am someone from the campaign said we weren't needed at the concert and not to bother turning up, so I phoned Caesar and said there was no point going over and that I'd meet him later.

As I was having my breakfast I set about writing some copy for back home. I was in my boxers and was happy in my own company. Then I heard rustling about in the room I hadn't slept in. Intrigued, I noticed someone get up and talk to themselves before approaching the door. I was a bit confused and wondered who the fuck had been staying in the same suite as me. The door opened and it was square necked Mark in just his briefs. "Hey dude," he said as he sauntered past me and got some drinks out of the fridge. I'd forgotten about giving my hotel key to a bloke I'd only met for ten seconds the day before. I was a bit put out because when I'm in my pants and in front of the computer I am a happy little soul, but it soon became apparent that I had to chat to this 'dude'.

He sat opposite me, me in my pants, him in his. I'm using the English description of pants here, but I would have much preferred it if I could have used the American one.

"What you writing Dude?" came the question. I explained that I was writing a story for my paper back home, but he didn't get the hint and carried on asking questions.

"Hey dude, how long did you stay at the party for? There were loads of chicks man, loads of chicks, did you meet any chicks, I was speaking to chicks all night," he said like a teenager.

I figured I'd be seeing a lot of this guy so I'd better start to like him. He was kind of endearing but certainly had a bit of insecurity in him. His girlfriend had dumped him just before he flew out from California to Miami and he seemed to be on a one man mission to "Find chicks, man". What was worrying was that after only spending the time it takes to eat a bowl of Honey Nut Cheerios with me he'd pinned his hopes on me and him 'finding some chicks' and using my suite to 'bang' them.

At the time that couldn't have been further from my mind, especially as I had a girlfriend and I couldn't be bothered wasting time playing co-pilot for some bloke with a square neck. Also, he seemed to think that he'd be staying with me until after the election, which freaked me out a bit because I thought my offer was good for one night only.

If he was English I would have run a mile, but I love Americans and listening to their experiences and views on everything. More importantly he had a car, and probably a credit card which would be helpful because I had to check into another hotel later that day. The phone rang and it was someone from the Miami Office asking if we were still up for volunteering today. I thought he'd had a change of heart over the Jay Z concert, so I said that we we'd go, to which he replied "Yeah, we'll get you volunteering there if you want, come to the office first though."

I remembered Caesar said he couldn't be bothered to drive to the concert anyway, so as Mark was in front of me I asked if he fancied going while I kept the office manager on the phone. Adding "There'll be loads of chicks there" seemed to do the job and he said he'd go with me. I told the enthusiastic manager that we'd be down in a few hours. I was buzzing because I'd missed Obama at the rally, missed Matt Damon at the march, missed Pharrell Williams at the phantom fundraiser and Fat Joe coming to the office but finally I would get to see some American celebrities including (of course) Puff Daddy, Jay Z and Mary J Blige.

We got ready and set out to find the concert venue. It was in Miami, not South Beach, in a poor neighbourhood called Hialeah. Mark reckoned it would take forty minutes to get there. I was starting to warm to Mark and was enjoying listening to his stories about previous 'chicks' and life in California. As well as being pleased I was getting a ride to the concert venue I was looking forward to being somewhere poor. I could get more information concerning the election and what it meant to the poorest in society, and do some digging around to see if there were any funny goings on at the voting stations.

We'd been driving for about forty minutes and Mark's story about being married to a Jehovah Witness in his twenties was well underway. Hanging on every word about his ex-wife being in the grip of her insane family I totally forgot to look out for signs - as he was driving I thought he knew where he was going. After all, it was his country.

We were looking for Atlantic Avenue in Hialeah, but we'd been driving for longer than we should have. We stopped off at a petrol station and before I knew it I was in conversation with a middle-aged black woman who was telling us all about how poor her neighbourhood was and what an Obama victory would mean to her. I took her name and number, thinking she'd be a great person to phone up to get reaction if Obama won, and asked her if I could use what she said for an article for an English paper.

"Be sure to send me a copy white boy!" she said with a hoot and a holler, then proceeded to give us totally wrong directions to the concert venue. Little did we know but we were only about a mile from our destination when she sent us back on the highway. After another hour in which we stopped off at McDonalds, phone shops, hardware stores and churches to get directions I phoned the volunteer coordinator to explain exactly where we were looking for. His attitude pissed me off and instead of sending us to the stadium, which we could probably have found with a little prompting, he kept on giving us directions to the office.

We finally found an Atlantic Avenue. As usual with American roads it was about 10 miles long so we went along both sides looking for the block that the office was on. Though the signs said Miami it certainly wasn't in the city and seemed semi-rural and nothing like a ghetto, but we carried on looking for the office regardless. However, due to the length of the road it was a hard slog. I was quite enjoying myself though - there are certainly worst things to do than cruising around America in a decent car, having an interesting conversation and listening to local radio. After I'd reconciled myself that we'd missed P Diddy and Co I was chilled out and in no rush to go anywhere.

We went up one idylic high street which was about as far away from a ghetto as there could be. Totally white, everyone driving BMWs and soft tops, it reminded me of Aspen. We were totally lost. Shortly after, however, we stopped off at a trailer park for directions. Mark locked the doors as we drew up to the entrance.

Three toothless creatures sidled up to the car. Their eyes were glazed and they were giggling to themselves. All wore dirty clothes and acted like the car on their land was the first they'd ever seen.

"Hello mate, any idea where the Atlantic Drive Obama office is?" I asked.

All three poked their heads in to the car, all white, two men and one woman. They seemed to be in their forties but their faces were contorted and strange. In my head the words "METH HEADS METH HEADS METH HEADS METH HEADS" were ringing out. Brilliant. Real life meth heads, something, like beautiful Latino women, we don't get in the UK as the cheap homemade drug has yet to gain a destructive foothold.

"O-BAMA, O-BAMA" the woman shouted about two millimetres from my ear.

Then the older looking guy took the lead, pushing his head in the window.

"There ain't no Obama office on this trailer park, boys. We don't get no politicians coming down here.

"Are you going to vote?" I asked automatically.

All three cackled, and then I realised it was a daft question.

"We're not allowed to vote, we're bad people," the matted haired blonde troll said.

"I've got a map in my trailer boys, come with me," the lead Meth Head said thoughtfully.

Before he'd finished Mark had said no.

"Wait here then, boys, while I go and get it," he said before wandering off into the park.

Within seconds the other two had asked for cigarettes which I was only too pleased to give them. I didn't like being stuck in the car as it reminded me of being in a Safari Park, not knowing who was watching who. I got out to stretch my legs and started chatting about life on the trailer park. I was in my element. This was the real America, the side you see on Dogg The Bounty Hunter.

This might sound strange but I quite liked the meth-heads. Compared to crackheads they seemed remarkably giggly and happy. I'm not condoning meth and I'm sure when the buzz goes they become house-breaking crazed criminals whose sole purpose is to raise cash for the next hit. On the other hand, they couldn't do enough for us and I don't think they'd ever met an Englishman before - in fact I don't think they'd met anyone outside of the trailer park before. They were also without hope, totally fucked as human beings. It's easy to think of black ghettos when thinking of the disenfranchised in America but poor whites get just as raw a deal.

These three, all dependent on Meth, all living a hand to mouth existence, all with kids who will most likely suffer the same fate, were about as far from the 'American Dream' as possible. They were fatalistic and made the point whoever won the election their lives would not be improved or changed. I pointed out healthcare reform could mean free medicine and care for them. They responded "The Man won't let that happen." I gave them more fags as I took down notes because I wanted this side of America reflected in my copy about the election.

K Jay I think his name was came back with the map and we put it on the bonnet as they pointed out where we were. We were on Atlantic Avenue, alright, but we were about 100 miles away from Miami. Me and Mark looked at each other in despair and then laughed long and hard before bidding farewell to the meth heads. I knew I'd never see any of them ever again, but I said a little prayer for them as we departed.

After a few more minutes of driving around looking for a way back to Miami my phone rang again. It was another very irate volunteer coordinator wanting to know where his 'two bodies' were.

I didn't lie. "We're on Atlantic Avenue mate, have we missed the concert?"

"What can you see on Atlantic Avenue. How can you have been on the same road for so long and not see the office?" he barked without mentioning the concert.

"Because we're lost" I replied in a deadpan way.

"OK, what can you see if you're on Atlantic Avenue?"

"We're at the entrance of a farm" I said, as we overlooked fields and fields of barley.

"A farm? What the hell?! You're the English guy right, what does a farm mean to you?"

"What does a farm mean to me?" I said, getting annoyed, "It's a place where a farmer lives, mate."

There was silence. I could hear the cogs turning in his uber-efficient brain.

"I have no idea where you guys are, but I can tell you one thing, there are no farms in Hialeah. I can't help you with directions and neither can anyone else in my office. You were supposed to be here two hours ago to go on the phones."

I repeated what he said for Mark's benefit: "We're supposed to be on the phones."

Mark's face was a picture. He grabbed the steering wheel, banged it twice and mimed the words 'No fucking way'.

I ended the conversation by saying: "Sorry, but I've no idea where we are. We'll try to make it".

They'd duped us with the promise of working at the Jay Z concert when all they wanted were another few bodies on the phone banks. It narked me more because we were volunteers who between us had travelled over 7,000 miles to help out in Miami, and we were giving up our time for free. I understood the pressure of the campaign but deceiving the people who are the backbone of the movement pissed me off.

We'd left the hotel about four hours previously and decided to head back to the South Beach office to help out there. I said: "I can safely say I will never be on this road again in my life." Mark looked into the distance at the fields and said: "Neither will I, brother. Let's get back to Miami. At least the place is full of chicks."

Facebook status: Steve Zacharanda is a bit relieved he missed the Jay Z concert, he was not lookin forward to telling thousands of ghetto dawgs they couldn't get in! get ya Sunday Mercury folks.

Adam enters Eden

The South Beach office was busy but not hectic as the day before. The usual suspects were there. Mark, Kale, Karim and Eric seemed to be ever present, and of course everyone found it rather funny I'd spent the day lost again and missed Jay Z, Puff Daddy and Mary J Blige. Karim found the concert venue and proudly showed me pictures of the superstars. It appears they didn't belt out a medley of hits but gave 10 minute speeches, but I suppose enthusiastic volunteers got closer to their heroes than ever before.

Mark was annoyed, however, because everyone there could have been working on the campaign and it was an unwelcome distraction considering polling day was less than 48 hours away. I couldn't have agreed more - I could have done a full day with Barry instead of circumnavigating rural Florida and holding court at Meth Head central.

I asked for a sheet of phone numbers and got stuck in for an hour. The important thing was to tell the people who hadn't voted that it certainly wasn't a done deal and that if they needed a lift to the polling station we could help. I pitied any female who got the short straw of getting Mark as a driver. They'd probably be taken on the scenic route if they showed any interest, or worse still a little bit of skin.

I liked to take the phone out and stand in front of the office when I was on the phones, especially as I now knew I was an attraction when I was using it. As I stood outside a woman approached me. She was about fifty and was wearing jeans, a pink t-shirt and a matching cap with a rainbow Obama badge in the middle.

"Are you with the campaign?" She asked.

Proudly I said "Yes"

"How's it going?" She asked.

Sensing I could recruit her I told her about how close it was and that we were all working harder than ever as the poll drew near. My little sales pitch for volunteers was smooth now. I explained how I'd come over on a whim to change the world and couldn't understand why so many people thought he would win when he wouldn't without them doing did everything in their power to help.

"Wow. Thank you for coming to America to help out, do you need any extra volunteers?" she said.

Bingo, another little contribution to the campaign by I thought. I said: "Of course we do, can you spare a little time?"

"There are about 40 lesbians around the corner and we can help out if you want" she said in a matter of fact way, like she was asking for a cup of coffee.

"Fucking brilliant!" I said without thinking. I immediately apologised for my language and said: "Well, we're ready and waiting, thank you."

I'd like it on the record that I managed to say that without betraying the fact that the image of 40 naked lesbians was flashing up in my brain.

"Great, I'll go and get them. By the way, I love your accent. Back soon!"

Half of me was expecting her to do a wolf whistle and lesbians would come running from every entrance and swinging down from the rooftops. Perhaps they were all parked in a special pink and purple lesbian love bus around the corner but wherever they were I had the job of letting the office know they were on their way.

Now it's not every day, or every job, or every political campaign that you get to utter these words to your bosses: "Mark, Kale, we've got 40 lesbians coming to help us out. They'll be here in five minutes." The office stopped and went quiet and more eyebrows were raised than in a James Bond box set. I think it was Ericka who quick as a flash said: "Adam, you only walked outside for five minutes, how do you do it?"I was going to explain that I hadn't gone lesbian hunting and somehow caught a job lot but then realised she was joking. Mark looked up and in his unflustered Californian accent said: "Yeah, great, we'll send them out door knocking", as if forty lesbians turning up was a daily event. Then again, in California it probably is.

Then a funny thing happened. All the men in the office started to perk up, jokes were exchanged and collars straightened. Square necked Mark ran to the toilet to freshen up and people dashed to check themselves in the mirror. Eric started to giggle to himself and Kale got his volunteer forms ready. It is a funny thing when men imagine lesbians. I'd take a guess that it's mostly in soft focus and that they are naked.

When I said 'forty lesbians' what every man heard in their brain was 'forty women', missing out the fact that they would all run a mile from us. However, we all waited nervously for the lesbian contingent to arrive. All eyes were on the door, and I could see everyone's mind racing. Would they all be like the lesbians in the pornos that most teenage boys cut their masturbating teeth on? Or maybe all super fit lesbian tennis players in mini-skirts with perfectly toned legs? Or even a battalion of hardnosed but beautiful female lesbian cops like Kima out of The Wire?

The waiting was over when the lady in the pink cap struggled up the office stairs. The whole office was in silence as she said: "Hi, I'm Pam. I'm with the South Florida Over 55s Lesbian Society (or something like that). How can we help?" With that every man pretended to be doing something else and the sexual tension was gone within an instant. One by one aging women in glasses, fleeces and all manner of different coloured jeans started to file into the office. I explained there wasn't enough room and some would have to wait outside whilst we allocated them to different areas of South Beach. They were great; funny, articulate and engaging people.

Several asked if we had any Gay and Lesbian Obama badges. Then it dawned on me the rainbow Obama badges were the Gay and Lesbian badges. I had taken a roll down with me to Lincoln the day before and gave them away when we were with Barry. There must have been hundreds of people walking around Miami happily wearing Obama badges which also told people that they were gay and proud. Well, you live and learn.

I'd forgotten I had to leave The Alexander Hotel that day and check in to the next hotel the Miami Tourist Board had set up for me, The Eden Roc. In fact Suzie's email blast had proved highly successful because I'd got enough nights at both Eden Roc and the Gansevoort South Beach Hotels to see me through to the end of my holiday. It helps to be a journalist when skint abroad.

I figured recruiting forty volunteers was a good enough contribution for the day and told Mark and Kale I had to leave. They were great about it, and again, had the right attitude to me and the other volunteers. I found square neck Mark and told him we had to leave The Alexander.

"Where are we staying next?" he asked.

"The Eden Roc Hotel," I replied, thinking that I was probably stuck with him for the rest of the holiday. Then again he did have a credit card, and a car.

We jumped in his Buick SUV, a nice motor, and he put his hands on the steering wheel, sighed and said with resignation: "Fucking over 50's." I laughed and pointed out the 'lesbian' was the bit that meant none of us had a chance even if they'd been teenage nymphomaniacs. I checked out of the Alexander and was delighted that there were no hidden charges and I got my $150 dollars back. As I left I remembered that I hadn't met the manager for the tour of the hotel as I had promised, which for a travel journalist was pretty shit.

The Eden Roc Hotel was about 300 metres down the road and looked fantastic, despite the bad sign of lots of workmen scurrying around the place. I'd primed Mark that I might need him to put his credit card down on the room if they made a fuss, and I was in no mood to hand over my $150 because it was all the money I had before I returned to the bank.

The hotel lobby was cavernous. Everything was shiny and brand new. The place even had that 'new' smell of wet paint. There was a beautiful glass bar in the middle of the lobby which had a real 1950s feel. The Eden Roc was the favourite haunt of the Rat Pack when they came to Miami in the 1950s and 60s.

I scoped the reception, and it was obvious the hotel had just opened and nobody knew what they were doing. I picked the youngest receptionist to check in with. She was gorgeous. Black, about five foot nine, a slender figure with long hair in a ponytail, she was nervously awaiting a customer.

"Hi Sir. Welcome to the Eden Roc, how can I help you?" she said with a smile which could have unlocked the heart of the world's most miserable bastard.

"Hello, my name is Adam Smith, and I am a travel journalist. The Miami Tourist Board has booked me in here."

She froze. Obviously the journalist line had scared her and she thought that if she messed up her guts would be for garters. It appeared that, as I thought, the place had just opened and she had just started. I put her at ease with a good old bit of British charm.

"Well to tell you the truth as a travel journalist I've checked into hotels across the world and I've never been welcomed by such a beautiful smile. You'll have a great career if you just be yourself, that's what great hotel receptionists all over the world have in common," I said before giving her a big smile.

She looked incredibly relieved and began taking my details whilst telling me the hotel's good points. She hadn't asked for a credit card. Perfect. I told Mark that we were in, although with the benefit of hindsight I should have got him to put his credit card down anyway, and got the bellboy to take our stuff up.

I found the hotel reception manager who had been watching the young lady check me in. He was Hispanic and about 50-years-old, and looked like he had been in the hotel game all his life.

"Hello, my name is Adam Smith and I am a travel journalist. Can I have a quick word about your receptionist?"

He took me to one side and had a very worried look on his face. Ah the joys of being a travel journalist, striking fear into the hearts of hotel managers everywhere.

"What is the problem Sir?" he asked.

"Well, I never know the right procedure because I'm always in different countries but I don't like handing tips over the counter to receptionists. Your receptionist has just given me the best welcome to a hotel in Miami, though, and I've been to a lot. Can you give her this tip from me please? Thanks."

I gave him $20 and relief washed over him. I know, smooth, and a good turn to what seemed to be a great young woman struggling on her first day. As well as the money, her boss might think better of her and give her a break. Would have I done it if she'd been pig ugly? I don't know. I'd like to think I would, it's the type of thing that can only bring good karma.

We got to the room and Mark couldn't hide his disappointment. "It's not a suite dude!" he said. It was a normal room, with a nice en suite and two double beds, which considering there was two of us was a relief. Anyway, it was brilliant because it was free, and considering money was running low that was without doubt the most important aspect of any hotel room I was going to stay in.

"Dude, what if one of us gets a chick," he said.

I laughed.

"What're the chances of that? It won't be me, because I've got a missus, and if you do and I'm out then feel free to shag away. Text me if you want and I'll stay away for an hour, then I'll be back and will expect a decent night's kip."

He looked crestfallen, a little confused and started to unpack his stuff. Thinking about it he probably had no idea what 'kip' meant. I didn't feel guilty. I'd only met the bloke the day before, so it's not like he was a best mate.

It was about 8pm and I decided to go to the office to see if there was anything I could do, as I knew what was coming next - Mark asking if we could go out and find some 'chicks'. I beat a sharp exit and got to the office about 8.30pm. There wasn't hide nor hair of any lesbian but the place was packed with lawyers. Legal people from across the country were flying to Florida to help out at the polls. It reminded me of the film Recount and brought home just how important these lawyers were. They could decide the election if it was close. Most seemed to be from New York and I managed to get some great quotes about why Florida needed so many legal people to ensure the vote was safe.

They couldn't wait to get to the polls and start arguing with officials who were stopping people voting. The '2000 robbery' was never far away from the lawyers' minds and tensions were really rising now as the election neared. The televisions were a blur of election news and campaign adverts and everyone in the office was getting more and more tired.

Then, as usual, something weird happened. I'd noticed a few of the lawyers had been asking for beer and food but thought nothing of it. There was a crate lying about so we were happy to oblige and there was a table of food that never seemed to empty despite how much we ate. Another couple of volunteers came in and asked "Where's the party at?". Again, we thought nothing of it, and anyway it was the time of night when all the office regulars were knee deep in paper work. All the phone and address lists had to be put together and sorted out. All the 'Voted', 'Not Voting', 'About to Vote', 'Need a Lift', 'Not Available', 'Phone Backs' and 'Don't Phone Back' markings next to the thousands of phone numbers and addresses had to be entered into a computer and sent off somewhere miles away, so the next day's lists could be sent back to us to start all over again.

Sometimes it was hard to concentrate because of the quality of international women coming through the doors. Every colour, age and nationality popped their heads in to the office. Some were with men and some without, and it was a novelty to start off with. As we were volunteers a bit of the Obama coolness was rubbing off on us when we spoke to the ladies as well, which was nice. But when you see such sights every day it becomes routine.

On this night there seemed to be a lot more volunteers from other parts of Miami turning up to the office, and they didn't seem to be asking for work to do but were happy just chatting about the election. It was great to hear about how Democrats in other areas were getting along. It was easy to be insular about South Beach but there was a whole city, state and country out there which would decide the election. I loved hearing about the local elections because they seemed so dirty and the volunteers were always local, which was interesting. They had to live with these results for years to come. Our man, who was on television beating someone up on an advert every five minutes, was doing well against the Republican incumbent.

Now the office was packed with people eating and drinking, and I kept on hearing the word 'party'. I asked one middle-aged guy eagerly filling his face with pizza what he meant by party.

"It's the South Beach office party. I've come for the party. It's a great idea, and it's great that they've put so much food and drink on" he said before taking another slice of pizza.

I was amused. I looked around and it made sense, all these volunteers I'd never seen before not doing any work.

I said: "Well I'm from the South Beach office. I come here every day and didn't know anything about a party."

He looked at me if I was mad.

"Look at all this food, all these people coming in and out every five minutes and all these women. How could this not be a party!"

I didn't have the heart to tell that it was like this every day, he was probably stuck in a call centre with a taskmaster demanding blood. Fair play to him anyway. There was no way I had the right to start saying 'you lot coming in here, eating our food, looking at our women, drinking our beer which we shouldn't have had anyway'.

"Sorry mate, I'm knackered so I'm not thinking straight. One question though, where did you hear about the party?" I asked.

"It was on the internal Obama website," he said.

"On the internal website?" I said.

He duly showed me on his Iphone. And there amongst a whole long list of other events across Florida: 'South Beach Barack Obama Office Party, off Ocean Drive, All Welcome'. I was laughing so hard my stomach was hurting because I couldn't wait to tell Kale and Mark. I'd noticed the pair of them looking at each other quizzically over the last hour concerning our guests. I hollered Kale. "Read that!" I said, pointing at the phone the bloke was holding.

Kale read about the party, blinked and then read it again.

"Jesus Christ. Jesus Fucking H Christ" he said, shaking his head before reading it again. "A fucking party, two days before the election?" Mark, did you know that someone has put up on the internal website that we're having a party in this office?"

Mark, who by now I'd worked out could have been told that Barack Obama was around the corner and needed to christen the toilet and still wouldn't have batted an eyelid, looked up from his pile of papers.

"Yeah? When's it starting?" he said in his wonderful Californian drawl.

"You're sitting in the middle of it Mark!"

He looked around at everyone eating, drinking and chatting away, shook his head and then put it back into his pile of papers.

Kale was still confused. "Someone's pulling our dick man. No-one from this office would have put that we were having a party in this office." A quick ask around and Kale was proved right. Someone had publicised a party in our office for a joke and people came, and we didn't even notice for an hour. I suppose that's why our office had to be the best in America.

We had so much fun and food but thanks to Mark and Kale we got the job done. It was good to give the lawyers such a nice welcome before they helped ensure the election wasn't stolen.

In the middle of all these lawyers came a stressed looking Karim, pulling his suitcases behind him. He was pissed off. "I've been thrown out of my hostel. I can't believe it"

"What for?" I said.

"For being an Obama volunteer. I can't believe it, I have nowhere to go."

It was the first time I'd ever seen Karim anything but cool.

"This guy, on reception, told me that they didn't want people like me in their hostel. When I asked what he meant by 'like me' he just said 'Obama'. Then he called me a troublemaker because I was asking if I could stay another night. I can't believe they told me to leave."

It was nearly 10pm. I knew why Karim came to the office, it became a second home for all of us. If in trouble, go straight to the office; it was unsaid but we all knew it.

Within seconds I said: "You can stay at our hotel if you want mate, there are two beds and either me, you or Mark can sleep on the floor." "Are you sure?" he replied. "Of course," I said without a second thought. After all, it was another way of helping the campaign. Karim wouldn't be able to enter all his data if he was on the streets. He looked relieved and agreed to stay. It would be a tight fit but, hey, a room is a room.

The office was buzzing and there was a Californian girl sitting in the corner. I noticed her watching and listening to me as I talked about eating for free in Miami and how as a journalist I had a few freebies lined up. As I was talking about my latest conquest she piped up:

"Do you know if the food is offset?"

"Offset?" I replied, confused.

"Yeah is it offset? Environmentally? Are the restaurants you've been eating at sustainable? For instance, are the tuna stocks replaced?" she said with the cold eyed stare of the earnest, eco-friendly zealot.

My mind instantly flashed to telling an American she was beautiful and her boss reprimanding me because 'beautiful was not a gender neutral statement', and another eco-warrior in Toronto bringing the whole tuna question into play at a dinner table full of lovely fish

"Bab, all I know is I've been eating for free, whether the tuna is offset or not I have no idea. It's not something that normally enters my head," I said.

Stony silence for a moment, and then she was off. For the next ten minutes she explained in every detail about the tuna stocks of the world. Now I am as green as the next man but food is food and free is free. She was a typical Californian environmentalist who was as idealistic as they come, and good on her. No leather, no meat, no anything except offset tuna. I couldn't resist telling her about the fois gras I ate in Toronto. Her face was a picture but I am glad there are people in the world like her fighting the good fight. Spending too much time talking about this stuff can usually put you off the cause though. I watched her as she picked through the office food, wondering aloud whether each product was OK to eat. I half expected her to pull out a microscope to look at the small print on the labels.

The conversation was thankfully brought to an end by the mention of the mythical Tap Tap bar. It was the Haitian bar a few blocks away that Mark, Kale and Nate would go to after the end of a long day on the campaign. It was now about 10pm and the t-shirts were put away, the printers turned off and the lights switched off, so we all headed down to it.

In a city of shiny bars, replica pubs, posh hotels and gleaming cafes Tap Tap was refreshingly shabby. The bar was small and the restaurant was closed. The barmaid was youngish, black and a welcoming smile. Behind her there was every rum imaginable. And in front of her was Nate Sherwood.

He'd had a tough day and was enjoying the rum. It was all very Ernest Hemmingway. I asked for a rum and coke and the fun began. Behind me the eco-warrior asked for a rum and coke but asked to see the coke bottle, she started the sentence 'Is this coke…?" and brilliantly the barmaid interrupted. "It's just coke, nothing more or nothing less."

As the shots came out and the eyes got bleary the phone behind the bar rang. We all looked at it. The barmaid picked it up. "Nate Sherwood? Yeah he's here." She passed the phone to Nate. "For you. It's the campaign I think". I was impressed. This guy was already one of the coolest people I'd ever met and now he's in front of me taking calls from the campaign in a rum bar. Nate took the call, listened then just said: "Yep, nope, yep, yep, ok, bye." That was it. Like I say, one cool guy.

The conversation turned to politics, and as Nate was there I started to ask him questions. I started with: "What the fuck is a super-sporadic? I've been looking for them all weekend." Nate explained that Super-Sporadics and the lesser known Super-Super-Sporadics were the key to election. This was a great piece of man management because he was hardly going to tell someone who'd spent days knocking the doors of or phoning Super-Sporadics without any luck that they weren't important.

It appears this group were people who previously voted Democrat, but that they were the most 'transient' members of society. Some were students, or even travellers. The Democratic top brass realised to beat the Republicans all the people who had ever wanted to vote Democrat had to come out and vote.

Normally, the labour intensive nature of finding Super-Sporadics meant they were always at the bottom of the list in elections. But not in this election, because they had people like me. In fact millions of people like me. In fact enough volunteers to send poor souls out with a list of Super-Sporadics in the knowledge that out of probably 100 addresses only 10 per cent would be still there. Add that 10 per cent up across America and that is a lot of people.

He ended his explanation with: "Most of our volunteers, Broooomie, don't get themselves arrested looking for Super-Sporadics." He had a point, but he'd put my mind to rest. If the Democrats were working to such a degree to win the election there was a good chance they would.

Nate was passionate about the campaign; in fact he was more passionate about the campaign than Obama. That fascinated me. I loved what Obama was doing but was cynical enough to know he'd probably balls it all up in the end - he's a politician after all. Nate gave me the best definition of the campaign and why it was so important to America:

"Man, this campaign isn't about Obama, it's about the people who are in the campaign. It is about the networks of people that have been created to make this campaign work. It is about neighbours talking to each other about their neighbourhoods for the first time. It's about these networks of people working together and changing the country from the bottom up. Obama is just one man, even if he is President he can't totally change the country because he is just one man. The only way there will be change is after he's elected, or not elected, these local networks of people who worked together during the campaign stay together. If they all disappear then it won't work. It's about the volunteers and the people man, it's about the people."

With that fascinating insight into the election a Chinese woman burst in and shouted "Naaaaaaate!" Everyone turned around in shock and watched as she headed towards a startled Nate. "I found yuuu," she said, almost crying. If someone's face could have contorted to literally say 'For fuck's sake' it was Nate's in the Tap Tap bar.

We all sat back and watched the scene. It became pretty obvious that this pretty twenty-something was besotted with the American hero. Who could blame her, I was? It was like been in the presence of greatness. I looked on with amazement as Nate tried to sort out the situation. She was obviously madly infatuated with him. She was laying herself on a plate for him but he took her outside for a sit-down. Trying not to be nosy but looking through the window, I saw him kindly but firmly tell her something which made her burst in to tears. I turned away in case they saw me. Five minutes later they returned.

He sat beside me and calmly said: "Where were we?", as if nothing had happened.

"What, before Natemania overtook the bar?" I said with a smile. "Are you crazy? She's lovely, you could spend the night with her"

I was expecting a smile. It didn't come. Nate looked at me in the eye. I thought I might have offended him, as you never know how some people are going to react when you bluster in to their personal shit.

"Adam, I have a girlfriend man, I love her man, so there is nothing to it." Then he uttered the immortal words: "It's cool to be faithful man, it's cool to be faithful man. Never a truer word has been spoken.

Before I could draw breath there was another grand entrance. "DUDE WHERE'S THE CHICKS, MAN?" It was square necked Mark, who'd guessed where I was. He had some good news. "Hey dude, I've got us an upgrade man." This is where alarm bells should have started ringing in my head, but with the peach rum and the general ambience they were nowhere to be seen. My radar for potential trouble was broken beyond repair.

"An upgrade?" I replied instantly, thinking of having a bigger room and maybe another bed for Karim. "Brilliant."

I thought I'd let him bask in his glory. "Yeah dude, you won't believe what I have got for us. Only the fucking ocean view VIP rooms, one each!!"

Again my brain's early trouble warning system did not kick in. In fact, I was happy as can be.

"Get that man a drink!" I shouted.

"Dude man, we have to go out and find some chicks man, they will be amazed by our rooms, they're awesome man," he said.

"Do they have two beds in each room?" I asked.

"Dude, two beds, sofas, kitchens and mine has a Jacuzzi, man" he said, not realising that he'd taken the piss by taking the room with the Jacuzzi.

"Fucking brilliant. Meet Karim. He's staying in your room with you" I said pulling Karim out of his conversation about tuna offsetting with the eco-warrior. Mark's face was a picture as he thought he wouldn't be alone with any lady.

I couldn't keep him in suspense. "Only joking, I'm not pulling any chicks, it's cool to be faithful. Karim will stay with me. You hear that Karim, you've got a bed for the night?" Karim seemed perplexed by Mark and all the talk of Ocean View VIP rooms but he was just happy to have a bed for the night.

The night carried on amid more shots of rums and more and more laughter. Mark was getting twitchy - there were no chicks and he kept on angling to leave with me. There was no chance I was going to go clubbing, but I had an idea. "Mark, meet my friend. She's from California, you two must have a lot in common" I said as I passed him on to the eco-warrior and returned to my conversation with Nate and Karim.

Five minutes later I eavesdropped into the conversation just as Mark was saying: "We're killing this planet I haven't eaten tuna for years because it's so hard to find offset tuna where I am." The guy had his faults but I couldn't help but like him. I'm sure he'd had a tuna melt the day before. "Hey Adam, we're going to a club for a dance," was the next I heard from him as to my delight the world's most ill-matched pair, him after snatch, her just wanting to talk about the size of a trawlers catch, left the bar.

I tried to sober up when I approached the hotel reception but I needn't have worried and got my new hotel room key straight away. I opened the door and we walked into a long corridor until the suite opened up in front of us. We gasped. It was perfect. Totally white and it looked like it had never been stayed in before. There were two big double beds side by side and a giant flat screen television and matching stereo. The windows opened on to a massive balcony which overlooked the ocean and the hotel's swimming pools complex below. The bathroom was as big as my room in the Argentinean hostel and had a bath as well as a power shower cubicle. There was a bowl of fruit and drink on the table with a note from the manager welcoming me.

Karim said: "Wow, I thought you were joking when you said you were a travel journalist. They must want to impress you, how much would this room cost?" I cracked open the red wine and ate a strawberry and then wandered on the balcony to look across the sea. Life was good. In fact life was brilliant. It felt better to have Karim with me, it's always better to share a great hotel room. Only hours earlier he was pissed off and homeless because he was being thrown out of a crappy hostel, tonight he would be sleeping in style.

I joked that we had the best room of any Obama volunteers in Miami. Except Mark of course, he had the next door room with the jacuzzi. The hotel wasn't even finished so there was a good chance that we were the first to stay in the suite. Even then I was remarkably incurious about how Mark had managed to get me upgraded from a bog standard double room to two brand new suites. Ignorance is bliss, as they say.

After demolishing the fruit and chocolates we put the television on and watched the news channels. It was wall to wall election coverage. Obama was looking tired and so was McCain, Joe Biden's teeth were fading and Sarah Palin still gave me a hard on. Everything had been said already, now they were just saying it again but not as smoothly because the exhausting campaign was coming to a close.

The election coverage was hypnotic. I loved CNN's Situation Room back in Britain but in America there were hundreds of programmes, over-enthusiastic pundits and sinister election adverts. As the Right was getting closer to defeat their attacks on Obama were becoming more and more strident. The attack adverts were on during every break. A new one focussing on Obama's black vicar was the closest to bone I had seen and it was on all of the time. Karim was troubled by it, but I thought it showed how desperate they were. In fact it wasn't McCain sanctioned anyway, just the work of an independent hate group.

We put Fox News on and gawped at it in amazement. The vitriol was staggering. "They won't let him win, you know that Adam," Karim said darkly. He thought there'd be another re-run of the 2000 election result but I was convinced the Obama campaign was too big to be defeated. I'm not a great believer in conspiracies. I believe in the conspiracy of the cock up. Massive organisations often struggle to deliver even basic services, so worldwide conspiracies where everything runs like clockwork are unthinkable. Someone, somewhere would almost certainly cock it up or blab about it to the wrong person.

"Yeah, but how many people can say they tried to prevent it Karim? We're here, and there are millions like us."

"What if he loses Adam?" Karim added.

The thought was so sad. After coming all the way to Miami to watch him lose would be terrible. I'd have felt guilty too, because in truth I'd been a pretty shit volunteer.

"What time are we getting in to the office tomorrow ?" Karim asked. It was the last full day before polling, but surely it wouldn't be as hectic as the Saturday because everyone was back at work. "First thing I suppose mate," I said. Then I remembered. "Err actually, I've got somewhere to be at 11am so I'll have to come in the afternoon." Karim looked at me, wondering what I could possibly have to do that was more important than getting Barack Obama elected.

What he didn't know was that I had a date with Destiny. Well, a date with a Florida billionaire actually. I'd been asked by Destiny to attend the opening of Miami's brand new skyscraper, hotel and leisure complex Icon. The billionaire who had paid for the project was going to be officially opening it with the French bloke who had designed it.

I was racked with guilt. I should have been helping Obama, but I figured as usual that everyone I spoke to I would urge to vote Obama.

I fell asleep about 2am, delighted to be in the most comfortable bed I'd ever slept in and happy that I was doing my bit for the campaign by putting two other volunteers up in the process. The next week would be the most insane seven days of my entire life.

Facebook status: Steve Zacharanda met an Obama fan called Mark let him stay at his free hotel, left him there and when I got back he'd upgraded to two free suits, now Karim is staying as well!

Adam banished from Eden

Monday, November 3

The phone ringing woke us up. It was Mark. "Hey Dude!" I put the phone on speakerphone so Karim could hear.

"Did you have a good night Mark, find any chicks?" I said, winking at Karim. Mark's tone changed: "Are you kidding me? You're kidding me right?"

Karim and I smiled.

"Adam, you're joking right, are you trying to tell me we didn't wake you up last night? You are trying to tell me that you didn't here THAT?"

"What?" I replied, trying not to laugh but having no idea what he was talking about.

"Dude, me and a chick were at it all night man, are you seriously trying to say you didn't hear us? You got to be kidding me. She was screaming and hollering all night man."

His disappointment was palpable.

"Is she there now?" I asked.

"No, she left about an hour ago."

"So you could be making the whole thing up then? How do we know you had a girl back?" I said, laughing with Karim, whose face was a picture. Needless to say winding Mark up about not pulling a chick was not the best idea because we got chapter and verse about what him and the 'chick' did.

Then my mind clicked. "Hold on. Is this the tuna fishing chick we are talking about?" I asked, remembering that the last time I'd seen him he was escorting her towards a taxi with a night at Salsa club beckoning.

"Man, no-way man, that chick was mad, she didn't want to dance with me in the club and then said she felt tired and went home, so I stayed on my own and got chatting to some chicks, you should have come man. You could have got yourself some ass man."

I laughed again. I would have loved to have seen the tuna girl as she slowly realised Mark couldn't care less about the environment and the only fish he was interested in was the red snapper in her pants. "I'm happy with my girlfriend" I said.

With that Mark banged the interlocking door. I opened it and in he walked, wearing only the hotel's dressing gown. He immediately gave me a high five and invited the two of us into his suite. I couldn't believe it. It was huge and even had its own jacuzzi and kitchen. The bed was giant size and I'm sure the carpet was lovely but I couldn't see it under Mark's strewn clothes. "The chick loved the room man." I was waiting for the 'thank you' but it didn't come. Then, again he got the upgrade not me.

I needed to go to the bank as I'd run out of money. Mark and Karim decided to wait outside as I went in to get the last of my wedge. As usual I was treated with respect and warmth by the North Beach HSBC staff. However, I ended up being passed back and forth from one idiot in an Indian call centre to another prat in the Swansea overseas banking centre.

At one stage after 20 minutes of giving my details to some semi-literate prick I discovered he was part of the 'changing details' part of the operation, and because he'd changed everything my account was on lockdown. Then after another 20 minutes talking to some bint in Swansea she told me that although there was £400 showing in my account she was not authorised to give it me.

The poor American banker whose phone I was using jumped out of his skin when I yelled: "I'm stuck in Miami trying to change the fucking world and now I can't get my own money because you useless dimwits can't do simple arithmetic or put me through to the right thicko in India. This global bank is a total crock of shite, I'm a journalist and I will forever slate your brand till the day I die. Why can't you all be like the American arm of your shite bank. And before you put the phone down I'll save you the trouble!" I calmly got up, shook the startled banker's hand and said: "No offence old boy." I walked out of the bank contemplating five days in Miami without money. Luckily, my angel from Stoke, Sam, agreed to lend me £300 and so enabled me to fight another day.

I had to get to Mary Brickell village for 11am for one of the swankiest opening parties Miami had ever seen. Destiny and Richard from Zakari PR had been quite insistent that I went along to the opening of the Ikon skyscraper complex. I was there for a few hours and immediately felt guilty for not campaigning as I had to listen to speeches from a fella called George and a French bloke. I did my bit playing the foreign journalist interested in the project, then phoned Mark for a lift. I'd just given up the chance of speaking to my first ever billionaire, for 'George' was one the most powerful men in Florida, Mr George Perez. The 'French Bloke' everyone was fawning over was none other than Philippe Starck, one of the world's foremost design geniuses. You win some, you lose some.

Facebook status: Steve Zacharanda sipped champagne and ate rum truffles with a billionaire but was rather underdressed and had no money..

The office was heaving. It was the last day before an election that would define a generation and change America forever. The free food was now becoming ridiculous, with tables piled high with pizzas, sandwiches, fried plantains, subs, burgers, tacos and a whole heap of food stuffs I'd never seen before.

Mark, Eric and Kale looked exhausted and I could tell tensions were rising because of Eric's tendency to give out terse orders. Mark and Kale had run the office from the start but Eric, who I'd now noticed had no hair anywhere, had more experience; unfortunately he often forgot that the people he was ordering around were volunteers.

As usual Karim had his head buried in his Mac processing figures, not lifting his eyes to avoid the tension, and Nate strode through the chaos like a serene blonde hero on a battlefield who didn't care about the arrows or bullets flying around him. Then he saw me and his expression changed.

"Suzie Sponder from Jewish Women For Obama has been trying to get hold of you."

My heart skipped a beat. I guessed it wasn't good news.

"She needs to speak to you. She wants to talk to you about 'the incident' at the hotel."

My mouth dried up.

"Incident?" was all I managed to say as the bile rose up my throat and into my saliva glands.

"Yeah, there was an incident at the hotel you are staying at. She sounds pissed man."

I thought back to the night before.

"Nate, me and Karim were with you last night. After we left Tap Tap we went home to bed, ask Karim."

I could see that he remembered last night but dealing with some shit volunteer from Birmingham's problems were the last thing on his mind.

"I'll call her now. What's her number?" I said.

I felt physically sick. It must have been serious if Suzie had taken time from her job to phone Nate about 'the incident'. I remembered the conversation with Mark when I woke up earlier that day. His words: "Yeah man, we did it on the balcony, someone even shouted up to complain," shot into my mind.

Shit. A customer must have complained to the manager about Mark having sex on the balcony and then someone at the hotel must have taken the trouble to phone the tourist board and complain to the Suzie about the journalist getting a free room and pissing off paying customers.

I began to swear profusely, then my knees went weak and I had to lean against the wall. Karim, with his beautiful sunshine way, walked past and asked what was wrong.

"Someone's complained about me shagging someone on the balcony to the tourist board" I spat out with venom.

"Hey, calm down. It wasn't you so you'll be ok."

I didn't have the heart to tell him then that he'd be homeless again tonight if I didn't sort this shit out. I couldn't wait to phone Suzie; some people put off hearing bad news, but don't. I want to hear bad news straight away because my overactive imagination means that whatever is in my head is usually a thousand times worse than the reality.

The words 'I've a bone to pick with you' are seared in my soul because my mum used to say it all the time. Whether it be uneaten sandwiches under my bed, lost travelcards or keys, lost dental braces, a lie uncovered or anything else she'd found she'd say 'I've got a bone to pick with you' and then not tell me for hours, leaving me stewing. Now as an adult I don't fuck around. Tell me now, or lose my interest. My own idiocy and stupidity is not a waiting game.

I left the office. I like to be outside for important conversations. I like to walk around and use my hands and bend my knees to gesticulate. I knew the approach. I'd blame everything on Mark. I'd done a good turn for a fellow Obama volunteer, for the campaign to help change the world, and through my naivety I had let everyone down - but it wasn't strictly my fault.

The phone rang out. I thought about putting the phone down after four rings then remembered Suzie wouldn't recognise the number anyway. It kept ringing, then that awful click. The click that means it hasn't gone to answer phone. The click that means it's time to perform.

"Hello, Suzie Sponder."

"Alright Suzie it's Adam, you wanted to speak to me?"

"ADAM! WHAT HAVE YOU DONE?!"

Shit. This sounded bad. I felt sick again straight away.

"Err, what have I done?" I said with a whimper.

"I CANT BELIEVE YOU'VE DONE THIS TO ME. I CANT BELIEVE YOU'VE DONE THIS TO ME ADAM, AFTER EVERYTHING I'VE DONE FOR YOU."

"Done what?" I said, keeping it simple. I didn't want to get into the shagging on the balcony because I now thought it might be even serious than that.

"Adam, I get you a free room and you threaten the manager to get an upgrade. This just doesn't happen to me. This type of thing just doesn't happen in my job. The manager of the hotel has phoned to complain. Do you know what that means? Do you understand? It was me who recommended you! I thought I knew you. I cannot believe how you acted. I cannot believe it. It just doesn't sound like you. My boss is chewing my ass for this."

She was speaking too fast, and I couldn't process what I was hearing to say anything back to her.

"You had a perfectly good room. You have to move out of there tonight."

Those words 'move out of there tonight' struck the fear of God into me. It was time to talk.

"Suzie, Suzie, please calm down" I pleaded. "I haven't spoken to the manager. I was campaigning yesterday, I checked in and left."

"Well the manager said that you asked him to come to your room and then demanded an upgrade and now you have the two best suites in the hotel. So how the hell did that happen? What room are you staying in Adam?"

"Errr...actually I did get an upgrade," I said before she had chance to say anything else. Finally the alarm bells started to ring.

"Shit. It was Mark."

"MARK?! WHO THE FUCK IS MARK?" Suzie shouted.

"Mark, the Obama volunteer I told you about. You said he was OK", said I, in a pathetic attempt to shift the blame to him and her.

"But the room is under your name. The room is under your name. Do you understand? Your name. Not Mark's or anyone else's, but your name."

For a split second I was going to mention Karim, just for a laugh, but this wasn't the time or the place.

"Your name. So you are responsible for whatever happens in that room. My position is not party political. I can't even say you're an Obama volunteer because my bosses will think that I've done you a favour because you're helping Obama. Which is not the case, because you said you were a - what were your words - 'a syndicated travel journalist who can reach a million readers'.

For the next five minutes I got taken apart. Perhaps it was the New York accent. Perhaps it was because I didn't have a leg to stand on. Perhaps it was because I am a total fucking idiot. I couldn't believe that I hadn't questioned Mark when he'd turned up at the Tap Tap bar saying he'd got an upgrade. I'd broken the cardinal rule of freebies. I'd caused trouble. I'd brought attention to myself. I'd left a bad taste in the mouth of people who had just tried to help me.

"And the manager of the Alexander Hotel phoned up to say you couldn't even be bothered to turn up to the tour of the hotel Adam. Do you know how that looks? No journalist has ever done this to me. And of all people, you. I even welcomed you into my home."

That last line really hit the spot. My legs were now as weak as American beer. Cunt is an overused and horrible word but I felt a complete one.

"I'll sort it out" I said with about as much conviction as a baghead says when he borrows a tenner and tells you he'll give it back tomorrow.

"YOU FUCKING BETTER SORT IT OUT. YOU BETTER SORT IT OUT NOW. DO WHATEVER YOU HAVE TO DO BUT SORT IT OUT ADAM. AND DON'T MENTION OBAMA."

With those fateful words the phone was unceremoniously slammed down. I was in the shit. I had no money for a hotel that night, let alone for the rest of the week. I had to come up with a story. I thought of the last words she said: "Do whatever you have to do but sort it out and don't mention Obama."

As well as the prospect of Karim and I being kicked out the night before the election I felt a deep pain at letting Suzie down. She had been a wonder during the trip and we'd been through so much, missing Obama and then campaigning with Barry and her daughter. I felt we had become friends. She'd invited me into her home and I had let her down.

I had to come up with a plan and quick. I thought about the facts. I hadn't spoken to the manager. The manager thought I was Mark. The manager had never seen me. I could blame it all on Mark, the idiot. My blood boiled at the square necked prick. The obvious excuse was the truth. I was doing a good turn for a fellow Obama volunteer and had been let down badly. But I couldn't mention Obama, so somehow I had to come up with an excuse for why some bloke was in my room and felt comfortable enough to pretend to be me and threaten the manager to get an upgrade.

By the time I got back to the office I'd come up with a story. It was demented. It was evil genius. It was fucking insane. But it was the only plan I had, and the only one that ticked all the boxes.

As I approached the office square necked Mark shouted: "Dude, what's happened?". "You, that's what's happened. You happened. You have totally fucked me up" I said whilst striding past him into the office.

I wanted to run my plan past Mark, Kale and Karim. First, I painted the picture. I told them what had happened and what I planned to do about it. Now, credit to these three wonderful human beings they didn't laugh me out of the office. They could tell it was serious. They'd never seen this Brooomie so angry. Good Mark's lip curled up in a smile and that was it. None of them betrayed the insanity of the situation. I like to think it's because they cared, or perhaps they were more worried about getting Obama elected in a few hours time. "Good luck, brother" said Kale as he put a sympathetic hand on my shoulder.

The first part of the plan was to get bad Mark onside so I couldn't rant and rave. He had to go along with the plan or it wouldn't work. If he started thinking he could tell the truth then the whole thing would come apart. I told him we needed to speak in his car, and outlined the situation:

"I'm totally fucked. Fucked more than I ever have been before. In ten years of travel journalism I have never been as fucked as this. Whatever you said to the manager yesterday means that I am about to get thrown out of the hotel and won't be able to stay at any other hotel after this. The manager has complained to the Miami Tourist Convention and the woman who sorted the hotel rooms out is getting shit from her fucking boss. And I have no money. So do you understand how fucked I am?"

After shaking his head he said in an angry tone: "Dude. Don't raise your voice. People are walking past. There's no need to be angry, we can sort this out."

Wrong answer.

"Sorry, but I'm fucked. What the fuck happened yesterday Mark?" I asked.

"Well, when I got into the room I thought it probably wasn't big enough for the two of us. There was no way one of us could bring a chick back. I phoned reception to speak to the manager to say I wasn't happy."

Dumbfounded at his lack of self awareness I just repeated: "You weren't happy?"

Mark continued: "I couldn't believe it when he came up to see me, but you see I'm not stupid. I'd phoned reception and asked what the spare capacity was in the hotel. Only 30 per cent of the rooms were full, so when he came up to see me I knew that 70 per cent of the rooms were available and there was no need for us to be sharing a room."

I should now have been spitting feathers but I was overcome with grudging respect and let him continue.

"You see me and my ex-wife used to go all over America when she was going to dentist conventions. She would always find out what the hotel's capacity was running at and then, if it was below sixty percent, she'd ask the manager for an upgrade because no would way that many new customers come through the doors that same night, so it doesn't matter if you move rooms. I told him I was writing an article about this place and thought we should get an upgrade. I learnt a lot from my ex-wife, we stayed in a hell of a lot of hotels."

The last sentence awoke me from my slumber.

"Did your wife pay for the rooms?" I asked.

"Yes, of course she did."

"Well, that's the difference because I got my one small room for fucking free. I don't have the right to ask for an upgrade because the hotel capacity is running lo…hold on, what do you mean you were writing an article? Did you pretend to be me?"

For the first time Mark now looked sheepish.

"Well, he presumed I was you and kept on calling me Mr Smith, so I just let him."

I palmed the guilt card from the bottom of the deck:

"I can't believe you did that Mark. That is a breach of trust, and it's totally ruined my holiday because now I'l have to stay in a hostel instead of a five star hotel later this week. Not to mention Suzie will complain to my boss back home about what has happened, and I'll be blacklisted from all hotels in America because Suzie will put me on the 'not to be trusted' list."

Since he was now attempting to apologise I figured it was time to outline my plan.

"I've got a plan." I said with an optimistic tone in my voice.

"A plan?"

"Yeah, a plan to get me out of this situation and a plan to make Suzie and her boss happy again. Please hear me out. If you don't go along with this plan my life is totally fucked."

"Go ahead" he said earnestly, having no idea what was coming next.

"Right. Listen carefully."

I took a deep breath.

"I am gay, and I've met you on the internet. This is the first time I've met you. This was meant to be a lovely weekend. You've turned into an abusive and bullying partner. You took it on yourself to upgrade the rooms, something I would never dream of. I am now mortified by the situation you've got me into and I am a bit scared of you. I want the hotel to throw you out, because, in gay terms you're too much of a bull for me to handle."

Silence. I could see it rolling around his head. My palms were sweating at the prospect of his answer.

"Woah. Woah. WOAH. Jesus fucking H Christ!" he said, getting redder by the minute. This wasn't the way I'd planned it. He gripped my arm rather tightly and stared into my eyes.

"Hey dude. I AM NOT GAY."

Then in a quieter tone to press home his point he said again: "I am not gay."

I thought it better to let him carry on.

"I am not gay, I've never been gay and I sure as hell will never be gay."

Then he looked out of the window and said under his breath: "Shit, I didn't even know you were gay."

Great. I had a raving homophobe on my hands who could scupper my brilliant 'being gay' plan. Then it started getting daft and before it clicked that he now thought I was really gay Mark started getting very agitated. "Who on the campaign thinks I'm gay? I've met some chicks man, they can't think I'm gay. Shit I'm not gay, man."

I thought I better step in. "Look, I know you're not gay. You know you're not gay. In fact nobody knows you're gay. The only person who will ever think you are gay is some bloke in a hotel you will never stay in again. What does it matter if he thinks you're gay? Mate, it's the least you can do. All you have to do is look crestfallen, pick your luggage up and leave the hotel. I'm going to be the one who's doing all the talking. Do you think I want to pretend I'm gay either?"

To my everlasting shame I said: "Look, I dislike gays as much as you do, but I've got to do this for my career, you owe me."

He looked a broken man. "Dude, have you told anyone else about this plan?"

I lied again. "I've not told anyone. I promise."

"So no one on the campaign will ever think I am gay?" he asked again. I scented victory. Like the feeling when someone opens their wallet to lend me £20, I was tantalisingly close to closing the deal.

"OK dude. But I'm not happy about this whole gay thing" he said.

Relief swept over me. "Thanks dude. OK, let's do it."

"What, now?"

"Yes now". I didn't want to go back to the office and risk a barrage of laughter at my improbable plan.

Throughout the entire journey Mark moaned about the situation and about how much of an ass the manager was. Worryingly he kept on saying he wanted to sort it out for me and do all the talking, but I stayed strong. I carried on throwing the guilt trips in and telling him I'd have nowhere to stay and my job was on the line. I was nervous but in a weird way looking forward to the challenge. Surely, the hardest part of all was convincing Mark of the merits of plan. By now I couldn't stand the sight of him and wanted him out of the hotel anyway. He would have to be the sacrificial lamb for me and Karim to stay.

Adam enters Eden - again

We pulled into the hotel car park and looked at each other.

"Are you really going to do this Adam? This is one of your British jokes isn't it?" Mark asked.

"Of course I'm going to do it. I have no choice. Suzie is relying on me."

Mark put his head in his hands. I couldn't help but laugh.

"What do I have to do?" he said.

"Nothing, just sit here and wait."

"You're crazy, man. You are crazy" he said as I jumped out of the car.

As usual it was hot and I was sweating but that would only play into my hands. I walked up the steps towards the lobby but realised I hadn't totally thought through the whole plan. I went for a little walk. I checked to see if I had my passport to prove I was me and not Mark, that I hadn't asked for any upgrade and that it was all a huge mistake.

I started to get into my part. Though I was going to pretend to be gay I wasn't going to ham it up with a camp accent and effeminate walk. The facts would speak for themselves. I was the real Adam Smith. I'd met someone over the internet and he'd gone mad. It was obvious I was gay, there was no need to ram it down anyone's throat.

Now, it's not something that I'm proud of but I can lie. I am a great liar. I can look you straight in the eye and tell you that you're black when you're white. I've had to be a good liar over the years, and I started young. I was scared stiff of my mother as a child, and to spare myself being screamed at I had to lie and lie often. I think I started as soon as I could talk. I knew which answer would make my mother lose her temper, so I always said the one which wouldn't.

My mum hated lying and liars. Top of the lying charts was my dad, who ran off with another woman that 33 years later my mum still refers to as Fanny despite her name being Bernie. I was two. She used to say: "You're just like your dad, the bastard, he always used to lie, couldn't even lie straight in bed he used to lie that much. I could never understand why he lied about even the smallest things. I'd say 'Bruce, have you posted that letter?' and he'd say 'Yes, I posted it today.' Then lo and behold a couple of days later I'd find the letter in his jacket. It just didn't make sense to me."

It made total sense to me. If dad had said 'No, I haven't posted that letter, I forgot all about it' he'd have got a load of grief, so it was just easier to tell a lie and post the letter the next day. I suppose it's just lying for an easy life, and I've always wanted an easy life, so it was always easier to lie than tell the truth and lying became second nature.

However, whenever I got caught out lying, which wasn't that often considering how many lies I told as a child, there was hell to pay. Needless to say the beatings didn't stop me lying, they just made more determined to tell better ones. As I graduated into adulthood I carried on lying, usually to girlfriends and usually for an easy life, to spare someone's feelings or to cover up a bigger sin. Teachers, lecturers, landlords, bank managers and bosses have been all been lied to as well, stories concocted about girlfriends losing babies, being mugged at knifepoint, finding religion and moving to Australia. Webs of deceit have been spun and often left untangled but as I entered my late 20s I retired from lying full time. Life is too short and hand on heart I can say I don't lie very much now - but all the skills are there.

Due to this complex relationship with the truth I cannot bear a bad liar. There's nothing worse than someone lying when they're a rubbish liar. If their story isn't straight and it's un-thought through it's the biggest insult of all. If you're going to lie make sure it's good and I believe it. Don't insult me by leaving us both standing there knowing you're lying but still going along with the pretence that it is the truth.

The secret lies with believing your own bullshit. If you're not going to believe it no one else will. If you're going to tell a big lie you have to walk in that lie's shoes to the bitter end. I told a wonderful girlfriend once I'd coughed up blood in the toilet at a restaurant because I wanted to get away and watch the football. When she moaned and didn't want me to go home I was even more pissed off because in my mind I'd coughed up blood, and imagine how pissed off you'd be if I you'd coughed up blood and someone was moaning about letting you go home early.

As I stood outside the Eden Roc Hotel I knew I was about to tell someone I'd never met before but who would have a big hand over the next few days a pack of complete lies, and I was fine with that. It felt like every lie in thirty two years had built up to this moment.

I knew I had the element of surprise. When the manager came out to see Adam Smith he'd be expecting Mark, but it would be me and I'd have a passport to prove it. I needed to look desperate, embarrassed, vulnerable and honest so the manager would take pity on me and let me stay in the hotel. I also had to get him to write an email to Suzie's boss saying it had been a big mistake and that Adam Smith was in fact a bloody lovely bloke. A tall order, I know, but that was the objective. I knew I had to pull out the performance of my life to keep this brilliant holiday on track and save face for Suzie.

I put my 'death knock' face so it looked like something was seriously wrong. It's the same face I used to put on when I had to speak to the relatives of a dead person. My voice goes up an octave and I sound ever so sorry to even be on the planet, let alone talking to you. I said a prayer, looked up to the sky for a second and then walked into the hotel.

The receptionist I'd tipped the day asked how she could help. I dropped the death knock face as I didn't fancy telling her I was gay or desperate so I asked her to get the manager as I had an urgent problem. I sat down in the lobby and watched people coming and going whilst thinking about the mess I'd got myself into. I tried to look agitated ready for when the manager arrived.

"Mr Smith?"

A female voice this time. I stopped looking at my shoes, lifted my head up and widened my eyes to give the 'ol' puppy dog stare'.

"That's me" I said with a quivering voice.

"Hi, I'm the duty manager. How may I help? Is everything OK?"

Obvious the physical aspect of my lying was already working and she had my sympathy.

"Everything is not OK I'm afraid. I've made a huge mistake and I need you to help me."

At this point I'd convinced myself I was in so much trouble I was about to burst into tears at any point and so was finding it hard to control my voice.

"Calm down, calm down, Mr Smith."

I fished my passport out of my pocket and gave it to her.

"Look, I'm Adam Smith" I said looking her in the eye. "I am Adam Smith"

"I know you're Adam Smith, I just asked for Mr Smith" she said, looking at the passport then back at me as if I was a total nut job.

I thought I better take control of the situation and get to the point about me being the victim of an internet gay bully-boy.

"I 'm a travel journalist and I've reviewed hundreds of hotels across the world, but this morning there was a complaint made about me from someone at the hotel to the Miami Tourist Convention. They said I'd been abusive to the manager and demanded an upgrade, something I've never done in a career of being a travel journalist - it just isn't the done thing. Now, this is where I made a grave error of judgement. I was involved in a messy break up from a long term relationship earlier this year and it cut deep."

For dramatic effect I stopped talking and took a deep breath before waiting for her to put her hand on my knee and say 'I'm sorry, go on", which she did.

"Well I started using dating websites and social networking sites to get to know people and I wanted to use my time in Miami to have a holiday romance. I met this guy online and..."

For dramatic purposes I then looked into the middle distance and paused.

"He just seemed so nice. So I asked him to stay with me at the hotel. But the last 24 hours have been some of the worst of my life and now I could even lose my job because of him. It's become a complete nightmare. I checked in yesterday, and went down to South Beach to get a flavour of the area. Whilst I was gone he must have pretended to be me and demanded an upgrade. He told me that he'd organised the upgrade as a thank you. This morning the Tourist Board phoned me to complain about my behaviour. They said I had been threatening and abusive and I might have to leave. I can't believe it. All I wanted was a discreet holiday romance."

This, to me, now seemed totally viable and I waited for her response. I looked her in the eyes. She stood up straight away. Which wasn't a good sign.

"I'll have to get the manager" she said.

"What? I thought you were the manager?"

"I'm the duty manager."

I felt robbed. I'd given my all for nothing.

"I'll get the manager. Don't worry though, I'm sure he'll be fine. I know the incident you're talking about I think he dealt with it personally"

I sat back and, remembering I was still in character, put my head against the wall and looked towards the ceiling. The proper manager would know that I was the real Adam Smith. What could go wrong?

I watched her walk across the giant lobby to the management suite and kept an eye on the door. Five minutes passed before the door edged open, and within seconds I was in a panic. The duty manager pointed to me and within five steps I knew the manager was gay. Now I faced the prospect of trying to trying to convince a gay man I was gay when I am not. This was something had I had not bargained for. This was an eventuality I had not foreseen. This could jeopardise the whole charade. I was going to be that 'bad liar' that I hate so much.

Not being gay myself I don't know if gays can spot one another a mile off but I doubt I'd set off too many gaydars in my time, mainly because I don't dress well enough. Then I remembered a mate of mine who used to chat gay guys up just to get free drinks when our money ran out. That gave me a little bit of hope.

I'd backed myself into an almighty corner. I couldn't escape from the lie because I'd told the duty manager and she in turn had probably told him everything. I decided to look scared and let him do the talking first. My heart was pounding as he approached and I was starting to feel rather stupid. My plan seemed to be in tatters. Maybe it wasn't as foolproof as I'd thought.

I thought 'In for a penny, in for a pound', and decided I was going to see this through to the bitter end. The manager was in his mid-thirties. He was a little overweight, wore a smart suit and had a shaven head; his was a very friendly face and he seemed a kindly soul.

"Hi, Mr Smith?"

I grabbed my passport out of my pocket and said: "Please look at this. I am the real Adam Smith. There has been a horrible misunderstanding and I am really, really sorry, and so very worried. Everything has been ruined. I am so sorry"

"Please Mr Smith, calm down, calm down. We will do everything to help your stay be as pleasurable as it can be."

This was a good sign. Perhaps I was overdoing the act but he seemed really concerned about me and asked someone to get me some water. I relaxed.

"Sorry. But there has been a massive misunderstanding. I am a travel journalist as you are aware, but I met my partner on the internet and this is first time we've met and I, well…err, let's put it this way, the reality wasn't what I was expecting when I said he could stay in my room. There is no way I would ever ask for an upgrade. I know the game. I've been doing this for ten years. I went down to South Beach and he said he had sorted out an upgrade. We now have two rooms, instead of one, and they're amazing but I was happy with what I had, and I thought he'd paid for the upgrade"

The manager's face betrayed nothing, he still had his strictly professional concern in place, just like my professional death-knock face.

"I then get a phone call from Suzie, who has been wonderful to me, at the Miami Tourist Board saying I had been threatening and abusive and had demanded an upgrade. I couldn't believe my ears. Honestly I don't think she believes me and I don't blame her I because I haven't told her about Mark. I have a wonderful job and this is the kind of thing that can ruin a reputation. I know I've made a terrible mistake but I was in a messy break up earlier this year and this has been my first foray into internet dating and I might have lost everything. You can see by my passport that I am Adam Smith. I would never be rude and demand anything. I'm a very reputable travel journalist."

At this stage I couldn't wait to get the whole thing over and done with, but I knew I had to stay to find out my fate.

"It was me who went up to your room yesterday, Adam"

"You?" I said with a big smile before blurting out: "So you know that I'm Adam then? And that I haven't been rude to any member of your staff?"

"Yes" he said.

I made a big play at being relieved. He carried on with a funny grin on his face, but he wasn't angry and that could only be good.

"Yes, I went up to your room and though this person was forceful I don't think I said that he had threatened me. I think there has been a misunderstanding somewhere because I didn't make a complaint about you, I just told our PR person what had happened because I had given you two suites."

Then something popped in to my head.

"Did you not think it was a bit strange that an English journalist from Birmingham had an American accent and was American?"

He turned his head to the side and brought his hands together in an exaggerated clap. "Well, I did think it was odd, but in this job you see a lot of strange things. Anyway, he did seem to know a lot about hotels, and he was very insistent about wanting a room of his own so he could get, how did he put it, 'some chicks'."

I repeated the word 'Chicks' in a mortified manner.

"And he was right. I did have spare capacity"

We both laughed long and hard as I decided whether this meant I should give up the gay ruse or whether Mark was just a heterosexual bloke who had pretended to be homosexual to get a free room from me. Mark would be the last man on earth to ever be mistaken for being gay, or at least he thought so. Another part of my fool proof plan that was anything but fool proof.

"So, do you want to stay in the room for the rest of your stay Mr Smith?"

Relief swept over me.

"I would love to. You could put me back in a bog standard room and I wouldn't mind. I just want to forget this ghastly 24 hours."

"And your friend?"

Now here was a quandary. It seemed as if I'd run into the world's nicest manager, and it looked like I'd be able to keep fellow Obama supporter Mark on board and in his room. Using the word 'friend' made me feel like I was giving up on my lie though, and the truth is I was sick of the sight of Mark. He'd taken the piss and had two free nights in a hotel because of me, and my bedraggled mistruth was still too important to lightly cast away.

I said: "No. He will be leaving. He totally ruined the first few days in Miami and I can't stand the sight of him. If you had been another manager I could have been out on the street. No, I made a big personal error of judgement due to private problems with relationships and now I've learnt another lesson. I thought we could be partners. I will tell him he has to check out today. Thank you. Thank you so much."

I put the puppy dog eyes on again. The first part of the plan worked, just, but I still had to get Suzie off the hook with her boss.

"I've learnt a valuable lesson about who to trust and who not to trust. Anyway, just one more thing. Could you email Suzie's boss at the Tourist Board and say it was a misunderstanding and that I haven't threatened anyone?"

"Of course I can Mr Smith. Feel free to stay in your suite for the rest of your stay."

Home free! This guy was a true gent, and all he cared about was the welfare of his customer, despite probably thinking I was totally insane. Perhaps it was because I'm a travel journalist and he didn't want any bad publicity, or perhaps he just saw a broken human being in front of him and wanted to help, but whatever the reason I remain indebted to him. I figured the hotel PR woman must have been the real bitch because I couldn't see this wonderful human being kicking up a stink. I was the one lying through my teeth, not him.

Then he said: "I have to tell you that your friend has incurred some charges on his room. What shall we do about them?"

"Charges? What kind of charges? Well, I'll tell him to come down and bloody pay them when he checks out. Some people are beyond belief" I said, shaking my head.

The manager looked embarrassed but looked me straight in the eye and said: "The charges included alcohol and adult movies."

With a deadpan face I repeated: "Adult movies?"

The manager, trying to suppress a smile, but still looking sympathetic, said: "Yeah, it appears your partner likes" - and here he paused for effect – "heterosexual adult movies."

The message was clear. I figured this was the manager having some fun and picking holes in the comedy story he'd just endured. I blew my cheeks out. As plans go, this had to be one of the worst of all time. Pretending that I was gay was bad enough, especially considering I was drooling over the receptionist, but pretending Mark, who couldn't go without five minutes without mentioning chicks, was gay was about as daft as it gets. I could never have guessed the manager was gay but it would have helped if Mark had tipped me off before I tried to become Quentin Crisp for an hour.

I ploughed on regardless, saying: "Never ever try and find yourself or anyone else on the internet my friend. No good can come of it. Anyway, enough of him, can you please ensure that I get a guided tour around this wonderful hotel? I'll let you into a little secret. A good travel journalist very rarely mentions in the hotels they stay in, but for you and for the Eden Roc, I shall make an exception". I grabbed his hand and said: "Thank you, this has been very embarrassing for me and you have gone above and beyond what I could ever expect."

"All part of the service, Mr Smith"

With that he smiled and walked off, thinking who knows what. I walked straight to the very grand bar, which was in the centre of the lobby and had a huge chandelier hanging above it, and tried to ordered a rum and coke on Mark's room; unfortunarely I couldn't remember what it was so I put it on mine instead. I knew Mark was waiting outside but I needed to relax and calm down before telling him he'd have to check out and pay for his heterosexual porn, which in my mind cast doubt on his story about being a sex god with a woman no-one saw the night before.

As rum and cokes go, that was one the best ever because of the relief that went with it. I had put myself and my reputation on the line to keep a roof over my head, and the bottom line was thanks to all these shenanigans Karim and I would be able to spend the next two nights in a splendid suite in one of Miami's best hotels. I felt as if I'd gone through 12 rounds with Mike Tyson. I can totally understand why method actors go mad after immersing themselves in a role for three months. I did it for an hour and couldn't cope with the stress.

I looked around and realised how beautiful the hotel was. As I've mentioned, it was Frank Sinatra's favourite haunt when the Rat Pack used to visit Miami and it still had that fifties refinement. I thought of all things they must have got up to in this fine hotel, finished my drink and headed off to break the news to Mark.

I jumped in to the seat next to Mark without a care in the world.

"What happened, dude?" he said with a worried look on his face.

"You could have told me the manager was fucking gay!" I said.

"Gay? I just thought he was helpful"

I looked him in the eyes as if he was mad.

"I think I've sorted it. Don't worry, he doesn't think you are gay at all thanks to you telling him you wanted a room to bring chicks back to and the fact that you ordered a load of heterosexual porn in your room". I couldn't keep a straight face and burst out in laughter and Mark joined in too.

"But, yeah, you've got to check out tonight and all you have to do is pay for your porn and drinks. I argued for ages that you shouldn't pay for the room because he shouldn't have given it you and he should've spotted a six foot two Californian wasn't a journalist from England."

"Thanks dude. I've sorted someone to stay anyway, so I'll be fine."

We shook hands and hugged, each of us still chuckling.

"Right, let's go back to the office and win this fucking election." I said. After that we never mentioned what had happened to each other again.

Facebook status: **Steve Zacharanda** has had to say goodbye to Mark after the complaint about 'the incident' to the Miami tourist board, just Karim and me now..........

Adam and the eve of history

I got into the office about 6pm and was determined to work as hard as I could to make up for missing the majority of the last full day of campaigning. The place seemed subdued. It was slowly dawning on everyone that within 24 hours the election would be done and dusted. Nerves were getting frayed and people kept on reminding each other of 2000, when Florida became the focal point for the entire world as lawyers argued over hanging chads and the result took weeks to be finalised.

I detected paranoia in the camp. There was a feeling that 'the man' or 'the Right' wouldn't let Obama win. Something would happen, no-one knew what, but something would prevent Obama winning. I don't think one person in that office the night before the election believed it would be fair. History had already shown that if there were going to be any dodgy goings on Florida would probably be the place.

It didn't help the television in the corner spewed out more and more alarming news of voting irregularities. There was the case of people with foreign sounding names being stopped at voting booths, or old machines not working in black areas, or people wearing any type of Obama gear being banned from voting. All this was interwoven with footage of the candidates looking more and more knackered on the campaign trail. They were now in bomber jackets instead of suits. Obama's grandmother dying also became headline news with every camera trained on his face to betray the pain in glorious High Definition colour, so that an equally tired looking news anchor could ask another tired looking person in the studio whether Obama had actually cried or not on the piece of film they had watched seconds earlier.

Every single advert was about the election and the anti-Obama ones were becoming hysterical. Always sandwiched in between was a pro-Obama advert saying how wonderful he was, though, so his war chest certainly was helping his cause in the battle for airtime. My favourite advert, the one that showed our Democratic candidate Mr Martinez beating someone up in the 1990s was on all the time, as was the advert linking Obama to his black racist pastor.

I'd never seen anything like it. When there's a General Election in Britain it's never as all encompassing as in America, regardless of how much is at stake. Perhaps it's because at home the election campaigns are kept short, but in America they're arguably two years long so when polling day finally arrive everyone is whipped up into a frenzy. Also, the law forbidding normal adverts in Britain from being used for political purposes ensures that the election isn't rammed down your throat every five minutes.

In Miami everywhere you turned there was something about the election. If you bought a cup of coffee in 7/11 you had to pick either an Obama or McCain cup to help the store's coffee cup election. If you picked up a paper, listened to the radio, logged on to a computer, the election would always be the first thing you saw or heard. If you just happened to be within spitting distance of a phone there was a good chance it'd ring, and that when you picked it up there'd be an automated message telling you one candidate would ruin the entire world if elected. For many ordinary Americans I'm sure the whole election experience is overwhelming and slightly obtrusive. Even gamers who spend their time on consoles were not out of the campaign's reach, as during this election Obama billboards even appeared in the cityscapes of computer games.

Yet the all important polls were changing all the time. One day away from the election and different ones said wildly different things. However, every poll in which Obama was leading seemed to come with a caveat about 'the Bradley effect'. This was basically short hand for saying millions of white Americans were never going to vote for a black man, but that they were too embarrassed to admit to a pollster they were racist and so claimed to be supporting Obama anyway. This didn't really make sense to me, as simply saying 'I'm voting McCain' is hardly a racially loaded statement. Nonetheless, the news anchors and journalists were always pushing the point that this election was too close to call because of all the racist Americans lying to the pollsters and going off to vote McCain in the privacy of the voting booth.

Volunteers were still bustling around the office, phone lists were still being compiled, data was still being put in to computers and t-shirts were still being sold, but more than any other day or night we were sneaking lingering looks at the television. We knew we'd done everything we could in our little corner of Florida, but we were buggered if we knew what was happening elsewhere. That little television was our window to the rest of America.

Kale's voice cut through the hubbub as one of the poll readings were being argued over on television. I'd never heard him angry before: "How the fuck can anyone be undecided one day before this election?" he said. "How after all this coverage on television and endless talking about the election can anyone, seriously, the day before the election not know who they are going to vote for?"

Kale was right. What kind of idiot, after being subjected to so many messages from every type of media known to man, could be undecided the day before polling day? What could possibly happen in a few hours to change someone's mind about who to vote for? Are these people just waiting in the hope that one candidate will produce a massive howler and say "I just love rough sex with a 12-year-old after breakfast" or "I'm all for abortion, in fact I've pulverised a few foetuses myself over the years", and therefore make their wavering undecided mind up for them? Or were the undecideds just sick to death of pollsters pestering them, so they gave them the one answer no pollster wants to hear: "I dunno mate?"

One thing's for sure, I'm always going to answer 'don't know' if I'm asked. There has to be some method in the madness. In fact I bet the people who say 'I don't know' to pollsters are the very same people who make the journey to the polling station just to spoil their ballot by writing something like 'none of the shitbags above'. You know what, more power to them, because democracy should have a place for the pro-active apathetic.

As polling day loomed I must have heard the term: "It's all going to come down to Florida again" almost as much as I heard "Have some free food, keep up the good work guys". That's why people like me, Kale, Mark, Eric and thousands of lawyers had descended on Florida, because if you're going to volunteer anywhere it might as well be a battleground where every vote counts.

The pressure on the voting apparatus was immense because the whole of America was waiting for the Sunshine State to mess it up again. It was hardly surprising, as the ramifications of the 2000 decision had changed the world. As Robin Cook, the former British Foreign Secretary, said when he resigned there was a distinct possibility there would have been no war in Iraq if those hanging chads had been counted for Gore. No Guantanamo Bay, no Abu Graib torture pictures, no relaxing of the Wall Street banking regulations, no sub-prime mortgage collapse. Who knows, Tony Blair might even have remained popular in the UK.

One look in those New York lawyers eyes had made me realise they were ready for a fight. I realise the Democratic top brass were not going to let this election get away from them, but then again without any of the above shenanigans there wouldn't have been an Obama candidacy and I wouldn't have been in America.

The feeling was that the voting officials and Republican supporting marshals would use any excuse not to allow voters in Democratic areas to cast their vote. They probably thought it was a safe bet that if someone had waited in the sweltering heat for hours to be turned away because they had an Obama badge on, they probably wouldn't bother to do it all over again. That's why the decision to let people vote in Florida in the run up to polling day was so vital because it would have been insane to try and do it on one day. The polling stations would never have coped. There were three or four hour queues most days so imagine all those people turning out in a single day. It would have been a recipe for a riot, as every simple mistake would have bern misconstrued as a conspiratorial act. Thousands of people could have been disenfranchised, which would have disastrous if the election came down to a couple of thousand votes again. It all seemed so cloak and dagger and was like nothing I've ever witnessed.

I spotted a replica ballot paper and started to look at it. I was confused, and I've got a politics degree, so God knows what an undereducated hick from a mid Florida trailer park would make of it. I counted how many boxes there were and came up with the mind boggling number of 49 places to potentially mark. There were 14 choices in the President and Vice President section, but as well as the Presidential election there was also the election for the House of Representatives, a straight fight between the Republican Lincoln Diaz-Balart and the street fighting Democrat Raul L. Martinez. There was the election for Public Defender, which had 10 entrants, and an election for State Attorney with eight candidates. Underneath all of this were the State Referendums voters had to navigate through, six of them in total. They ranged from college funding, an amendment to the State Constitution about illegal immigrants' land rights, waterfront property law and tax law. However, the most controversial one was Amendment 2 on the Florida State institution:

This amendment protects marriage as the legal union of only one man and one woman as husband and wife and provides that no other legal union that is treated as marriage or the substantial equivalent thereof shall be valid or recognized.

In as much as marriage is the legal union of only one man and one woman as husband and wife, no other legal union that is treated as marriage or the substantial equivalent thereof shall be valid or recognized.

There was a simple yes or no next to the question. I read it once, twice, three times and still thought it was bizarre and a little bit nasty. I'd seen how much this one issue had divided people at the polls and it seemed a perfect way of creating strife and prejudice. It was pure cynicism to hold the gay thing on General Election day because an unprecedented number of black voters would be at the polls and, due to historical and cultural attitudes, would probably vote against gay marriage.

I didn't take any notice of the other referendum results but sure enough that was the result and now gay people are virtual second class citizens in the state of Florida. On the same night California repealed an earlier decision to approve gay marriages. November 4 2008 was not a good day to be gay in America.

I still felt Obama would win but my optimism was waning by the hour. However, the sheer amount of people turning out to vote had to be a good sign, and especially the massive amount of black voters voting for the first time. Surely no-one would risk the fall out of cheating Obama out of a fair victory. Then again, my argument was somewhat diminished when Mark decided to change the channel to Fox News to see how they were reporting the election. I can't deny I like a bit of Fox, I find it hilarious. Of course, it's frightening that millions of people really believe all the hyperbole.

The night before the election everyone on the channel looked like they were on the brink of insanity. They looked like they knew the game was up and Obama would win, and I could imagine a mass burning of files behind the scenes, just like when revolutionaries are at the gates and everyone starts destroying evidence. We were open mouthed as we watched Ten Reasons Not to Vote for Obama by Sean Hannity. Even the title showed any flimsy veneer of objectivity had been stripped to show an intrinsic hatred of Obama. The reasons were as daft as they were dangerous, from him being best pals with a terrorist to his being a devoted disciple of Reverend Wright hell bent on bringing anyone white to their knees. I can't deny it though, I did get everyone's point that there were people in America who would do anything to stop Obama get into power, but after what I'd witnessed on the campaign trail I thought this nasty bunch were certainly in the minority.

The night before the election was the first time I heard anyone openly discuss Obama losing. The campaign had been so amazing, so life-affirming, so original, so all encompassing, so successful at uniting people of all ages and colour and so positive no-one spoke out loud about the prospect of losing. Everyone probably thought about it, but just like everyone probably thought about Obama getting shot it was a taboo subject not to be mentioned out loud.

Kale, who had given up six weeks of his life and had driven across America to Miami, said it first. "I can't even contemplate Obama losing, not after everything we've been through." Karim, who had flown across the Atlantic to help out, looked at the floor and added: "I don't want to think about it. But I don't think they will let him win." Mark, who had worked 12 hours every day for free for six weeks and had no job to go to after the election, pitched in: "We've done all we can here but who knows what the rest of the country is thinking." Then I, who'd spent the rent money to try and help my hero but had proved a pretty shit volunteer, tried to lift the mood with a cod piece of demographics: "Look, this is the first election when the majority of the black people in America will vote, and they will vote for Obama. I reckon he will win".

No-one was convinced and Mark just handed out more phone numbers for us to call in a bid to wring out the last few voters from the lists. "Let's hope we find a few undecideds! That would be like phone list gold!". With that line I went outside into the evening sun and sat on the Ocean Drive beach wall looking at the sea as I phoned everyone on my list. As usual most of the people didn't answer but those that did all seemed a bit pissed off that we were phoning again. First I had to ask if they'd voted, then if not why not, if they needed a lift to the polling station, if they had all the right documentation, and if they had voted who did they vote for. Those who voted usually said they had voted for Obama.

A laid back black dude came on the line sounding as happy as can be. "Hey man. Obama is going to win, have you seen how many people are standing in line? They're all voting Obama man. I don't need to vote."

Though totally likable this type of voter was Obama's biggest enemy. I kept calm and said: "I really wish I was as confident as you my friend. I'm in the campaign and we are all shitting ourselves thinking we're going to lose. Imagine if it's a rerun of 2000 and it goes down to the wire and you didn't vote. How are you going to feel?"

That guilt trick worked, but I used other tactics to get people to the polling station. I persuaded one guy to go and vote because I told him the queues were 'wall to wall pussy' and that loads of people had hooked up in the lines whilst waiting to vote. "The trick is to watch who goes to the back of the queue and wait for some hot chicks to come along. Join it behind them and you have an hour or so to work your magic." "Shiiit, that's what I am talking about. I'll be there, brother."

This wasn't an official line, just my own method. I exaggerated to people and said queues wouldn't be long on polling day because thousands had already cast their vote, when in fact everyone was expecting huge queues the next day. Several people said they couldn't get time off work. A lot of bosses wouldn't let their employees go out and vote because of how long it would take. I couldn't argue with that and thought 'I bet if I was American I'd be the voter who left it to the last minute and missed my chance'. After all, back in England I very rarely voted because I haven't been on the Electoral Register for years in an attempt to dodge some of the bastards I owe money to. However, in that hour sitting in the sun I persuaded at least seven people to go out and vote. My spirits were lifted and I went back to the office a happy man.

I tucked into a massive beef sub, piled my plate full of coleslaw and a very generous portion of fried plantains, cracked open a bottle of Cherry Coke and sat back to watch the goings-on in the office. Ericka was selling t-shirts hand over fist. Karim had his head buried in his laptop inputting data. The big bearded local campaigner was rooting through the lawn signs for his candidate and tossing the Obama ones aside. Kale was sitting next to the printer and playing Scrabulous on his laptop while he waited for more directions from whoever was important at the end of the fax line. Mark was returning to his huge pile of papers after obviously having another nip of the not so secret whisky bottle in the toilet, Claire was marking off numbers and compiling lists, and Eric was glued to the television looking worried.

As usual there were customers who were just milling about in the middle of the office talking shit about which colour t-shirt suited them and whether to buy a 'Cat Owners for Obama' badge, little realising they were in the middle of an election campaign office where everyone was stressed out. I couldn't help but think the South Beach Barack Obama Office was my favourite place on earth. I loved everybody in it. Everyone looked so tired but so determined and I loved the look on the face of everyone who walked in and couldn't really grasp whether it was a t-shirt and tat shop or the serious nerve centre of the campaign. As it approached 10pm the office started to empty. Everyone hugged one another as they left and promised to be there early the next morning. Ericka was deep in conversation and could tell I was listening. She was ordering t-shirts for the next day. "Hey Adam, where are you from?" she asked.

"Birmingham Ericka, more trees than Paris and more canals than Venice."

"We haven't got a t-shirt from Birmingham, do you want one saying 'UK' or something?"

"I am a Brummie"

"Brooomey?" she said.

"No Brummie. It's spelt B-R-U-M-M-I-E"

Ericka repeated "B-R-U-M-M-I-E-S" down the phone and then said: "I don't know either. He's from Birmingham, England, I can't really understand a word he says."

I couldn't help but laugh. Ericka was great. A veteran campaigner, every so often she'd let herself believe and say: "I've not seen anything like this since Kennedy." She'd often bring her dog into the office and get so busy she forgot he was there. I could see her eyes glaze over when I spoke to her; she just couldn't grasp the accent, but still pretended she understood. She must have made the campaign thousands of dollars selling t-shirts, tapping in to the zeitgeist and giving people their very own piece of Obama. She had one hell of an operation going if she was ordering t-shirts every night for the next morning.

We locked up and Kale agreed to pick Karim and I up at 6.30am the next day. It was going to be a long day because the polls on the West Coast would close hours after the East Coast and we would be on the phones to voters out West after our polls closed. Karim and I were knackered and were thankful we'd managed to stay in the hotel. Before we went to sleep we both watched television, flicking between all the news channels to see if anything major had happened in the last three or four hours. We were both nervous, but American television is hypnotic and we watched transfixed, eating up every graph, poll and pundit's view on the next day's events. I found it hard to fall asleep. I was so excited but I finally nodded off thinking about Obama winning and what the party would be like in 24 hours time.

Miss America 2004 Ericka Dunlap and Me

Me enjoying visibilty duty outside the polls

Sam and me at the Versace Mansion

Nate and Barry

Bringing Muppets for Obama to the party

The one and only Kosher King Jelvis in the office

Me and my mate Barry on Collins Avenue

All the ladies loved Barry

Maartje capturing me capturing history in that jumper

Me and Wu-Tang-Clan surrogates celebrate Obama winning

Without a care in the world: Obama wins!

Karim, Kale, Me, Mark and Willard on the last night

The State of Play on November 4 2008

Now, to understand what happens in the rest of the book I think it's about time I tell you what was going on in my life on the day that Barack Obama stood on the verge of history. I was 32-years-old. I lived in a bedsit with a load of Africans in Handsworth and was constantly broke. I'd made bad decision after bad decision concerning women and money over the last 15 years, which had resulted in me having no proper fixed abode. However, despite descents in madness, being a pubaholic and having to deal with a mother who was in and out of mental institutions I had one constant – being a journalist.

In 2000 I was selling insurance for Direct Line and was on over £30,000 with bonuses, all set to buy a house and become a fully paid up member of the rat race. One day, however, I saw a job advert for a trainee reporter at the Lichfield Mercury and sent in a well written and rather embellished CV, then grandstanded the interview. I got the job, which had an £8,000 salary, and said goodbye to any chance of owning my home and hello to a life on the breadline. It is without doubt the best decision I have ever made.

Loving every minute of it, I carved out a reputation as a competent hard news hack, although I was a bit reckless and enjoyed a night on the piss too much. I was told that I was an 'old school journalist', the type who got his stories from the pub and who ignored rules because they thought their conduct should only be called into question if their stories weren't up to scratch. Shagging colleagues and accountants, crashing pool cars, sleeping in the office to ensure I was on time, borrowing money from MPs to take women out on the town, abandoning bangers in office car parks and a whole host of other misdemeanours - I'd done them all, but at the same time I'd produced a lot of copy and some front pages.

This somewhat maverick approach had been fine on the Lichfield Mercury, Sutton Observer and Great Barr Observer. However, when I started work for the Birmingham Mail in 2005 let's just say I didn't impress the top brass – well, some of them anyway - despite being the only journalist to be in the middle of the Handsworth riots when it got really dangerous in my first week. The editor Steve Dyson made it clear he didn't like me because 'I projected an image of myself in the newsroom', or in other words I had a big personality and he wanted an office of yes men and women.

Mr Dyson and Andy once told me I'd be sacked the next day during one of my spells on probation, then didn't bother speaking to me again for a month, letting me come into work every day thinking the axe was going to fall at any moment. OK, I'd been late a few times, my local ASDA had complained about me stealing petrol and someone else had complained that I'd fallen asleep during an interview, but I've never forgotten been dangled on a string about my probation being signed off.

Luckily two other news editors, Steve Swingler and Jim Levack (who I'd been sat next to in order to be found out) both realised I was a good operator and demanded I be put out of my misery, so eventually my probation ended.

However, the paper was going downhill and as one of the only Brummies in the newsroom and the only one who still lived in a poor area of Birmingham I bore the brunt of the readers' frustrations. Every time I went to the pub, shops, or bookies someone would tell me: "Adam, your paper is shit. It's boring. I don't buy it anymore." I tried to defend the paper but I agreed with them and when the cost cutting programmes began I couldn't defend it anymore. Every journalist will tell you why they think their own paper is crap, but my main gripe was that I just didn't think it reflected the Birmingham I knew and loved. Brummies are funny people and love to chat about the absurdities of life, and there was nothing in the paper that could ever raise a smile. It *was* boring.

I loved my job though. I like to think I'm a born journalist, and I couldn't imagine doing anything else. I have to admit as well, my head is so big it knocks the chip off my shoulder. I'm known as 'Adam the Journalist' in countless pubs and clubs in Birmingham and I've never being accused of being a grass, which is an achievement. I'm the first to admit if I'd been in a stable relationship, living in a stable home environment, I might have fulfilled more of my latent potential, but fuck it.

Journalism is different from other professions. Obviously the pay is ten times worse but there are some key differences from being a teacher, policeman, doctor, lawyer, dentist etc. One is that as a journalist you can sleep with whoever you come into contact with professionally. A policeman can't try it on with a victim of crime but the journalist who pops round the house for an interview afterwards can do. My pulling power went through the roof when I became a journalist. OK, it only took about a month for the bird to realise I was skint, but as an opener 'I'm a journalist' is up there with being a pilot where I'm from. Unlike other professions a journalist can never be struck off by an official body like a doctor can be by the General Medical Council, and a journalist can get a whole host of freebies. I forewent the chance to buy a house to be a journalist so I could try to get free holidays, free meals, free clothes, free CDs and free pints of Strongbow on a daily basis.

Those are a few reasons why journalism has often been full of off-the-wall characters, but I'm sad to say the characters are dying out with every round of redundancies.

There was more to it than that though. Helping people who need help and bringing the rich and powerful to task is wonderful. Sadly, over the last ten years the job has become a shadow of its former self. Each journalist has to write more stories than ever before, and as the story count increases so does the number of press releases that journalists receive. However, despite constantly moaning about the paper what happened in August 2008 came out of the blue, and suddenly I had one of those big life changing decisions to make. The kind of life-changing decision I always seem to get wrong.

Trinity Mirror, who owned the paper, decided to sack everyone on the spot and ask us to apply for our own jobs. The way they chose to do is was by getting the editors to tell us all we were all off to the promised land of modernisation and everything would be better. We were all lured into a conference room and told that the future was fantastic. I was running Credit Crunch bingo, in which fellow journalists guessed how many minutes it would take before one of the bosses would use the term 'credit crunch'. I won with 2 minutes.

The bosses talked a lot about 'silos' and a load of other bullshit management speak. We all knew what was coming; as journalists we're trained to see through the bullshit and it was an insult that our own bosses tried this with us. After telling us all we were moving to a new (cheap) office and a 'new dawn' of journalism was on the horizon we were told to pick up a consultation document as we left the building. I didn't even bother opening mine and it was only when one journalist read it in the pub that we realised the 'consultation document' doubled up as a job application. Steve and co didn't tell us to our faces that we'd have to apply for our own jobs again. I was fuming, and took it way too personally. I got drunk and wrote a load of abusive messages on the editor's blog, I wasn't the only one.

The small print showed there would be 65 fewer people to do the same job, and that we'd have to move out of our city centre office into an out of town call centre without even enough parking spaces for the journalists. Basically the bosses wanted to force as many journalists as possible to throw in the towel and apply for voluntary redundancy.

As a member of the union I pushed for a strike and let myself get wrapped up in the whole office politics of the situation. We were being shit on, and as a matter of principle I wanted to leave, even though I'd been rubbish at every single job I'd ever done except for journalism. When the cream of the company said they were leaving, again out of principle, I did the same. Two people whose advice I listen to, my dad and Tom Watson MP, both said I'd be mad to leave because at the end of the day I was a journalist and shouldn't give it all up because of frustration.

Nonetheless, I was certain, so I volunteered to leave a job I'd worked most of my life to land – being a journalist for my hometown paper. The day we all had to say whether we were staying or going was very emotional. Friend after friend handed their notice in and so did I. I walked out of the office and into the Queens Head pub opposite where all 'the departed' were looking forward to the future.

I had taken a massive chance. It was calculated to a degree. I figured I'd get sacked anyway if I'd stayed because the company would be looking to save cash in any way they could and I didn't think I'd last long in the new call-centre. It was now or never to launch my own media company.

I'd decided to set up a PR company called Cheekie Media and resurrect my magazine Goggle-eye. A year before I'd launched that title, a men's magazine for Birmingham. The entire story of the magazine will have to be told another time, but the long and short of it was that as founder and editor-in-chief I produced (in my humble opinion) probably one of the best publications ever to be printed in Birmingham. Funny, edgy, full of rather delightful women and interesting features, its content really did reflect the hilarity of Brummie life. Over 15,000 free copies were delivered to pubs and clubs across Birmingham.

All this was done not with a bankers' loan or an overdraft facility, but with a £20,000 investment in Scottish banknotes from a great bloke I met in a pub. Unfortunately my business partner, who everyone warned would rip me off but who I'd set the magazine up with and liked a lot, decided to spunk all the advertising revenue on women, class A drugs and God knows what else. The only way to describe him, as well as being funny, fearless and insane is that he could sell ice to the Eskimos, but after negotiating the deal of the century wouldn't bother getting out of bed to deliver the cold stuff to them.

The money had gone and my partner was nowhere to be seen. However, I was convinced Goggle-eye could be resurrected and planned to use my redundancy money to kick start the magazine. The fact that I technically owed £20,000 helped with my decision as well, but I believed, and still do, that Goggle-eye can be a massive success.

Over the previous year I had also branched out into PR. I'd knock out a press release for a friend's nightclub, pub or company and charge about £150. I figured if I did this full time I could make a decent living and as the other Birmingham PR companies were so poncy I thought I might feasibly make a killing. I knew I never wanted to work for any PR company but I figured owning my own company should be different and pay the bills, so Cheekie Media was born.

That was my thinking in late September 2008 when I handed in my notice. In early October, the Great Crash of 08 happened. Obviously this stacked the odds against a new PR company and the Second Coming of Goggle-eye. A friend of mine had agreed to invest into Cheekie Media after he was made redundant, so I set off to America knowing that any publicity I could get for Goggle-eye and Cheekie Media would be priceless as I didn't have any cash to pay for any.

By now I was having serious second thoughts about leaving the paper but I knew there was no turning back. Every time I heard the news another thousand people were being made redundant, so it chipped away at my confidence in a decision to leave a job with a pay packet of £25,000 to set up my own business. That's the trouble with 'voluntary redundancy', it's you that makes the decision to leave so it's all on you, regardless of the fact there was a good chance I might have been sacked later anyway. If it all went tits up then I was going to be left with that horrible 'I shouldn't have left' feeling whilst being totally skint.

I had a plan to do a leaving YouTube video. The video would be of me, Gurdip and anyone else who wanted to be involved clearing their desk and leaving the paper for the last time. The haunting theme from The Hulk, *Lonely Man,* would play in the background with a caption 'Dedicated to every journalist who lost their job in 2008'. I thought it would be a great way to leave the company and get a point across to the nation's journalists, who we were being sacked left, right and centre.

I'd been using the moniker Steve Zacharanda for years when I wrote music reviews and as there are about five other Adam Smiths in journalism, most of whom have had bigger careers than me, I wanted to do something that would get the name more widely recognised. I'd booked my holiday months before and I was therefore on official holiday whilst in America. I was going to do three days work when I returned and that would be it, I'd be an ex-employee of the Birmingham Mail. I desperately wanted that front page about Obama. 'Adam Smith – in Miami', though, so I knew I had to send some copy back to the paper on the night of the election even though I wasn't getting paid for it.

Another big factor that contributed to the way I felt on election day was my girlfriend Nicole. We'd being seeing each other about four or five months but we both loved each other dearly. She was beautiful, only four foot nine but had the heart of a lion. Her regal coffee-coloured face was framed with electric blue hair. She was perfectly spoken, very arty and the owner of the world's best smile. She was kind, clever, daft, sexy and caring, but she had mental health issues and a boatload of physical illnesses which only made me love her more. She had a certain magic to her - perhaps it her artistic bent or her strong spiritual beliefs. Whatever it was, she had me wrapped around her little finger. However, despite my love for her, it never entered my head not to go to Miami.

I knew if I was in England on the night Obama got elected I would have been like a bear with a sore head. I would have hated myself, I would have hated whoever was sitting next to me, and I would certainly have hated anyone who had contributed to me not going. To be fair Nicole was fine before I went, probably because she, like everyone else I knew, presumed I'd never get my shit together to go to America.

We'd kept in touch whilst in America. Her voice on the phone was the most tender one I could ever have imagined and I craved it, despite how much it cost in transatlantic calls. After two weeks apart she was sending me emails about how much she loved me, which wasn't like her to say the least. Perhaps I shouldn't have gone to America as I was building a future with someone I loved, but I looked on this trip as the last anywhere on my own because we'd be inseparable when I returned.

OK I didn't tell her I'd picked Miami months before I met her because my ex-missus Sam lived there, but hey, what she didn't know didn't hurt her. I'd never have done anything to jeopardise what we had together. I loved her more than words could describe and she was the sun that I span around. She had so much power over me; she could win any argument because I loved her so much. I'd had string of failed romances and a head full of regrets but I was finally with someone who I wanted to spend the rest of my life with.

I was proud that I'd actually followed through on an idle day dream and volunteered for Obama, though. Whatever happened in the next 24 hours I knew I'd done something that millions of other people back home hadn't even thought about, let alone would have gone through with I'd have something to tell the grandchildren about, if I ever had any. In fact I was as happy as I've ever been on that fateful day before America decided if Obama would be its President.

Election Day

Tuesday, November 4, 2008

The alarm went off at 6am and the television was on within seconds, not that we needed to be told it was polling day by perfectly manicured presenters in a studio thousands of miles away. This was the day where every second counted. This was the last day of hope. This was the last day of not knowing whether we could change the world.

I couldn't decide which of my Obama t-shirts to wear. I ended up wearing the yellow one with all the flags of the Caribbean on it, putting the beige number in my laptop bag. I figured I'd need more than one because it was going to be a hot and sweaty day. I could see in the corner of my eye Karim every so often looking quizzically at me. I think he was amazed by the sheer skill I demonstrated in being able to lose something within seconds, find it and then lose it again within a matter of minutes - whether it was my phone, mp3 player or money. I decided to take my laptop to the office because I planned to blog throughout the day and had to write the article for the next day's paper. Karim said with a massive smile: "Let's do it!"

We tumbled out of the lift in high spirits, especially as it was 6.30am and I was delighted the beautiful receptionist was on duty. For all I know she might have thought I was the raving loon who either was gay or, for reasons unknown, pretending to be. However, she smiled a smile that belonged to someone who knew that you'd tipped them before.

"Good morning sir. You're up early today."

"It's never too early to early to change the world baby! There's only one thing you can do for me today, and that is to make sure you vote for Barack Obama. Your country is counting on you. Don't forget to vote, promise me!" When she'd said yes I joined Karim, Kale and Mark in the car.

We all high fived and within two minutes our holiday song came on the radio: 'TI – Whatever You Like'. We all sang the anthem's chorus together with our hands in the air, including Kale who was driving at the time. Technically it went 'You can do whatever you like, baby, you can have whatever you like, baby you can go wherever you like', but I always changed the lines to 'I can do whatever I like'. I wound down the rear window and let the morning air blow in my face as we drove down Collins Avenue, savouring the moment.

I'd never been up that early in Miami and the weather was perfect. The sun was coming up but it wasn't swelteringly hot. We piled into the office and I made for the food. Somebody switched the television on and everyone started getting ready for the rest of the volunteers to arrive. Worryingly, it looked like there weren't going to be enough placards so we set about making some of our own. I had a sudden flash of inspiration. On mine I wrote: "Palin is a Dinosaur Denier – But McCain is Prehistoric".

I was extremely proud and showed it to Mark and Kale, who looked at me as if I was mad. "She doesn't believe in evolution guys! Hence dinosaur denier" I said, trying to explain the joke, but the pair shook their heads in unison. "We get it Adam, but the prehistoric bit might offend older voters," Mark said. The next few posters I hastily made were just bog standard 'Obama – Biden' signs, but I wedged my 'Palin is a Dinosaur Denier' into the wall so there'd be a chance of someone seeing it and enjoying the joke.

Election Day 7.30am: Facebook status: Steve Zacharanda is GONNA CHANGE THE WORLD TODAY! And is armed with his 'Palin is a dinosaur denier' placard.

There was lots of work for everyone to do on election day. Those promised a lift to the polling booth had to be picked up on time. We had to dispatch the lawyers to the polling stations to stop any funny business, and volunteers had to be outside to give people encouragement to keep waiting in line. The fax machine still spewed out sheets and sheets of names and numbers to phone. Mark decided that Karim and I would be placed on 'visibility' duty. I liked the sound of being visible; after all, you wouldn't want to be put on invisible duty would you.

Kale and Mark were talking about the main intersections on South Beach and North Beach. It was about 7.30am and I guessed that they wanted us to be walking advertising hoardings during rush hour, and I was right. We snaffled two of the official 'Obama – Biden' boards and jumped in with Kale.

I noticed there didn't seem to be much fervour on the streets. I'm not sure what I'd expected, but the morning of Tuesday November 4 2008 didn't seem different to any other day in Miami. This made it all the more strange, and it felt like the calm before the storm. We jumped out on a pretty impressive intersection which led to one of the main bridges from South Beach to Downtown Miami. After suggesting we stand on either side of the road to be more 'visible' Kale thanked us for helping out and told us he would be back 'in a few hours'.

It quickly dawned on me that visibility is a pretty boring job, but I killed the boredom by waving at all the motorists. However, there wasn't much interaction because the vehicles were going too fast to see the whites of the drivers' eyes. I then realised I'd forgotten my MP-3 player and radio. I'd become a massive fan of the Paul and Young Ron Radio Show on BIG 105fm since being in Miami and really wanted to listen to them do their exploding egg presidential competition. Whichever microwaved egg (McCain or Obama) didn't explode first would win the election. This was essential radio but I missed it.

After about an hour I was starting to go out my mind with boredom and my arms were aching holding up the signs. Every so often Karim and I would wander over to each other in the central reservation and have a chat. I wanted to talk at the same time as doing 'visibility', but he quite rightly pointed out that more people would see us if we stood apart. Then again, he'd remembered his Ipod.

I wanted someone to talk to but as usual on American main roads there were almost no pedestrians, so when any approached I desperately tried to make conversation. I spoke to a teacher for a while who was well up for Obama but who didn't think he would win, and I also chatted to a big black guy who was rooting for Obama but wasn't registered to vote. There was a bit of a lull then, but after half an hour of no human contact a young man appeared at my side as if from nowhere. I must've been daydreaming or talking to myself because I hadn't seen him standing quietly beside me.

Impeccably turned out, this guy was about five foot five and didn't have a hair out of place. I guessed he might have been gay just because of how pristine he looked. His tanned skin was even all over, he was perfectly shaven and unlike the crumpled mess I was there wasn't a crease on his t-shirt or shorts. He had the features of a male model, as his nose was perfectly straight and his aviator glasses fitted him so well they looked like they were sprayed on to his face.

The trouble with sunglasses is that you can't see where anyone is looking, so I thought as he was standing next to me I'd introduce myself.

"Hello mate. I'm Adam"

"Adam! What a lovely name, my name is Pietro," he said offering me his perfectly manicured hand.

He was softly spoken but every syllable and vowel was perfectly pronounced and I detected a European accent.

"I saw you and I thought I would come over and say hi and support what you're doing with your Obama poster."

I was touched. It was a wonderful gesture and I was glad of the company. He was an Italian who was living in Miami so we had shared European heritage, and what's more I love Italian food. Pietro was also a pleasure to talk to; funny, intelligent with a wicked sense of humour, it was nice to meet someone who could get a double entendre or two as well. He knew the South Beach club scene better than anybody and invited me to an election night party that would go on to the early hours. I shuddered as it dawned on me the day and night before me would last an eternity. Pietro made my visibility shift a joy, and people like him were why I loved the Barack Obama 2008 presidential campaign. After about an hour my new found Italian friend made his excuses and left after ensuring we'd become friends on Facebook.

After three hours or more on visibility duty Kale pulled up. We'd covered the whole of morning rush and the traffic had died down. The heat was gradually edging past 100 degrees and as the intersection was exposed I was worried I'd faint with heat exhaustion. In fact I was happy he'd remembered to pick us up because if he hadn't we would have been there all day.

We parked near the office and as we were walking I noticed a brilliant election poster stuck on the lamppost. The simple poster was split into two – the top half with a picture of McCain and the bottom with a picture of Obama. At the top it said: "Who Sucks Most – Vote With Your Gum". There were three pieces on Obama's side but McCain was covered in gum, which was a great omen.

The office was bustling but it wasn't bedlam as I'd expected. I noticed there was a traffic jam outside as volunteers with cars were coming to the office to get their lists of voters who needed a lifts. Everyone seemed positive unlike the night before. Mark said: "It seems quiet out there, that has to be a good sign."

It wasn't even 11am and I was shattered. Standing around holding up placards is tough work in the heat. However, as Napoleon said 'An army marches on its stomach' and my nose twitched as the smell of piping hot pizza wafted through the office. A delivery just sauntered through the volunteers and put it down on the food table. As I was tucking into a piece of pizza with enough red meat on it to give me an instant heart attack Erika called out my name.

"Adam! Adam? The English guy? I've something for you."

"Here I am!"

The office went quiet as she stood over me.

"Thank you for all your help Adam. You have this, and don't worry about the cost, it's on the house."

Then she held it up – a sky blue 'Brummies for Obama' t-shirt. It meant the world to me because I knew it was unique. Unsurpisingly there had been no Brummies for Obama t-shirts before Ericka asked me where I was from, and now I'd be wearing it in the wider world. Karim, Mark and Kale all cheered and clapped. It was a lovely gesture, as she didn't have to ask for a bespoke t-shirt for me. Perhaps as a veteran of elections since the 1960s she knew when it was over everyone would scatter to the four winds, so this might be the last she ever saw of me.

I love that t-shirt, and always will. I felt I must have made an impression if the mother of the office, who couldn't even understand a word I said, had ordered a brand new t-shirt slogan printed for me. Brummies for Obama had been added to the panoply of interest group for Obama t-shirt. As I had a spare few minutes I decided to celebrate by uploading a blog to the Birmingham Post website:

A Slice of Life in the Obama Campaign

By Adam Smith – in Miami

'Hi I've got 100 lesbians outside, can we help?' the elderly lady said with a smile when she entered the Barack Obama Miami South Beach Office.
'Err, great, bring them in? I replied.
And in came the South Floridian Pensioner Lesbian Convention Committee, I think that what they were called anyway, and they were lovely.
They wanted lots of the 'rainbow' Obama stickers.
'Yeah, the Rainbow ones are the Gay and Lesbian for Obama stickers, everyone knows that'.

Ah not me, I just jumped on a plane a week before and turned up at the Miami South Beach suited and booted armed with a CV! I've been giving Rainbow badges out to anyone and everyone. This Barack Obama campaign has to be seen to be believed.
It is, like, you know, totally awesome, man.

Our office has every black, white, mixed race, latino, young, old, clever, stupid, funny, serious, laid back and intense people giving their time up for free. For Obama.

I know in my heart he will let me down, he will disappoint me, he is, a politician.

This campaign is not about him. It is about US. The volunteers. People like Kale Williams, aged 27, who has been working for free for six weeks and will have to drive across America to get home. People like Dustin Hoffman lookalike Will, who is Jelvis, the Jewish Elvis, The King of Kosher, who dresses in his Star of David jumpsuit and walks around Miami beach singing 'Ba-rock the vote Baby, shake, rattle and shalom baby. It is Karim, the London living Belgian who jumped on a plane from London and spends all day entering data on a computer and got thrown out of his hostel for supporting Obama.

It is about the black lady who remembers segregation in her native Kentucky and has worked on every election since and never thought she would have the chance to vote for an African American candidate. It is about the 40 Danish students who turned up to help.
It is about Ophelia, the mother who got suspended from her job for Obama, and then every day stood outside the polling station holding an Obama sign getting honk after honk as well as being called Babykiller.

It is about Suzie and Ceaser who drive from place to place to see who needs help.
It is about Mark Spear, who has no idea what he is going to when the election ends.
This is about Ericka, who has to listen to people decades her junior, chat rubbish as she calmly builds a business empire for Obama selling every type of t-shirt in the office.
This is about the friendships that we have made and will stay forever, it is about the networks and teams of people who want to change.

No-one put it better than the coolest political operator on the East Coast. Nate Sherwood, who runs the South Beach operation in a way that is simply fantastic.
We are volunteers, we are told to do our jobs but we can put our own spin on it.
Drinking a rum in the Tap Tap bar, reflecting after a day where thousands of doors were knocked on his patch.
He said: "People don't get it, this campaign is not about Obama, it is about the people in it.
"He is a just a politician, he can't change the country on his own, we are the ones who can change this country.
"What this campaign has done is brought people together, the important this is

that these networks, these teams that have changed politics and worked so well, stay together to really change the story."

To me Obama has given me an experience that money could just never buy, in the future he probably will do stuff I disagree with. But I will never forget this moment, the hope, the belief, the unity, and if he wins and it all goes wrong, c'est la vie, baby. Like my ex-loves, I will remember the good times and not how the relationship ended............

"What do we do now?" I asked Mark. "Don't know, we've got everything sorted – we've got lots of people giving voters lifts and the polling stations are covered too. What do you want to do?"

Karim and I looked at each other and shrugged, but then I noticed Barry out of the corner of my eye and as the office loudhailer was finally free there was only one thing to do. "Shall we take Barry down to Lincoln Road with the loudhailer and tell everyone to vote for him?" It was a simple idea but it struck a chord. Karim had been hearing all my tales of going on the town with Barry, so he was up for it. We carefully put the cut-out in the back of Kale's truck and we headed off towards Lincoln Road.

I was in my new t-shirt in the front seat, flicking through radio stations looking for hip- hop. I didn't have a care in the world. And then my phone rang. I looked at the number and realised it was from back home. My stomach turned and I couldn't help think that it was bad news.I wasn't wrong.

"Hello?"

"Hello," came back a broken voice. I had to turn the radio down to hear her.

It was Nicole, but I'd never heard her like that before. I'd heard her happy, dismissive, annoyed and excited but never like that. She spoke beautifully but all life seemed to have drained from her voice. She was upset, and I was thousands of miles away. I started to panic.

"What's wrong bab? Bab?"

I was getting more and more worried and Kale and Karim went quiet, realising something was wrong. I asked her again and at last she answered. I could tell she was holding the tears back. "I'm going to lose the flat." Far from being worried, I was just mightily relieved she hadn't been raped or told she'd got cancer. "I've had a letter that says I'm going to have to move out. I don't know what to do, I'm so worried. I'm going to be homeless. I wish you were here Adam".

I would have given anything to be across the world and holding her as she cried, to tell her I loved her and that everything would be ok. However, I couldn't comfort the woman I loved because I was 2,000 miles away in a pick-up truck with a cardboard Barack Obama, a Belgian-Moroccan and Californian. Not one to be overly worried about any kind of official letter I figured she was over reacting, but I couldn't let her knew I thought that.

Kale and Karim were looking at me to see what I'd say next as they still didn't know what was happening. I took a deep breath and made the type of speech you can only make to someone you love. There was no point getting into the specifics, like asking how she could be thrown out when she was living in a council flat on housing benefits. She just needed to hear a man who loved her tell her everything would be ok. I took a deep breath and went for it.

"Bab. Please calm down. We're going to be ok. Everything is going to be ok. I'll be back on Saturday and nobody can do anything until then, can they? What's the worst that can happen? The council can't just kick you out that quickly. If it's a matter of days I'll give you the number of an MP mate of mine and he'll hold them at bay. Is it a matter of days?"

"No" came the whimper across the phone line. I felt like a pilot who'd prevented his plane nose diving into the ground and could now concentrate on climbing back up into the sky.

"If you have to leave your flat then so be it. I'm getting my redundancy in a couple of weeks so we'll use that to move somewhere. Me, you and Nathan baby, it will be perfect. I love you more than I love life itself and I promise I will never let you be homeless. I love you and Nathan too much. I'm so sorry I'm not with you now, but please don't be upset. I love you more than anything. I love you, Nicole, and if you love me too then everything will be ok. Do you love me?"

"Yes, I love you Adam."

"Do you believe that I love you Nicole?"

"Yes, I know you love me Adam"

"Does Nathan love me?"

"Yes, Nathan loves you Adam."

"Well, everything is going to be cool then isn't it baby? Everything is going to be cool. Please believe me, please believe in me. I'm with Kale and Karim baby. Kale, Karim how much do I love my missus?"

Like all good men in that situation, without missing a beat the pair shouted: "He loves you baby, he never shuts up about you!"

She laughed through her tears, giggled and then said sorry for bothering me. A weight was lifted off my shoulders. "Me, Kale, Karim and Barry are changing the world today baby! Love you!" I put the phone down and let out a massive sigh of relief.

Kale and Karim were staring at me as if I was mad.

Kale said: "Dude, are you for real?"

"What do you mean?"

"Are you for real? All that stuff you just said?"

"I meant every word lads, she's the one."

"Shay's the won?" Kale repeated with a mock English accent.

"No, she's the one" I said, starting to laugh.

"Did she believe all that bullshit?"

"I meant every word"

Karim piped up: "How old is her kid Adam?"

"Kid?"

"Yeah. Nathan."

"That's her dog mate."

"HER DOG!" they both shouted at once.

"Yeah, what's wrong with that? I fucking love that dog."

Kale then preceded to do an impression which he would repeat later on YouTube of me going: 'Kitten, kitten I love you kitten, we're going to get a flat and everything is going to be ok, do you love me kitten, do ya?' What should have been a very private conversation had taken place in front of two people I'd known for two weeks, but I was fine with that because they were and always will be good friends. That's why I loved them taking the piss out of me.

I don't know what they must have thought of me. A day didn't seem to go by without some sort of disaster erupting and me having to some heavy duty fire fighting, but I suppose that just showed what an achievement it was for a fuckup like me to manage to get over to America in the first place. Anyway, I was happy again. The fact I'd promised to spend all my redundancy money on helping her move didn't matter because it would mean I'd have somewhere to live when I got back after not paying my rent.

Barry is back on the town

Lincoln Road was deserted as we headed towards the old theatre I'd stood outside on Saturday. I experienced a tingle of excitement as I'd finally got my hands on the office loud hailer. That alone was exciting enough, but to have Barry with me again as well as Karim meant I was in my element. I was of course also sporting America's first ever 'Brummies for Obama' t-shirt.

We set up stall in the centre of the pedestrianised street and waited for the masses to come, but this time they didn't. Again, I don't know what I'd been expecting to happen on election day but it certainly wasn't this. The whole place seemed subdued. Then again, Miami South Beach is party central, so perhaps it's not surprising there wasn't much action in the morning; it's the kind of place that doesn't come alive until after midnight.

I needed the loud hailer because the road was deserted and so I had to hail anyone who walked anywhere near us. The response was underwhelming; in fact more than one person thought that we were charging for photos with our cardboard Barry. The loudhailer gave me another option though. It meant I could crouch behind Barry so it looked to passers-by like he was freestanding and was talking all by himself.

This was great fun, and Karim would be in the bushes laughing at people's responses to the talking Barack Obama. I spotted a good looking couple in their thirties. They hadn't seen the Barack Obama to their side. I shouted through the loud hailer: "CHANGE!" The couple jumped out of their skin and looked straight at Barry in disbelief. "I WANT CHANGE!" They didn't move so I thought it was about time for the punchline: "I WANT CHANGE – I HAVE A $10 NOTE AND I NEED CHANGE FOR THE CIGARETTE MACHINE". They didn't laugh, and that really annoyed me.

I mean I'd gone to all the trouble of flying to America, crouching behind a cardboard cut out of Barack Obama, doing a passable impression of him through a loudhailer and then delivering a rather funny punch line which played on the constant talk of change that had defined the election. How on God's green earth could they not laugh? Or if not laugh at least show a flicker of human emotion, even if it was just a shaking their head in disgust.

I wanted to run up and kick the hell out of the idiots, but instead I peeped behind the Obama cut out and just shouted: "Don't be scared guys – it was just a joke". They didn't even reply, just flounced off down the road probably comparing notes about the acidity of their matching moisturisers. That was the final straw for me for Lincoln Road, and as it was mostly bars and restaurants that wouldn't open for a few hours we decided to go to Collins Avenue.

I love Collins Avenue. It's a thoroughfare that runs straight through South Beach. Ocean Drive may be full of famous art deco hotels and bars that tourists head to immediately, but Collins (though it still caters for tourists) is where the people who live and work in South Beach hang out. It has plenty of bars, shops, fast food joints, cheap hotels and chemists and no matter what time of the day the place seems alive. There are pretty women everywhere as well.

After nearly three weeks I felt part of the furniture. The advantage of having a good memory for faces is I knew shop assistants, tramps, policemen, street sellers, barman and hotel bell boys to say hello to and pass the time of day with. They probably knew me as the 'Crazy UK Obama fan who no-one understands'.

The intersection of Collins Avenue and Lincoln Road was heaving with traffic and people. There were all types: young, old, rich, poor, black, Latino, white, ugly and beautiful going about their daily business. I said to Karim as we set up stall: "This is going to be like shooting fish in a barrel baby!" then hollered through the loud hailer. "Come and get a photo with the Next President of the United States of America!"

Obviously I did my "CHANGE" gag a few times to get a laugh as compensation for the wooden, humourless couple on Lincoln. It was nice to know my comedy bones hadn't deserted me because many people found it funny, except maybe Karim who must have heard the same joke about 30 times in one hour. Karim has a wonderful way about him which instantly puts people at ease, especially women. He kept his cards close to his chest in Miami but he's the kind of guy that will end up marrying a beautiful heiress to a fortune that also does groundbreaking charity or scientific work, saving the planet on the side. You know the type.

On the streets of South Beach we were on fire with the ladies. I've never seen so many come to have their photo with Barry. I bet the majority did it to see how they'd look as a couple. I was always on hand to say with a smile: "You make a lovely couple" or "Michelle had better watch out." We had competition though. In fact it looked like we'd moved in on their territory.

About 20 feet from us there were two hip hop dudes that were peddling 'official Obama CDs'. They didn't have a loud hailer but every so often they would break out into some freestyle rapping, something Karim and I couldn't do. I could tell they weren't happy about having a card board cut out and a Brummie with a loudhailer outshine them on their corner. We started giving each other funny looks but I couldn't keep it up. I've seen enough episodes of The Wire to know arguing over turf brings nothing but trouble.

I went over to introduce myself and Barry. Despite the boiling heat the smaller one of the two was dressed in heavy camouflage slacks and matching jacket, underneath which he had a black and yellow Wu Tang Clan t-shirt. When I got closer I noticed he had about four Wu Tang rings on his fingers and a massive Wu Tang silver medallion around his neck. His multi-coloured cap was on backwards and he had braces on his teeth. What was there not to like about him?

His friend was leaning up against the wall feeling the heat. He had a huge belly and an even bigger Wu Tang Clan t-shirt draped across it, with a baggy cap on. He was happily sucking the straw of a McDonalds soft drink. We exchanged pleasantries and I asked to see his Obama CD. He pulled out a CD with a paper sleeve which had 'Barack Obama – Yes We Can' scanned on to it. I looked at the track listing and it seemed to only contain music either by or inspired by The Wu Tang Clan. Not a band you'd immediately associate with the Presidential hopeful, I but one that I have a soft spot for never the less.

"I'm from the campaign, is this official Barack Obama merchandise?" I asked, trying to keep a straight face.

"Yeah man, this is the proper shit man. Obama man. Obama our man."

The bigger one chipped in: "This is the real shit man."

"Ok brother, I'll have one. How much?"

"$15"

"$15? No chance. I'll give you $5, a free photo with my man Obama here and I'll endorse your CD."

"Deal."

We all shook hands and they had their photos taken with Barry. To keep my end of the bargain I hid behind Barry and in the loud hailer shouted "Get your official Wu-Tang Clan Obama CD right here." After giving them a potted musical history of Birmingham when they asked what a Brummie was I left them to their own devices. Now I know these guys were just using Obama to sell their CDs but I couldn't help but think fair play to them. All publicity is good publicity on election day, and who knows, the Wu Tang Clan vote might just swing it for Obama in 2012.

Back on the street Karim and I noticed another approach worked to get younger people in for a photo with Barry. "Get the Facebook and MySpace profile picture that all your friends will be jealous of!" This last line was the killer one with the under 30s and the advent of camera phones meant that almost everyone who walked past could be enticed into our Barry photo fest whilst being given a gentle prod about their voting intentions too.

I loved watching how people posed with Barry. Some, usually the guys, would take it very seriously and would puff out their chests and ensure their profile was right, where as others drape themselves over him and do their own gang signs for the photo. We were having fun but doing our bit for the campaign because every hour counted from now on until the polls closed at 7pm. I couldn't give our stickers and leaflets out quickly enough and the good people of Collins Avenue certainly seemed pro-Obama.

If anyone asked about the photos we were taking on our own cameras then I explained that we were doing a YouTube video – 'Barack Obama's Big Day Out in Miami'. In fact Caesar did do one in the end and it now serves as a wonderful memento of all the people we met.

The one thing I found hard was I wanted to speak to everyone for a lot longer, but as there was always a queue we didn't have time. Then again it kind of made us look more important and popular than we actually were. By this point I was getting knackered again. Whilst Karim was in his element chatting to two Venezuelan women about the campaign I thought I'd leave him to it and just rest against the wall with Barry watching the world go by. A woman shouting "BRUMMIE!" snapped me out of a great daydream I was having about giving Obama a guided tour of Perry Barr.

Two pretty students who I could tell were from England were standing in front of me, one ginger and the other dark haired. "I can't believe there's someone from Birmingham here helping out Barack Obama. Please take a photo of us with him". They were both from Nottingham University and I think one was a Brummie herself. They were both Obama fans, which was nice but wouldn't help him get elected. At this stage it was on the voters that we had to use our charm.

Karim turned around after saying goodbye to the Venezuelans and bumped in to the two students, striking up a conversation with them. I was glad to give Barry over. After he'd taken their photos Karim staggered over to me looking both bewildered and bewitched. Both of us were now pretty tired; it's hard work being so bloody upbeat all of the time and trying to be quick witted and on the ball. We also had to be street smart because we had to stop a few people stealing our 'Obama – Biden' signs, and I knew there would be hell to pay in the office if Barry ever got stolen.

As the heat continued to wear me down I remembered we had no lift back to the office which was about a mile away. I couldn't be bothered to walk all that way with my 'Muppets for Obama' sign, complete with wooden stake, so I planted in the grass verge of Collins Avenue and left it. I look back and curse myself because I'd just tossed away a piece of history as I couldn't be bothered to carry it in the heat.

Karim and I took Barry into McDonalds and tucked into some ridiculously cheap burgers. I thought the £1 menu was cheap in the UK but in America they sell burgers on for 59 cents on some days. The pair of us were feeling the strain as we'd been up since 6am and it was now nearly 2pm.

"The women in this town are crazy, man," Karim said out loud as he looked into the middle distance; "I've never met so many women in one day". We chatted about which were the best, the worse and the most enchanting women we had met in the last few hours. I have to admit I do have a soft spot for Latino women after a wonderful dalliance with a Dominican Republic beauty in New York, and Miami is full of such stunners. They were all the more wonderful because you don't get them in Britain so they seem all the more rare and exotic. Karim was a fan of Latinos too. I envied him; he was young, free single and could speak loads of languages.

I couldn't complain as I was in a relationship with the woman I loved so meeting ladies in Miami was great because I didn't feel any pressure to pull them as if I was single. I love women so I can appreciate all of them – young and old, rich and poor. I love making a good first impression and getting a smile that they wouldn't have had if hadn't been for meeting me.

We couldn't even finish our burgers without being interrupted by people asking about Barry. I can understand how celebrities feel now. Being with Barry was like being with Brad Pitt, Samuel L Jackson, Jelvis and Perez Hilton all rolled into one. We steeled ourselves for the journey back to the office but we needn't have worried - it was a joy throughout. Normally it would have taken 15 minutes but with Barry it took nearly two hours. The more enthusiastic people I met the more energy I seemed to get to carry on.

We took Barry into hairdressers, we were dragged into tattoo parlours, we were ambushed by a legion of Cuban children and we even got a round of applause from some pensioners when we passed a polling station. As we were ambling along the pavement a massive screech filled the air that made us duck for cover. My first thought was of a drive-by shooting.

"OBAMA!" came the cry from what sounded like a woman being strangled. A Mercedes pulled up in the middle of road and the driver's door was flung open. All I could see were two long female legs pointing towards the sky, and my mouth dropped open as I followed the thighs up to see the skimpiest of panties and nothing else. The passenger door opened and another woman jumped out. They ran towards us. There were both Latino, one in a mini-skirt and the other in just a bit of chiffon, both obviously on coke and still out from the night before.

"Oh my Gawd, I thought it was Obama," said the bikini clad girl, chewing gum way too fast. "What are you cute guys doing here with Obama?"

"It's election day love. It's kind of a big deal, baby!" I replied, not knowing where to look because of all the naked flesh in front of me. Karim and I tried to act cool but it didn't really work as these two were like a whirlwind, touching Barry and us. They could probably tell from our faces that we were dumbstruck and they had the kind of confidence and tactile ways that only lap dancers seem to have. Their make-up was thick and their perfume too strong but both oozed trashy sex appeal. Within seconds I felt an erection swell in my pants and prayed no-one would notice.

We took their photos, then let them take ours as drivers started to honk their horns because the Merc was marooned in the middle of the road. These two beauties overtaken by Obama love kissed us both goodbye and then they were off, swearing and flashing at the irate motorists as they went. Karim just shook his head in disbelief. "This town is crazy, man."

As we edged closer to the office I was tempted to stash Barry underneath my arm like a surfboard but I couldn't do it. That simple piece of cardboard meant a lot to me. He was my very own Barack Obama. Further up Collins Avenue we found a wonderful avenue of trees to walk under which shielded us from the scorching sunlight. We slowed down to snail's pace because it was so nice not to be exposed. I was dripping with sweat and was worrying about the prospect of a chafing situation again. I didn't look like the cool unflustered Miami folk surrounding me.

As we strolled beneath the trees I noticed something out of the corner of my eye in the distance. After focussing on the trees ahead I realised someone was behind a tree crouching down taking photos of us. I immediately felt uneasy. Obviously I didn't know who it was and started to worry it might be the officer who had warned me to stay off the street a few days before. The last thing I needed was to be locked up on election night.

I kept my eye on the shadows behind the trees. When we were about 10 yards away the musical sound of people speaking French rang through the air and three people jumped out from behind the tree. I recognised one of them. She was a female photographer I'd seen hanging around the office. She was well cool; she worked for Guyaweb, a Guyanan website, and was quite small with a shock of black Afro-hair that frizzed in all directions and an endearing goofy grin. I suppose Karim, Barry and I walking along must have made a great shot, although it might have been a lot better if it'd been totally natural with us unaware of the camera.

She was with a good looking couple, a handsome black guy and a pretty Latino girl, who both spoke French as well. They came towards us taking photos. I was glad to have Karim with me because he can speak about ten languages. For the next 15 minutes we posed for photos as the photographer took all sorts of shots and made us stand in all different positions pulling different poses. She seemed amazingly laidback in a way that only black, French-speaking Guyanan photographers can be. I imagine her going all over the world representing Guyana brilliantly.

She was amazed I was a journalist but I couldn't speak her language to capitalise on our shared profession. I found myself doing that very embarrassing English thing of talking slower and louder to someone who doesn't understand the language, as if by magic that would make them understand. She just kept on saying "Mister Broooomie journalist loves Mr Obama."

It was a lovely moment. None of us were American but we'd all been drawn to Miami to see history. We said our goodbyes, but only after we'd found out they were going to watch the results come in at a big Democrat party at Jungle Island. The two of us finally got to the office just as there was a huge row brewing outside because someone, somewhere had parked their car and blocked the road off so that the volunteers couldn't pick voters up to go to the polling stations. Normally I would have watched the arguments unfold and maybe picked a side, but I was so tired I just wanted to sit down. Karim was the same. Being with Barry was tiring work.

Election day, 3pm. Facebook status: Steve Zacharanda is knackered already, standing on intersections waving signs, walking around with cardboard Obama, getting people to vote, now in the world's most mental office.

As I was tucking into a plate of pizza, fried plantains, coleslaw and beef sandwiches I heard the unmistakable sound of English voices. Privileged English voices, and lots of them. My heart sank. I go abroad to get away from English people. The voices got closer. They sounded southern. The door opened and six men burst through, all in their twenties or early thirties, all with tidy haircuts and spectacles, all with shorts and white socks and expensive phones and cameras hanging around their necks. They were organised, eager and obviously on a working trip abroad. I tried not to take any notice in the hope they would pass by and leave me be. Fat chance of that.

"Giles (or something like that), look at this – Brummies for Obama." Giles came over and they both looked at me. Every bone in my body wanted me to say "What the fucking hell are you looking at?" but as I was in the office within earshot of Ericka I didn't. I just waited until they spoke to me instead of looking at me like I was in a zoo.

"Brummie – how funny, are you from Birmingham?"

"Yeah, how did you know?"

"It says on your t-shirt"

"Oh, so it does. Well spotted"

"We're all with the Labour Party. Are you with the Labour party?"

"Do I look like I'm with the Labour Party? I'm with my own party of one mate. I jumped on a plane a few weeks ago and I've been volunteering ever since"

"We're with an MP too"

"Wow, sounds a right laugh, I've been volunteering with the Jewish Elvis"

"So you're not Labour then?"

"I used to be. Not anymore"

I bit my lip, I didn't want to wash our country's dirty linen in front of all the Americans in the office, and as I hadn't had any alcohol I didn't automatically go into a rant about the war, the lies, the attack on civil liberties and my own pet hate - the posh Labour Party apparatchiks who joined the party when it looked as though the Tories would be dead for a generation and who sneer at the working class the party was formed to defend. Call me old fashioned but give me an angry young man straight from the pit or the shop floor over some public school hotshot. Labour is supposed to be the party of the working man, but if the working class man or woman can't even progress in the party because someone with better qualifications and more expensive hair gel is blocking their way how can Labour represent the very people it's supposed to look after?

As I say, this wasn't the time or the place to have a row about the Labour Party, and these guys were helping Obama out, although I suspect were trying to get tips for elections back in Britain. To break the awkward silence I namedropped Tom Watson just to show that I wasn't a total clown. I didn't mention he'd got me and Miss America into the House of Commons. They wouldn't have believed me anyway. Thankfully another Giles, Tarquin or Harry blustered in with a load of sheets that Mark must have given him. "We've got our orders boys – we've got to go to all these addresses, let's go." With that they all checked their Blackberries and probably synchronised their watches before disappearing into the Miami sun.

I think my ingrained inverted snobbery made me take an instant dislike to them or perhaps it was the snide remarks about being a Brummie. Perhaps it was a bit of self-loathing because they were probably better volunteers than me, or that I was no longer the only Englishman in the office. Putting aside my dislike of the posh boys, Mark was happy to have some eager volunteers so that was good enough for me. After watching CNN for twenty minutes I decided to stand outside the office with Barry for a while.

As Kale and I were chatting outside the office a tall guy with a droopy moustache came ambling by. Kale asked: "Hey Sir, have you voted yet?" The man, who looked Mexican and towered over the two of us at about six foot three, was crestfallen when we mentioned the election. I could tell he was embarrassed but he plucked up the courage to say: "I, err, can't, err vote. I made a mistake when I was younger and I'm now classed as a felon, so I can't vote."

Kale said sympathetically "Too bad brother," and shook his hand.

"I would have definitely voted for Obama though guys. I have two jobs now and I've got my life back on track but I still can't vote."

I sensed an opportunity. I said: "Hey mate. I can't vote either because I'm from England. That's why I'm volunteering so I can tell my grandchildren that I helped Barack Obama get elected. Why don't you do something for the campaign, then you can say that you helped him get elected too. Don't let not being able to vote stop you from taking part in history"

This guy, who must have been around 40-years-old, was visibly touched. He looked at the floor then at me and then at Kale.

"What, you'd let me help out on Barack Obama's campaign?" he said.

I jumped in: "Of course, mate. It's election day and we haven't got enough people. Can you spare an hour of your time?"

"I can spare two. What do I have to do?"

I'd heard in the office that the volunteers at one of the polling stations were getting tired and wanted to be replaced. I said: "Wait there brother, I'll get you a sign to hold up at the polling station. All you have to do is walk up and down by the polling station holding the sign up. It'll show that we have a presence at the polling station and will stop any Republican funny business."

The already tall guy seemed to grow two foot taller. I could tell he was chuffed he'd be able to do his bit. I nipped into the office and phoned the volunteers to tell them to keep an eye out for a six foot plus Mexican who'd be coming to help out. The trouble was, I couldn't find any new signs. I didn't want to send him out with my Palin is a Dinosaur Denier placard and the only other one was a 'Save Energy' sign that Erika had brought back from some demonstration a few years ago. I gave it to my new volunteer who seemed even more confused than before.

"You can't let him out with that placard. It has nothing to do with Obama," Kale said. I was getting desperate because I didn't want this Mexican to miss out on helping the campaign. Also, I didn't want to have to go down to the polling station because I was knackered. I then remembered the 'Obama – Biden' sign that I had hidden away to bring back home with me as a memento. For the second time in a day I gave up a piece of history, handing it to our new felon volunteer. I gave him a speech about how much we needed volunteers and stressed that he'd be making a difference. I ended my little motivational chat by looking him in the eye and said: "Welcome to the campaign brother. Obama is counting on you."

We shook hands and off he walked towards the polling station, holding the placard above his head as he went. I don't think I explained that he didn't have to hold it up until he got there, but he had the walk of a man who knew he was making a difference and I didn't have the energy to run after him and tell him. Kale was leaning up against the wall laughing at me.

"What?"

"Where do you get all your bullshit from dude?"

"What bullshit? I meant every word."

Still laughing Kale said: "Well I can't say a thing because you got a volunteer and I don't know how you talked him into doing visibility in this heat. I'm just glad for your sake that it's election day because the press would have a field day if they knew that Obama was recruiting convicted felons."

I laughed along with him because I didn't think it was the time or the place to say I'd been trying to recruit felons for the last two weeks. It was dawning on everyone that we'd done everything we could and that now it was down to the people. This, judging by some of the people who came into our office, was worrying. Everyone who came to buy a t-shirt or other memorabilia was asked if they'd voted. One twenty-something woman was adamant she had voted. And then she let it slip.

"I clicked yes for Obama"

"What do you mean you clicked?" I asked.

"On Facebook, I clicked on Obama, and I voted that way."

We stared in silence at this woman. She thought she'd taken part in democracy because she had voted in a Facebook poll. No matter the country, never underestimate the stupidity of the general public. I think it was Eric, who after nearly fainting regained his composure and told this nice but dim woman that she'd have to get to a polling station (and quickly) or she'd miss out on the election. However, there's an argument to say that she was ahead of her time and that in 10 or 20 years time we'll all be voting via our phone or computer.

Ode to Joy rang out and I grabbed the phone.

"Is that the office?"

"Yep, South Beach Office"

"Are you with the campaign?"

"Yep. How can we help?"

"We're being overrun with Republicans and there are loads of arguments down here. Can you come over and help?"

It always seems to be that last phone call of the day that brings trouble, but I got the name of the polling station and headed down there, getting Kale to drop me off. It looked like a fire station and there were loads of people milling around. After I got out of the car I realised I was in the area where I'd nearly been arrested. My stomach turned when, within seconds of arriving, a beefy male policeman called me over and said: "Have you come to vote?"

"No I'm with the campaign and I was told there was some trouble down here."

"Well the fun and games are over, so you needn't worry," he said sternly.

It seemed that the polling station had run out of something or other and that people were getting turned away from voting. By this time it had sorted itself out and people were voting again. I wanted to find a Democrat lawyer to check everything was ok. Instead I got Richard Burton and Elizabeth Taylor's son, looking resplendent in peach hot pants, arguing with a parked car. As Don King says: "Only in America."

I've no idea what he was so angry about, but he drew me into his argument. He looked about forty, had a white tank top on, loads of jewellery, peach hot pants and round spectacles. He also had one of the campest voices ever and he kept on saying to me:

"Police brutality. Police brutality. Would you believe it?"

"I would mate. Believe me, I would" I said.

"Wow, what an accent? Are you English?"

"Yep"

"My mother is Elizabeth Taylor"

"No shit?"

"Do you want to know who my dad is?"

"Michael Jackson?"

"Michael Jackson! You're funny. No, Richard Burton"

"So you're the love child of Richard Burton and Elizabeth Taylor? What are you doing in Miami?

"I live here, darling."

Of course I've no idea if he was the real love child of Richard Burton and Elizabeth Taylor but I took him at his word all the same and did a short video with him, which I'm embarrassed to say I didn't save properly on my shit camera. However, one thing I was not prepared to do was argue with the police with him.

"Come with me, I want you to be a witness when I go and speak to this brute of a policeman who manhandled me."

"Err...no chance. I'm a big fan of your father's work but I've been in trouble with the law myself this week and I'm not even supposed to be standing here."

Now it's not every day you meet the offspring of the first ever celebrity couple, and I'd have loved to have spent time with him, but this was election day and every minute counted so I shook his hand and said goodbye before laughing out loud. Imagine the stories he would have had; it was just a shame that I'd met him at the worst possible time.

I was still looking for someone from our campaign when a blonde woman in a sedan pulled up beside me. She looked all a fluster and I knew she was going to come and speak to me. She was in her mid-twenties and dressed in a business suit.

"Excuse me sir, can you tell me what has happened here please?"

"They stopped people voting I think, but Richard Burton and Elizabeth's child is over there, he knows."

She got her notebook out.

"Are you a journalist?" I asked.

"Yeah I am, but I'm only new and I've been sent out here and I'm not sure if I've got a story."
My old journalist's instincts clicked into action and I thought I'd give her a helping hand.

"My name is Adam. I'm the leader of the Barack Obama International Brigade, which is made up of volunteers from across the world who've come to Miami to help"

She took my details down and again asked what had happened.

"Have you read anything about the International Brigade?" I asked, waiting for the penny to drop.

"No."

"Well, don't you think you might like to ask me about it because you've got yourself an exclusive. I'm a journalist by trade and I was going to write it myself but I thought it would harm the campaign. As voting is nearly over you can have the story!"

"Wow? Would you do that for me?"

"Yep."

"Where do I start? How do I do it? This is the biggest story I've ever had."

I got in her car and near enough wrote the whole bloody thing for her.

"This is your introduction - Volunteers from across the world have been descending on Miami to help the Barack Obama win the Presidential Election. This is your second par – Foreign nationals from Britain, France, Belgium, Denmark, Morocco and other countries have been working in South Beach trying to get the vote out for Mr Obama. This is your third par – There are believed to be over 50 of them and they call themselves the International Brigade. Do you know who the International Brigade were?"

"No"

"OK, you better take this down then: The International Brigade were communist sympathisers from across the world who went to fight in the Spanish Civil War". I then gave her a paragraph or two of my spiel, describing how I'd ended up in Miami and what I thought the election would mean to the wider world. I could tell she hadn't taken it all down because she couldn't do shorthand.

"That's a massive story. The right wing press will pounce on it because it shows there were foreigners helping sway your election. Your news editor should be chuffed. And, I said, I's exclusive."

It certainly was exclusive because I'd made the International Brigade up, but the story was very sound.

"I'll get you a picture of us if you want?"

"That would be great."

I could tell she was nervous. There's nothing like being on your first job as a journalist with the News Editor breathing down your neck, but I've had loads of old journalists cover me in the past and I try to help young pups as much as I can.

"Are you going to say thanks then?"

"Oh, I'm so sorry, thank you so much"

We exchanged phone numbers and I said she could phone me anytime she wanted for quotes or if she got in trouble with the story. I decided to go back to the office as the polling station was packing up and the last ten minutes had been that bizarre I needed a cigarette. By the time I got to the office I was dead on my feet again. I'd been up nearly 12 hours and the heat was really taking it out of me. I was thinking about going back to the hotel for a quick sleep before the results.

As I was watching the television Nate Sherwood came into the office. He was doing a tour of all the offices he was responsible for. With his customary Hollywood leading man smile he said: "How's it going South Beach office? Are we winning this election or what?" His confidence put me at ease about the election. After all, this was the finest political operator in the Eastern United States.

"How we looking, Nate?" I asked.

"We got people outside the polling stations, we got lawyers in the polling stations and we've got you guys ringing voters and knocking on doors. We're doing fine man, just fine"

"What about the rest of the country?"

"Who knows, are you gonna stick around to phone up the West Coast voters when our polls close?"

"Of course brother, I'm in it until the death" I replied.

"Great, let's get some espressos. Are you coming Broo-may?"

I followed Nate to a cafe. I had no idea what he was ordering but I figured he must be onto something good to look so unflustered and fresh despite being at the end of a long election campaign. He smiled and offered me a six inch glass filled with what must have been super-concentrated expresso. I nailed it. And then felt the rush of blood to my head. It was like having electric shock treatment.

"Shit me, Nate. How many of them do you have a day?"

"As many as I need brother," he said, adding as an afterthought: "It blows my mind man to think you've come from the UK to volunteer Adam." As he said that I felt on top of the world. I'm not sure if it was the concentrated coffee and maybe the hint of alcohol that was probably a key part of the espresso, or if it was hearing such kind words from someone I near enough idolised.

"Thank you Nate. I know I'm not the best volunteer, people can't understand me, I've spent hours lost and I nearly got arrested but I think going out with the cardboard Obama really suits me. I love it"

I wasn't fishing for compliments. Honestly.

"Adam, you gave up everything and came here. That alone inspires people in this campaign, and I love listening to you on the phones now I understand what you are on about."

We had another high octane espresso and headed back to the office. Nate said as we ambled back: "Hit the phones for a few hours now Adam. This is the last push". Before I'd gone for to the cafe I was dog tired but now I wanted to take on the world. A few words of encouragement and mainlining caffeine was all I needed and Nate had spotted that.

I took a chair outside with a sheet of numbers to attack. Within a few minutes Kale, Mark and Karim had done the same and we set about delivering the final push. All the numbers I had were in Colorado. I'd been there on a press trip and felt confident because I could say that I'd been to Denver, Canyon City and Aspen. "Isn't Colorado a Republican state?" I asked out loud, to no-one in particular. Mark lifted his head and said: "It's election day, no state is Republican today. We've got people in every state trying to turn them blue".

With the sun on our faces we all set about phoning our lists of Colorado voters. The atmosphere was more jovial as we knew this was one of the last jobs we'd do for the campaign. It was easier because we didn't have to fill in the fiddly sheets about whether these people had voted or not. It was too late to input data. Every so often Kale would do his impression of me on the phone to Nicole. It was all the more amusing because he couldn't get my accent at all:

"I canna believe your gonna get kicked out of your flat kitten, I can't believe it, but everything is gonna be grand kitten, we'll get a flat and everything will be ok. I miss you miss you sooo much, Kale tell her how much I love her Kale, 'he don't miss you at all'. No tell her how much I miss her Kale, tell her!"

I've never used the terms 'grand' or 'kitten' in my life but it was hilarious all the same. I didn't think I'd ever have as much fun on an election campaign again. I looked at the people surrounding me. After hours, days and weeks working on the campaign and partying afterwards I could call them my friends.

Mark could cope with any scenario thrown at him no matter how scary or strange. His facial expressions made him look he was permanently just about to grin but he had a serious side too. He'd travelled the Far East with his girlfriend, who he loved dearly, and then given up six weeks of his own time to help Obama. Then there was Kale, who is named after a vegetable like his forefathers before him. His painting and decorating business had folded and he'd petitioned all the rich people he knew to sponsor him to go to Florida to help out in a swing state. He was on the run from an intense Jewish volunteer who he'd had a tempestuous affair with during the campaign. Then Karim, a Belgian of Moroccan decent, who though still in his early 20s seemed to have the kind of CV that I'd make up but that was actually true. He'd worked with the Belgian Deputy Prime Minister and was aiming to be a big cheese in the world of human rights litigation. I was the oldest of the lot but the way we all took the piss out of each other and laughed at each other's jokes made it seem like we'd known each other for years. All of us were thousands of miles from home but had been brought together by a man we'd never met and probably never would – Barack Obama.

The good people of Colorado didn't seem to mind me calling and telling them to vote. Knowing these people were going to be the last of countless voters I'd phoned up in the previous weeks I enjoyed it all the more. Again, I really do love talking to Americans and had many a great conversation with the people I'd phoned up out of the blue. Though working on the phones can be hard, selling Obama is not as soul destroying as selling insurance, and I'd slowed down I wasn't getting as many confused people on the other end of the line. A woman who sounded like she was in her thirties answered the phone.

"Hello, my name is Adam and I'm calling on behalf of Barack Obama, just to see if you've voted in the Presidential election today"

"Where are you calling from?"

"Miami, baby!"

"Wow, that's a hell of an accent to be from Miami"

"I know baby, I had a car crash two years ago and had to learn how to speak again. I've no idea what this accent is"

"No way, and you're volunteering for Obama?"

"Yep, he's the best candidate for people who have had life threatening car crashes. Have you voted yet?"

"Of course, it would be wonderful if we turned Colorado blue! Thanks for the phone call, have a good day"

How can you not enjoy a conversation like that!

The office was still a magnet for Obama fans and sitting outside we had the best seats in the house to see the various women walk past us. A red Hummer pulled up. The tinted window came down and a black woman in her fifties poked her head out. She had the confidence of a woman who can afford a Hummer.

"Yo guys, is this an Obama office?" I shouted back: "Yeah Baby! This is the Miami South Beach Barack Obama office! We're gonna change the world!"

She laughed and introduced herself to all of us. I noticed there was someone in the other seat and asked her who it was.

"My daughter," she said.

"Does she want a photo taken with Barack Obama?" I asked.

"Hell yeah."

She jumped out and then we waited for her daughter to. All our jaws must have hit the floor at the same time because of the vision of beauty that emerged from behind the bumper. She had her haired pulled back, perfect golden brown skin and a smile to die for. She was wearing light blue jeans and a cream top, but though she'd obviously dressed down she couldn't hide her assets. She looked in her early 20s but seemed quite shy as well. She was beautiful, but she didn't realise quite how much - a perfect combination.

We all fell over ourselves to introduce ourselves. There's nothing quite as funny as men trying to impress a gorgeous girl. Even Karim was puffing up his chest.

It appeared that her mother was Jamaican and a big cheese at an airline. I was out with Barry and the camera in a flash. They were both so friendly. Karim was in there lightening quick and within five minutes had the mother offering him reduced flights. The daughter was so demure it was awe-inspiring; she kept giving little self-effacing smiles and giggling at our awful jokes. I'm not sure how long they were there for but the first photo I took of them was in daylight and in the last one it was pitch black.

"What are you guys doing for the inauguration?" the mother asked.

Mark was the quickest off the mark and said: "We don't know if he's going to win yet."

"Sure he will. Look, we've got a place in Virginia so if you guys are coming for the inauguration we'd love you to stay at our place. We've got the room haven't we?" she said to her daughter.

 "I'm sure we can fit you in, even if we have to share rooms"

Within a second we'd all agreed to go to the inauguration in January. Needless to say none of us did take the offer up three months later, but on that night in November 2008 anything seemed possible. The daughter must have been outrageously beautiful as even Karim was admiring her and he had the highest standards I've ever known. As I was spoken for I started living my fantasies through him: "Right, the way to get her is through email. She'll love the fact that your European, she'll probably come over and see you. You can do this, Karim"

Karim said sardonically: "Yes we can".

Dressing for Victory

It was approaching 8pm. The polls had closed in Miami and we'd exhausted our sheets of Colorado voters to call. The office was emptying of volunteers and thoughts were turning to the night ahead. As our Guyana friends had told us, there was a giant Democratic Party event at the theme park Jungle Island just off the causeway. There might even have been some free drinks on offer for volunteers, but after the previous party I wasn't going to hold my breath. The Tap Tap bar was also holding a party and I fancied going there because it would be a bit less formal than the official party. There were Kale, Mark, Karim, Claire and myself left in the office.

Claire was one of the only local volunteers in the office and she knew the town like the back of her hand. She was in her twenties and had that well built American look. I don't mean it in the bodybuilding sense, just that she was a woman who looked the picture of health and would probably remain so for the rest of her life. She had ruddy cheeks, a big smile and an athletic body.

We decided to go back to where we were staying, get ready quickly and head down to Jungle Island because Jelvis and all the North Beach volunteers would be there. I think the general view was that it was a better place to watch history unfold as well. I had no idea what time the result would be announced, but everyone was talking about the importance of the first exit polls which would be announced soon. My stomach was tightening with every hour that passed thinking about whether Obama would win or not.

As usual we put the television on to see what was happening, but as the polls hadn't closed yet on the West Coast there was a lot of talking about anything and everything except concrete evidence about who was going to win. As Karim went to the shower I jumped on my laptop, thinking it would be the right time to write the majority of my copy. I was going to hedge my bets and write the story as if Obama had won the election. Now you must understand, I'd never have done this if I'd been working, but I was on holiday and as soon as Obama won I wanted to party instead of spending ages thinking up introductions and trying to get quotes.

I still wasn't sure if the Birmingham Mail would use the story the day after so I wrote the story, used the quotes from the black lady I'd met the week before about what it would mean to her to see Obama win and left some space for quotes from Obama and McCain with a few paragraphs about the actual result. The introduction and body of the story was done and dusted within about twenty minutes and I figured I would send it after the speeches which, if they were between midnight and 2am, would mean my news desk back home would get the copy before they got into work at 7am. I didn't want to spend more than twenty minutes of my night writing because I wanted to let my down hair down with my newfound friends after a tough campaign.

I jumped in the shower and by the time I'd had a shave CNN were predicting that Obama had done well in a series of key states. We both let out a screech of delight when the key battleground state of Pennsylvania was called for Obama with a big swing. We both knew the importance of Pennsylvania in the race for the White House. Throughout the election it was top of the news agenda and none of the pundits thought Obama would win as handsomely as he did.

We watched as Maine, Maryland and DC fell to Obama, all of which were expected, but we were waiting for Florida. Then it buzzed across the screen: 'Florida too close to call'. I was a bit crestfallen but I couldn't help be pleased the drama would be drawn out. I wanted to be at the party when Florida was called. It would be a seminal moment for everyone in the campaign and I wanted to be jumping around, not in a hotel room in my pants getting ready to go out.

Karim seemed more relaxed than I'd seen him. He was repeating the word 'amazing' as Wolf Blitzer predicted state after state would go blue. He was looking forward to celebrating an Obama victory but still wasn't letting himself believe until he saw the final result. As we got ready we both knew this would be a night that we would never forget as long as we lived.

I couldn't decide what to wear. It wasn't that I was spoilt for choice, more that I was scratching my head wondering what to put on given the chronic lack of clothes I had available. My decent tops were either dirty or in a crumpled mess at the bottom of my suitcase. I'd worn all three of my Obama t-shirts throughout the day and wanted to put something clean and smartish on for a night which I figured would end up in a nightclub in Miami. I plumped for my blue and white striped top which was at least clean because it hadn't been worn all holiday, so I set out to party in one of the coolest places on earth in a top I'd bought for £10 from Tesco the year before. Little did I know that within 48 hours millions of people would see me and forever associate me with that blue and white Tesco number.

Election day. 8pm. Facebook status: Steve Zacharanda is ready to party like its 1999. Jungle Island full of thousands of Democrats then a Haitian rum bar. He deserves it, kind of ☺

Kale, Mark and Claire came and picked Karim and I up and we headed down to Jungle Island full of joy at knowing we would witness one of those moments in world history that people remember forever. Jungle Island is a huge theme park just off the Miami Beach causeway and it was a job to find a car parking space because it looked liked the party was well underway.

We finally found the conference room where the Democrats were holding the party. The sign said: "Tree Tops Ballroom – "Obama Victory Celebration" which filled a superstitious Brummie like me with dread. The words 'tempting fate' ran through my mind. I soon forgot about that when I walked in to the ballroom. It was long, in fact about 50m long. There were American flags and Democratic banners hanging off the walls and the place already was full of volunteers, press, activists and party workers.

There was a stage at the front of the room with a massive American flag behind it and giant screens showing CNN. People crowded around televisions waiting for results to come through, and those not looking at the televisions had their heads buried in their mobile phones hoping to hear more positive news about the election.

It was impressive. There seemed to be about a thousand people there, all looking like they'd won the lottery but were waiting to have their ticket validated. There were two differing sets of people: those who thought Obama would easily win, who were probably volunteering for the first time, and the other group, who wouldn't let themselves believe he'd won until they could see the result with their own eyes. They were campaign veterans scarred from 2000.

What struck me was the diverse nature of the crowd. The people there were black, white, Hispanic, Asian, young, middle-aged, old, all hoping a new America would be born in a few hours time. I wondered how white and middle-aged the McCain parties would be and was glad I was on the right side.

People had brought along their placards and wore their campaign t-shirts too. As well as the Obama fans there were all the supporters of the Democratic candidates in all of the local elections. Jelvis was in his civvies, but still managed to look like a star. The North Beach volunteers were there, as were the lawyers who didn't look as happy as everyone else. They were probably praying for a decisive result, fearing they'd be stuck in Florida for the foreseeable future doing battle with their Republican opposite numbers.

I couldn't help but think that we'd got there too late but then I remembered why. I clapped Kale on the back and said: "How many of these lot do you reckon were phoning Colorado after the polls closed?"

"Not many Broo-may, not many" he said with a smile. "Cos we're the Barack Obama South Beach Office baby! First in, last out, that's how we roll", I shouted as we headed into the breach.

Like any Englishman abroad I immediately scoped the joint for the bar. I was disappointed, very disappointed. I couldn't see one anywhere. I started to panic. I'd just worked a monumental shift for the campaign and wanted an alcoholic drink. The best drink is the one after a long day trying to change the world. I was also determined to have a drink in my hand when the election result was announced so that I could toast the new president of the United States of America.

I started delving in and out of groups of volunteers in a frantic search for the bar - some people had drinks, so I knew there had to be one somewhere. I noticed a table of booze and breathed a sigh of relief. There were two women in catering uniforms behind it serving drinks as quickly as they could. I joined the back of the line and noticed no-one was exchanging money for the drinks. My spirits rose as I assumed the drinks must be free, as a thank you to everyone who had volunteered for the campaign. How wrong I was.

When I finally got to the front I asked for a rum and coke. The part-time bar lady looked at me as if I was stark raving mad and said loudly, for the benefit of everyone in the line, "These drinks are not free, sir." With a healthy hint of sarcasm I replied: "Of course they aren't free! Why on earth would the Democratic Party buy drinks for the people who've been working for free for weeks on end for the campaign?". I looked at her face and at those around me and realised this approach wouldn't work. I let out a laugh to show I was joking.

"I've got money"

"Sorry, sir, you can't buy a drink here. You need tokens and you need to wait in that line buy them..."

I jumped in: "Let me guess, then wait at the back of this line to get my drink?"

I wanted to shout: "Fucking tokens! To buy drinks? What a complete and utter disgrace, what twat made that decision?" I stopped myself from going into a rant about how, on such an important night, they'd managed to come up with the most arse about face way of serving drinks to the troops. Instead I tutted, shook my head and walked to the back of the token queue. I was getting anxious. I kept looking at the screens and then at the people watching the results come in. I didn't want to be the idiot waiting in a queue or in the toilet when Obama became president. I wanted to be with Kale, Mark, Karim, Claire, Nate and Jelvis – the people who had made it happen.

As I inched along the token line I kept an eye out for Kale and Mark because I knew that they too would have gotten around to thinking about getting a beer. Sure enough they appeared through the crowd, just as pissed off as me that the drinks operation was being run like a school disco. As I was nearing the front I attracted their attention and told them I'd get their tokens and to wait in the drinks line.

By the time I got served I was delirious with waiting.

"How many tokens would you like Sir?"

"Seven."

"Seven?"

I said: "Yes, seven. I've worked all day for Obama and I want a drink. Now I know how much of a palaver it is to get one I need several because I don't want my first few drinks ruined by the nagging fear that I'm gonna have to line up for hours to get another one. I just want to party."

"Seven it is then, sir."

Luckily I had enough money to pay for them because I'd have looked like a right idiot if I hadn't. I had the tokens. Now all I had to do was get the drinks. I joined Kale in the queue and gave him four tokens for himself and everybody else's drinks. At this point I wasn't even bothered that I was pushing in, and for an Englishman with patient queuing seared in his soul that is saying something.

The woman recognised me straight away.

"Sir, what would you like to drink?"

As I handed her three tokens I said: "You really should have put some signs up about this token thing, I've been waiting for twenty minutes now to get a drink. I'll have three double rum and cokes please."

She looked at the token and said: "But three double rum and cokes..."

I glared at her and after seeing the expression on my face she stopped what she was saying, said "Sorry for the delay," and poured the drinks. I later found out that one token only entitled me to a single. I'd only wanted one bloody rum and coke but because of some idiot who couldn't organise a piss up in a brewery I'd ended up with three double rum and cokes. Lives can change on such mundane mix ups and mistakes. And mine did.

America starts turning blue

I quickly found Nate, Jelvis, Karim, Mark, Claire and the others from the office and immediately relaxed knowing I'd got my drinks and had a front row seat for history. "Florida is too close to call," said Mark. My stomach tightened and I realised how hard it must have been in 2000 to wait weeks to find out who had won. That was why we were all in Miami though, because we all knew Florida would be a tightly fought battle. I was more optimistic about the national picture, but anything but victory in our state would have left a bitter aftertaste.

I imagined when Obama won it would be like New Year's Eve after the clock strikes midnight with people dancing, hugging and shaking hands. I still wasn't totally sure when that moment would happen. I'm used to British General Elections in which the polling doesn't stop until 10pm and people still put a quaint cross on a piece of paper to pick their candidate. All the pieces of paper are bundled up, put in boxes and driven to the election count where the result is declared about 5am in the morning.

In America, obviously, it is done differently. Different states do it differently as well. People punch their votes into high tech computers, so obviously the results are collated quicker than in the elections for the mother of all Parliaments in Westminster. The trouble with computers however, and this is a personal theory, is that someone, somewhere controls the computer and one day might distort the numbers one way or another. As Stalin said: "It's not who votes that counts, it's who counts the votes that counts".

The overwhelming feeling was that Obama was going to win. Everyone had seen the exit polls and when certain states declared a wave of jubilation reverberated through the room. Up to now it had been quite reserved though. However, when Ohio was called for Obama the room went crazy. I knew it was a big swing state but people were celebrating as if it was the whole election. There was a roar of O-BA-MA and groups of people either side of me were jumping up together. I couldn't help but be caught up in the fun, high fiving people and letting anyone who wanted to hug me hug me. For the first time I let myself seriously believe he had won. I downed one of my double rum and cokes so I could concentrate on shaking hands and looking at the faces of jubilant Democrats.

Kale had told me the electoral college number that Obama needed to win and I kept stealing glances at Obama's count as it edged towards the 270 that would make him President. As well as the national result we all wanted to know whether we'd done our job and won Florida. I could tell Nate was getting nervous about the result. He knew within hours everything would be laid bare: how many people had voted Democratic in firstly Florida, then Miami and then South Beach. He obviously wanted to deliver his patch for Obama. There would be a list somewhere with the results on and his name next to South Beach. For a moment I wished I'd worked harder for the campaign, for Nate and for Obama.

I was watching Nate drift in and out of conversations as he kept an eye on the stage at the front of the room. Suddenly his brow furrowed and his eyes sharpened. I followed his gaze and spotted a few suited officials fiddling with the microphones. The room suddenly went quiet as we awaited the result. I crossed my fingers as others bit their nails and held loved ones to their chest. We were about half way back and couldn't hear exactly what was being said, but within seconds it was obvious we had helped Obama win Florida. There would be no recount. Florida had turned blue, and all our hard work had paid off.

Within seconds we were all in a circle hugging each other and jumping up and down. I looked at my friends' faces and they were filled with unadulterated joy. Kale had a daft grin on his face, Karim was laughing out loud, Nate was shouting something at the top of his voice I couldn't hear in the din. Mark was 'whoop whooping' and Claire was bouncing up and down, so frankly I wasn't looking at her face. Me? Well you'd have to ask the others what I looked like but I must have said 'Fucking brilliant' about twenty times in a row. Soon the whole room was chanting 'O-BA-MA' and people were jumping on chairs to shout and scream the chant that defined the election. The woman on the stage looked as if she was still reading out results, probably the local election results, but no-one cared. It was party time.

The states kept on coming. Virginia saw another round of shouting and screaming, and then it happened. We passed the 270 mark. I couldn't tell you what state it was or what time it was but the sheer communal elation told me Barack Obama had just become the 44th President of the United States, after the most remarkable election in a generation.

I've never seen such spontaneous happiness that didn't involve drugs in all my life, and I doubt that I ever will again. I thought when Florida was announced the place had gone crazy but when the winning mark had been passed it was pandemonium. It's fascinating to see how people deal with unadulterated joy. Some shout, some dance, some sing, some need people to hug their friends, some want to kiss the partner they love, some cry and some take a moment to take it all in. In all probability most people do all of those things within an hour – I know I did.

Just minutes after Obama's victory I did something I'd never have dreamt I'd do just a couple of weeks before. I gave The Jewish Elvis, Jelvis, a massive bear hug and a kiss and told him I loved him. He took it in his stride as every superstar should when an overemotional fan invades their personal space, and I really meant it. I mean, Jelvis? The guy made my campaign. It wasn't just him though, I loved everyone at that moment and told Kale, Mark, Claire and Karim I loved them because I did. I still do now because I shared that unbelievable moment with them.

The lights were bright, so I could see everyone's individual expression in the sea of happy faces around me. One heavy set guy in his fifties was just continually jumping up and down on his own. Every time I looked back in his direction he was doing exactly the same thing. I wondered what was going on in his mind. In every direction there were people crying with joy. It was beautiful.

I looked at the massive TV screens and saw the pictures of people going crazy across America. Waves and waves of goose bumps rushed over my skin and the hairs on my neck stood for attention for minutes on end as the enormity of the situation hit me. Against all the historical odds a mixed race man was President of the United States of America. The good guys had won, and just to see so many people go crazy in the streets was fantastic. It was one of those all too rare moments in which you see young and old celebrating like there was no tomorrow, and all because of politics.

I could tell this night was never going to end and that no-one would be going home early because the adrenaline would have stopped any sane person sleeping. Music would blast from the sound system in no particular order and for no particular reason, but every time there was quiet you knew something important was happening. A hush descended across the room and all the televisions showed the same image – John McCain. He was just about to concede in this most historic of elections.

McCain was speaking in Phoenix and everyone in our room was waiting to see what he was going to say. His wife was at his side as well as Sarah Palin, who looked gorgeous in a shiny blue power suit. A cheer went up in the room when he said he'd just phoned Barack Obama to congratulate him on winning the election. However, the reaction in Arizona was very different. As soon as Barack Obama's name was mentioned the all white audience began booing. Everyone around me started to laugh because the Republicans were obviously hurting.

To McCain's credit he motioned to his supporters to shut up and went on to give the best speech of his life, clearly aimed at uniting America. Within a few moments he was acknowledging the enormity of a black man being elected to the White House, 100 years after the uproar that greeted President Theodore Roosevelt inviting Booker T Washington to dinner, and referencing the 'cruelty of those times'.

After about three minutes of the speech I had a panic attack. I realised I hadn't being taking notes. I went to grab my notebook but realised I didn't have one, then searched for a pen in my pocket and realised I didn't have one of those either. My worries passed though; I assumed I'd be able to pick up the exact wording of some of his most important quotes on the BBC or CNN when I compiled my report. I smiled as I thought about the number of times someone had said to me "What, a journalist without a pen?" and again, not for the first time in America, I thought 'Oh, fuck it, I'm not being paid to be here.'

Instead of worrying I just savoured the moment and took in every word of John McCain's historic 10 minute speech. What I found fascinating was that none of the Democrats around me mocked the old war hero. I think people realised he was a good man and not a Republican in the image of George Bush or Karl Rove. However, when he said that there was nothing more he could have done to have won the election I disagreed. He could have played the race card, like many racists in his party wanted him to, but he resisted because he knew it could have torn America apart. He might have won more votes, but he must have known that if the forces of bigotry were unleashed in his campaign it could well have opened a Pandora's Box of racial tension. For his courage and his decency, to me John McCain is an American hero. I felt goosepimples cover my skin as I watched his speech. It was a perfect way to concede an election.

When he finished speaking a round of respectful applause went around the room and everyone near me commented on what a great speech it had been. It was all the sweeter because it meant that Obama had really won. Even the most pessimistic conspiracy theorist in the room couldn't have denied that Obama was going to be President. I took the last few gulps of my rum and coke and again congratulated myself for being in America at that moment in history, before heading off to get more drinks. I was overjoyed that Kale was coming the other way with a double rum and coke for me. I gave him another big hug, as much for the drink as for the fact that we'd helped Barack Obama win the election of elections.

Obama's electoral college vote stood at 333, and every time another state went blue a cheer went around the room and people partied harder realising the Democrats were on course for a landslide. I thought about my prediction for the Sunday Mercury in which I'd said 'Whatever happens, it will be too close to call', and laughed as I realised that my political radar was probably not as sharp as I'd hoped.

Officials were periodically wandering on to the stage to talk and punch the air. There was still a crowd around the stage but those towards the back of the room seemed to be having their own party. However, when all the screens stopped showing different pictures and every single one beamed out the picture of an empty stage in Chicago there was a surge towards the front of the room as everyone awaited the new President Elect of the United States of America.

Barack Obama's acceptance speech would be the defining moment of the entire night. I found my South Beach comrades and we all waited for the great man to appear. This time I had a pen and paper at the ready, but I decided not to try and do shorthand because I wanted to enjoy the moment. The victory party was at Grant Park in Chicago and there was a gasp in the room as the cameras panned across a massive crowd that seemed to go back for miles and included every colour and age. When the cameras turned back to the stage it was obvious the secret services had built a Perspex box to stop the assassination threat that dared not speak its name.

This really was an incredible moment in the life of America and by extension the world. It wasn't just the voters in Florida, California, Virginia and New York that were now glued to their television sets. People all across the world were ready to fall back in love with America.

The room cheered wildly as Barack Obama, Michelle and their two daughters walked onto the stage and towards the podium. He stood in front of the microphone. You could have heard a pin drop in the room in the seconds before he opened his mouth. He said: "Hello, Chicago". The camera switched angles to show the giant crowd, many of whom were fervently waving the stars and stripes.

The reinvigorated politician continued: "If there is anyone out there who still doubts that America is a place where all things are possible, who still wonders if the dream of our founders is alive in our time, who still questions the power of our democracy, tonight is your answer". A massive cheer erupted in the room but quickly died down before he carried on speaking. I stood enraptured, staring at the man who'd inspired me to drop everything and fly thousands of miles to help him to change the world. I put my pen and paper in my pocket. I wanted to soak up every last second of this speech.

When Obama mentioned John McCain the crowd in Chicago cheered, and those in our room did the same. As a ripple of applause went through the room, I clapped too, and thought back to the Republican rally when McCain had to stop his supporters booing the name of their new President. Obama paid tribute to his wife Michelle and I thought about Nicole. Maybe with a good woman behind me I could also change the world. I bet Obama wouldn't hadn't have got where he did without the support of his wife, the love of his life.

Of course, he also thanked his army of volunteers. He said: "But above all, I will never forget who this victory truly belongs to. It belongs to you. It belongs to you. It belongs to you, Adam from Perry Barr. Thanks for helping me. I'll be in touch to lend you some money, brother". OK, the last line was in my head but when he said 'you' I felt as if he was talking directly to me, and I suspect everyone else in the room felt the same thing. A lump came to my throat and my eyes started to moisten. When Obama added: "This is your victory" another cheer rippled through the ballroom and everyone started to high five each other. They soon lapsed into silence, waiting for him to speak again.

The camera panned to a crying Jessie Jackson, who had been there the day Martin Luther King had been shot, and the crowd let out another cheer. Obama continued:

"This is our chance to answer that call. This is our moment. This is our time, to put our people back to work and open doors of opportunity for our kids; to restore prosperity and promote the cause of peace; to reclaim the American dream and reaffirm that fundamental truth, that, out of many, we are one; that while we breathe, we hope. And where we are met with cynicism and doubts and those who tell us that we can't, we will respond with that timeless creed that sums up the spirit of a people: Yes, we can. Thank you. God bless you, and may God bless the United States of America."

With that the speech was over and the partying started again, everyone cheering, dancing and hugging each other. I wished Nicole was with me, I wished she could have experienced what I was experiencing. I promised myself I'd bring her back for the inauguration and propose to her. I wasn't going to be melancholy on such a wonderful night though. In fact just having a loved one, no matter how far away, made me even happier. There wasn't a thing in my life at that moment that I would have changed, and those moments don't come along very often. I savoured it so that my soul would be stronger the next time everything went to shit.

I got myself another rum and coke, this time without all the hassle with tokens because even the sour-faced barwomen were partying now. I thought about leaving Nicole crying outside her tower block, about getting the flights getting mixed up, all the trouble in customs, my first night with Sam and how amazing she was, the hotels, the faux gay affections. I thought about how I'd nearly met Obama, about Jelvis, Barry, the wonderful office and all the friends I'd made. I had one man to thank - Barack Obama. If he hadn't have had the audacity to run for office, I would have never have had the audacity to try and help him. I looked to the sky and thanked God for helping me. I was meant to be in Miami that night. I had to be, so many things had gone my way which shouldn't have.

I looked at a beaming picture of Obama's face on a fat woman's stretched t-shirt, and felt a surge of pride that I'd helped him get to power. I couldn't help but think of the old black woman in the office who'd seen men lynched in her village in the Deep South, and I said out loud: "A black man is in the White House. Fuck me, anything can happen."

I went for a cigarette and noticed the media centre, if it could even have been described as that. It jogged my memory and I realised that I'd better send my election copy. I grabbed the car keys from Kale and went to get my laptop. When the night air hit me I immediately felt a little woozy. Not drunk, just woozy.

The media centre was nothing more than lots of plugs, power points and extension cables stretched out on the floor of the terrace next to the convention room. I found a space, plugged my laptop in and started to hook up to the internet. I knew what I had to do, I had to find the copy I'd written and insert some quotes in to the story. I remembered quite well the choice quotes from John McCain and Barack Obama, but I thought I'd check the BBC and CNN to insure the quotes were correct.

As I was cross checking I noticed someone beside me. I looked up and it was the Guyaweb photographer. She was speaking to herself in French and seemed to be all of a panic. I couldn't understand what she was saying but I could tell she couldn't get something to work on her computer or her phone. In her ever-so-cool French accent she said: "Hey journalist, can I borrow your phone?" How could I refuse a damsel in distress? "Of course, but it's not a works phone and there's not much credit left so you'll have to be quick."

I handed her the phone and she spent a minute screaming down the phone in French. She smiled her goofy smile, handed the phone back and then started tapping away at her computer. How I wished I spoke French, because at that moment I'd have loved to have learnt more about the funky photo journalist from Guyana.

It took about 10 minutes to cross reference my quotes with the BBC and CNN websites and I set about checking my copy to see if it could be improved. I knew the Birmingham Mail didn't print any news story not written in 'their style', which was pretty boring; no flair or imagination was allowed when writing news. This might have been an advantage when writing whilst tipsy, but I'd completed the majority of the copy in the hotel beforehand.

As I was spellchecking my copy I noticed another woman standing above me. I recognised her. She was the Dutch internet journalist that had been hanging around the office, I'd watched her interview Jelvis a few times and we'd exchanged pleasantries, but as far as I knew I hadn't told her I was a journalist. She was tall, looked to be about 40-years-old and had the aura of an experienced travel journalist.

She crouched down said: "Hi. My name is Maartje, I'm making videos about the election. What are you doing?"

"Hey Maartje, I've seen you around. I'm a journalist from England who is volunteering for the Obama election, and I'm sending some copy back to the office for tomorrow's paper," I said.

"Cool, can I make a video of you?"

I didn't give it a second thought and replied immediately: "Of course you can, I'll speak slowly so people can understand me!"

With that she pulled out what looked like a normal digital camera and started filming. I waxed lyrical about the South Beach Obama office and being part of the International Brigade, and explained that I was sending copy back to my paper despite being half cut. I followed up with a mock Dutch accent, then mentioned I was copying quotes from the BBC and before sticking two fingers up at the camera and saying: 'I've just resigned from the Birmingham Mail, Birmingham Post and the Sunday Mercury. I'm launching my own magazine, Goggle-eye. Fuck you, I'm doing what I want to do".

She pressed the stop button on the camera and we both looked at each other in silence for a second or two. We burst out laughing. "That was brilliant. You're a funny guy Adam, thank you so much! Is that true about leaving your job?" Drunk on Obama's victory, life itself and several double rum and cokes I felt on top of the world and I was proud of my performance in front of the camera so I took a chance. If Barack Obama could win the election then why on earth couldn't I make Cheekie Media and Goggle-eye a success? A publicity stunt would be the perfect springboard to success.

I said: "Put it on YouTube and you'll have shitloads of views. I'm a well known journalist in England and loads of people will be interested in me resigning like that"

She smiled, a smile that suggested she knew I might not know exactly what I was saying, and said: "Are you sure?"

"Yeah man, fuck it, put it on YouTube tonight"

We both laughed again and she said: "You're so right in what you said about America there Adam. Thanks again, make sure you have a good night."

I said "No worries, baby," before shaking her hand to say goodbye. Karim wandered over and sat next to me. He'd been watching me being interviewed.

"How you doing buddy, who was she?" he said.

"Some Dutch bird making videos about the election. She seems pretty cool, man. I'm gonna send my copy and be back in to party"

He got the hint and left and I set about putting the finishing touches to my article. I remembered that I had to send it to the editor of the Southampton Echo, Ian Murray, who I'd met on a press trip to Colorado a few years beforehand. I'd asked him if he would take my copy during the election as a back up after the lukewarm reception I'd got from my newsdesk. I knew I was a little drunk so I spell checked it about three times before I pressed the send button; also for good measure I sent it twice to ensure it would arrive safely. This is what I sent (including all of the grammatical errors):

Adam Smith In Miami

THE UNITED States of America has elected the remarkable Barack Obama as their first African-American President.

Barack Hussein Obama, the son of a black Kenyan student and a white American woman, swept to power after millions of voters gave him a mandate for change.

Just 52 years after Rosa Parks started the Civil Rights movement by refusing to give up her bus seat, millions of Americans from all different races flocked to polls to elect Mr Obama.

In front of a crowd of 125,000 in Chicago, the President said: "I believe in the America that says to every challenge "Yes We Can', the road ahead will be long. Our climb will be steep. We may not get there in one year or even one term, but America I have never been more hopeful than I am tonight that we will get there.

"And I promise you we as a people will get there,"

In a magnanimous speech John McCain accepted defeat and said: "I deeply admire and commend and President Obama."

Half of America woke up to a new President but the other half stayed awake to see history unfold in front of their eyes.

Sheila Ettienne, aged 65, a black grandmother from Miami Gardens, wept with joy when she saw the results come in.

She said: "This is the best night of my life, I never believed that I would live to see this day, I cannot believe America has voted to put a black man in the White House.

"My grandchildren didn't believe me when I told them our people were slaves and we were regularly lynched in America.

"People died so that black people could vote, Martin Luther King had a dream, and he died for it, and Obama wouldn't be there for his and others sacrifice."

Mr Obama put together an amazing coalition of rich, poor, black, white, left, right, urban and rural voters.

His campaign broke records raising more cash than any before and attracted volunteers from across the world.

Miami South Beach Obama co-ordinator Nate Sherwood said: "This campaign has been successful because we all own it, it is not Barack Obama's campaign it is everyone who got involved.

"He inspired us all but he cannot change the country on his own only the people can, this is a wonderful day for America."

Barack Obama is the first president since Ronald Reagan in 1980 to sweep a massive amount Congressmen and Senators to power with him, giving him a massive advantage when he begins his presidency in January.

A new chapter in world history has begun, and whatever happens, people in America will never forget this moment.

Not the greatest story but it did the job and was written in the Birmingham Mail style. I had filed copy on location during at an American Presidential Election, and I thought I deserved an extra drink to celebrate a high point in my journalistic career. I comforted myself that I would write a brilliant feature about the election the next day. I packed up the laptop and took it back to Kale's car, bumping into Karim, Kale, Claire, Mark and Nate and jumping into the middle of amidst a hail of high-fives. "I've just told my bosses to fuck off on some Dutch TV video channel," I said. Everyone laughed. I didn't give my little performance on camera a second thought that night.

Time to party

Revellers were still celebrating in the ballroom. There was dancing, endless O-BA-MA chants and countless eyes reddened with tears of joy. I wandered around the party aimlessly but happily for a while, bumping into fellow volunteers, listening to speeches, watching the TV, getting more drinks and just enjoying victory.

As I stumbled through the crowd I bumped into the New Labour delegation. Needless to say none of them were as pissed as me. We exchanged pleasantries and all agreed it was an amazing moment in history and one which we were privileged to see. Then the subject turned to English politics. Freed from the shackles of the politeness of the office and the prying ears of Ericka I let rip. I can't remember what the gateway question was, but knowing me it probably was something as inane as 'So are you voting Labour this election?' However, I think it was more likely along the lines of whether I'd be volunteering for Labour in next General Election. I thought I'd give them a piece of the mind of the common man, as in my experience most political nerds haven't a clue.

With a glass of rum sloshing around and my arms and hands gesticulating in all directions I went off into a lengthy rant about politics, which believe me is not a pretty sight. It doesn't happen very often as nearly all the people I know couldn't care less about politics, so I don't have the chance to make an arse of myself as often as I should.

My love of politics was born in the Miners Strike of 1984; as an 8-year-old I listened to the fascinating and never-ending arguments between my Communist ex-miner Grandad and my Thatcherite policeman dad, who was coining the overtime scrapping with striking miners. That's why I firmly believe politics should be argued about endlessly.

I could sense their perplexity as people around me heard what I was saying. After all, the whole room was happy and I was the only one looking pissed off. I said: "I fucking might have volunteered for Labour, but that was before you started lying to the country, declaring illegal wars, arse-licking the rich and forgetting the poor, turning the country into a surveillance state, giving bailiffs the chance the break into my home and taking the piss with my civil liberties. I think I'm what you might call Old Labour pal. Don't think I haven't told one of my best friends, who happens to be one of your MPs, everything that I just said. I bet you've come here to see what tricks of the trade Obama uses so you can use them in our election. Well, it won't fucking work because Labour is in power. You might use the internet better but how can you use the whole argument for change? Labour's had their chance and fucked it up. They don't deserve to win and believe me if they do, they'll be out of power for a generation, believe me he next election is the election to lose"

With that drunken point made I stumbled off without saying goodbye and left what was probably a nice group of middle-class Labour Party activists to enjoy their night without some drunken idiot reminding them of the all the problems they wanted to forget.

I loved bumbling around looking at people crying, hugging and staring into space, and trying to imagine all the stories they had to tell. I didn't have a conversation for about half an hour because everyone was just going from one person to the next hugging and high-fiving before finding someone else to share their joy with. Whenever I thought people couldn't look any happier a cameraman would come along and people would go headlong into happiness overdrive. As well as shouting "O-BA-MA" into the camera revellers would start dancing in different daft ways. Four black men of about sixty were standing in a line doing some kind of synchronized boyband dance, and in front of them three 'Cuban Women for Obama' were in the middle of a pretty raunchy routine. Eventually both groups joined together and after some awkward dancing started a conga line. I couldn't remember the last time I'd done the conga but I doubt if I will ever experience one with as many different colours, ages and nationalities again. It was simply bliss.

These days people party for any old reason, but can there be any better reason to bust a move than knowing that the world will be a better place? Obviously I was elated but I could never have been as happy as an American because they'd lived the last eight years under George Bush and many of them, when they heard I was from England, said that they were delighted because they believed the world wouldn't hate them anymore. I must have said: "Tonight my friend, the world has fallen back in love with America," about a hundred times.

"Right on dude!" shouted one burly Latino bloke as he slapped me on the back so hard my heart nearly shot out of my chest. One volunteer in her twenties just burst in to tears and said "Thank you so much" before burying her head in my chest and sobbing uncontrollably. After giving my sweater a soaking she tearfully explained that Obama winning meant that the prospect of having health insurance was a reality for the first time in her life. She said would start a family now because Obama had won. I got a little emotional myself thinking how this election would change this blubbing woman's life.

Other party guests had other reasons to celebrate. A big, swarthy looking man wearing an Obama top and shorts jumped in the middle of the two of us, whilst making a strange shape with his left hand, and said: "We've thrown the Republicans out man. We did it man, we did it man, America is great again!" At the back of the room I saw a group of women, all of whom looked to be in their

20s and 30s, surrounding one man who I couldn't help but think must have been a lucky bugger.

Then one of them stepped aside and I realised who he was. It was square-necked Mark. Unbelievably, he was surrounded by 'chicks'. Our eyes met, and as I walked towards him I could tell he was a little nervous in case I ruined his shot with the bevy of beauties. We shook hands and laughed together. "You good Adam?" "I'm good Mark. It was all worth it to see Obama win." "You're damn right dude. You're damn right" He didn't introduce me to his women, so we shook hands and said "see you around" at the same time, safe in the knowledge we'd never see each other ever again.

I would've liked an apology or a 'thank you' but despite almost ruining my entire holiday I couldn't dislike the man on the night Obama won. I didn't want to leave a bad taste in anyone's mouth and I didn't want to ruin his chances of the perfect night. By this time it was a free for all on stage with anyone and everyone talking shite down the microphone. However, there was one nice touch when some local wag put a cardboard Barack Obama behind the microphone. My heart skipped thinking it was my Barry from the office but it wasn't because I'd hidden ours away that night. Everyone cheered when he appeared and people rushed to have their photo with the great man.

Whilst outside having another cigarette, Caesar phoned. I was glad he didn't share his auntie's anger about my escapades. After lots of shouting and cheering down the phone he started asking where I was going after the Jungle Island party. I didn't have a clue and he couldn't understand a word I was saying anyway. I'm sad to say I never had the chance to get back to him because the French speaking journalist had used my last bit of credit. To be fair, I knew Caesar would have had a great night anyway.

It must have been about 2am when people started drifting off and I found all my friends to find out our next destination. Nate, naturally, was taking charge. He seemed so happy. The more he drank the taller and more languid he became. The prevailing view was that we should go to a hip-hop club and it just so happened that there was a place on Miami Beach. I stuck to Nate like glue because I didn't want to lose everyone on this night of nights.

Drunken Democrats were falling out of the ballroom singing songs I'd never heard before, and every time I caught someone's eye they would start talking about how happy they were. Jungle Island isn't the easiest place to navigate so as I waited for Nate to say goodbye to the never ending queue of people wanting to touch him I enjoyed watching drunkards stumbling up and down different staircases, totally lost. I'd love to know how many of them woke up in Jungle Island the next day after passing out.

We finally got into a taxi and headed off to the club. The taxi journey was, as Americans say, 'awesome'. There were just a few of us so we could really enjoy having a chat about the election win without other revellers jumping amongst us and starting random conversations. Nate kept on saying he couldn't believe how much Obama had won by and he had a massive mandate for change because he'd have both the Senate and the House of Representatives on his side.

As the taxi sped towards the club I couldn't help marvelling at the sheer number of people on the streets celebrating. Though it was in the early hours there seemed to be hundreds of people milling around at intersections. As we slowed down it became obvious that everybody had taken to the street to celebrate. The majority of the revellers seemed to be black, but there were lots of young whites and Latinos. No-one seemed to be going anywhere but every time a car passed they shouted 'Obama' and demanded a honk.

We hung out the windows and shouted 'Obama' back, feeling like the world was about to change. The taxi driver said South Beach had come to a standstill with people standing on their cars waving flags and climbing through the top of their sunroofs with Obama posters. He just kept on saying 'It's a crazy night man, it's crazy night". There had been spontaneous parties on street corners as soon as the news was announced, with hundreds of cars lining the streets, horns beeping and music blasting out. The police had tried to move everyone on but gave up because of the sheer numbers of people partying in the street.

I borrowed a phone and rang Nicole. I wanted to speak to her when she got back from her nightshift. She seemed so happy to hear from me and that Obama had won. I put the phone up in the car and said 'How much do I love Nicole?' and they all shouted 'He loves you, baby" and with that we said goodbye. I couldn't have been happier. Obama had won, I was in Miami, I had a woman that I loved and who loved me too and I was with great people on the way to a club.

We jumped out of the taxi and headed towards what looked like a broken down fence leading into a derelict housing block. It reminded me of everything I'd ever seen about the start of hip-hop in New York in the 1970s. A tumbledown cityscape is the perfect back drop for hip hop. We came into a scruffy courtyard with graffiti covered walls and a staircase which went up to a door. It was open enough for us to see the shapes of people beyond it.

I could hear the bassline of speakers above me and my stomach turned over. I love a grimy nightclub. I pushed the door open and entered. It was packed, mostly with black revellers. There was netting on the ceiling and sweat running down the walls.It was very different to the other nightspots I'd been to in Miami.

They were all very smooth, cool and filled with beautiful people. This place was full of real people having fun and not trying to look like a million dollars.

Modern hip-hop blared through the speakers. I thought I'd died and gone to heaven. The room was quite small and there looked to be about 200 people there, every one of them smiling and dancing. I shook Nate's hand again with admiration for picking such a great place to party. As I headed to the bar I started seeing more faces from the campaign. Jelvis was there, as were the lawyers, who were now partying hard because they were officially off duty. Kale, Karim, Claire and Mark had also arrived before us and were downing drinks whilst edging closer to the dance floor.

Everyone I greeted gave me broad smile and shook my hand or hugged me. It was brilliant. I felt like a conquering hero. The partying Brummie had arrived. There's no better feeling than walking into a great club playing great music with a bit of cash in my pocket, then seeing loads of people I know and love and who are happy to see me. I hit the bar hard, ordered several rum and cokes and began chatting to everyone I knew, laughing and joking, reliving moments in the campaign and reflecting on the glorious thing we'd taken part in – getting Obama into the White House.

Everyone was so happy. Gradually talk turned to our own lives, and then it was like any other night, friends making each other laugh and swapping ever more outrageous stories. The music started to take over the night. When the first few bars of our holiday anthem ('Whatever You Like') came out of the speakers Mark, Kale, Karim and I all linked hands and sang to the sky.

Tune after tune came across the sound system, and well, it doesn't happen very often, but I thought I'd drop the A-bomb. I cleared my mind of junk and just let the music take my body over, pulling out some dance moves forged in Birmingham but at home on this grimy dance floor in Miami. For over an hour I just danced away in bliss.

When I got deeper into the dance floor I saw the two Wu Tang Clan fanatics from earlier that day. They were in the same clothes and looked more at home in the club than standing in the shopping centre. They must have had about 40 articles of clothing, jewellery, rags and other accessories, which in a weird kind of way made sense. They recognised me and we greeted each other like long lost friends. I called Karim over to share in the joy. We all took photos with each other, some of which I have to say are my favourite photos of me in any period of my life.

"You cool man, you cool?" said the small one with the braces on his teeth.

"Course I'm cool brother, Obama won!" I replied.

"Me know man, me know man"

"How many of them CDs did you sell then mate?"

"All of them! It was off the hook."

I said with a smile: "Were they bollocks official Obama CDs! But who gives a fuck man! Obama won!"

We hugged again and he gave me a huge grin which looked dazzling because the lights were reflecting off his braces: "You're cool man."

I can't deny I felt proud and said: "I know mate, I am cool. Well tonight I am, the rest of the year I'm a fucking idiot".

The crowd was so friendly and everyone was talking about Obama. We were partying hard for politics and it was great. Two man mountains stood in front of me and shouted 'O-BA-MA' at the top of their voices, then did a thunderous high five that caused such an impact it sounded like a bomb had gone off. When I told them I'd come from England to volunteer one each of them in turn grabbed the back of my head, brought it into their bosoms and hugged me hard. I could hardly breathe as my cheek was squashed against a t-shirt and I could feel sweat entering the pores of my skin.

When the embrace ended we high-fived and they told me they were best friends who, after marrying their respective wives, didn't see much of each other. They'd decided to volunteer for Obama one night a week so they could be together and have a beer together afterwards without their wives knowing. I couldn't help but laugh and admire the pair of them. They seemed to be just as delighted to be out at 3am as they did about Obama becoming President. One of them started crying and this set the other one off. I couldn't believe my eyes. These two grown men were properly blarting in a hip-hop club. What a night. What emotion. What a fantastic moment to be in America.

Little did I know but in the streets of every major city there were scenes reminiscent of my sweaty Miami club. The pictures and videos of Americans pouring onto the streets to celebrate Obama's victory are on the internet for everyone to see. For one night only the poorest sections of society felt like they'd changed the country that they'd thought cared nothing about them.

The toilets at the club (which I've recently being told is called Purdy's Lounge) were refreshingly bad. The walls were covered in graffiti and the floor was gloriously awash with piss and soggy toilet roll. I only realised how bad they were when I was woken up sitting on the bog in the cubicle. My vision was blurred but I heard the unmistakable banging of a toilet door just centimetres from my head.

"Hey Dude, how long you gonna be?" came the call from beyond the toilet door.

I'm not sure when I hit 'the wall'. Perhaps it was after my 15th double rum and coke or maybe after one of the Tequila shots people kept on giving me. It had obviously caught up with me up when I'd sat down on the toilet. The banging continued and I looked down to see if my trousers were down at my ankles. They weren't. "Not long mate, sorry," I spluttered before wobbling to my feet. I looked down into to the disgusting putrid toilet water and knew what I had to do for the good of the night. I put my fingers down my throat and waited to gag before pulling my fingers out of the way of the cascading sick. After I'd been sick once my body convulsed as I heaved, but my body had nothing more to give. Reinvigorated, I checked my sweater for splashback and wiped my mouth before exiting the toilet in a Hugh Grant 'Sorry about that, chaps!' way. I washed my face in the sink and took a mint gum from the basin by the door.

Freshly sick, freshened up and chewing gum like an angry cow I was ready for my second wind, so I set about drinking again. About 5am the horrible moment happened and the lights come on, which meant it was time to go home. Well, normally but Obama's victory night was different. Quite a few of our crowd had disappeared and Mark and Kale reminded the last bleary eyed remnants of the South Beach office that we were on the guest list at another club in South Beach, open until 7am.

Kale, Mark, Karim and I jumped into a taxi and headed off to South Beach. I remember laughing all the way through the journey, about what I've no idea. We were all still high on victory. There was a queue but we strolled straight to the front and we were let straight in. The club was typically South Beach, full of beautiful people who were 'too cool for school'. It was upmarket, high class. The drinks were expensive but the music was laid back dance and I immediately wished I was wearing better clothes, had more money and something to keep me awake. I knew that falling asleep in the toilet in this club was not an option.

The perfectly groomed women and men were all in their own worlds and I doubted whether I would be chatting to many of them about Obama. However, the four of us bought drinks, joked around and enjoyed looking at the mighty fine women on display. The club was quite big and it was good just to walk around people watching. However, there came a stage about 6.30am when I could feel the room spinning. Only Karim and I remained, and we were going through the motions a bit so we made the decision to call it a night.

We jumped in a taxi and headed back to the hotel knowing we had wrung out every drop of enjoyment from the night that Barack Obama had been elected President. It was time for bed. We strolled bleary eyed through the reception of the Eden Roc, nodding hello to the receptionists and porters as we went. I spotted the hotel manager, the one that I'd pretended to be gay to the previous day. My heart skipped a beat. Out of the corner of my eye I saw him do a double take and then look at me and Karim. I couldn't help what I did next, it was just a way of proving I wasn't lying about being gay. As the lift door opened I playfully put my arm around Karim's shoulder and whispered in his ear to make it look like we a couple.

Now, Karim didn't realise what I was doing, but for the sake of a really daft lie I let the manager think that I'd picked him up and that I was taking my young Moroccan lover back up to the penthouse room. I'm not proud of it, but well, shit happens! Who knows, from one gay man to another he might have thought 'Good on him'.

When we got in the room we didn't even put the television on – we knew the news already. I'd been up 24 hours and had been through the full gamut of emotions. I was now ready to sleep for hours, so by the time my head had hit the pillow I was fast asleep. What I didn't know was what was happening on the other side of the Atlantic.

Meanwhile, back home....

Wednesday, November 5

After meeting me Maartje from CousCous Global had gone back to her hotel room and uploaded two videos of me on to YouTube. One was entitled 'Birmingham Mail – Obama Afterparty' and the other 'Birmingham Mail – Hard News Crying'. At 10.45am in England, which is 5.45am in Miami, someone posted a link to the video on Steve Dyson's 'Editor's Chair' blog on the Birmingham Mail website. The snowball had started to roll. The following is taken directly from the blog:

Editor's Chair blog – Birmingham Mail website

I see there's an ambassador for your paper in Miami at the moment (link to vid)

Steve Dyson Thank you for bringing this to my attention. Nuff said.

Steve Dyson Hmm. Having now viewed this link and video, I must say that this was not a very wise interview for AS to have given. He hardly shows himself in a very good light. I can only assume that his comments were the results of inebriation. Needless to say I will be looking into this. Therefore there can be no further comment from me on what is now an internal matter.

Bootless and Dizzy Eyed How can it be an internal matter, when it's plastered all over YouTube?

Just after midday the journalist's trade website Hold the Front Page put a story online about me and the video, and a couple of hours later the Press Gazette was featuring the story of the drunken regional journalist resigning in Miami.

The shit well and truly hits the fan

I was awoken by the maid asking if she could clean the room. I shouted to her to come back later. The loudness of my voice sent a pain shooting through my brain. I could smell a haze of pungent rum centimetres from my face – again. It took about five minutes to finally open my eyes for the first time. The night flashed before them: the booze, the hip-hop dive, the posh Miami club and the victory party. I was pretty happy I hadn't made a total arse of myself.

About a minute later I thought 'Err…naused, knobhead' when I remembered giving the New Labour crew a load of grief. Then I remembered the Dutch woman with the video camera and I opened my eyes wide open. "Shit". The questions started running through my mind. Had I been live on air? Had she put it on YouTube? Had anyone seen it at home? My eyes focussed on the ceiling as I thought about the possible ramifications if she'd put it online.

I smiled. She thought it was funny so I guessed other people would; it was probably no big deal. In the scheme of things, with Obama winning the election, a video of a drunken journalist would most likely sink without trace in the deepest echelons of the internet.

The curtain was closed but the room was still full of sunlight. I wanted to get up but instead did a sideways roll to get closer to the floor. After some perfunctory stretching I went to the balcony to look at the ocean and the sunny skies. It felt great not to have to work at the office. I sat and looked across the waves, drinking a coke and wondering what to do. I didn't want to wake up Karim yet as it was about 2pm. I thought about logging onto Facebook but I couldn't be bothered to interact with anyone. I opened the room door in the hope of finding a paper outside to read about last night's monumental events.

The Miami Herald had the simplest but most beautiful headline: 'Obama Wins'. I promised myself I would never lose the paper (I have) and that I'd buy several more copies for posterity. Every single shop in Miami was sold out within hours. I loved leafing through the paper, enjoying a great day to be alive. Karim came ambling on to the balcony. "Hey man, we can enjoy the balcony man, what a view!" I showed him the front page and he smiled and simply said: "Yes we did".

After a while I relented and went onto Facebook to update my status:

Facebook status: Steve Zacharanda has a hazy recollection of sending copy then resigning from his job live on Dutch TV, then dropping the Hip-Hop moves with crying Americans, YES WE DID!!!!!!!!!!!

An instant message popped up from Emma Culwick, the Birmingham Mail's chief reporter. "Adam – what the hell have you done?" A pang of worry shot through my body. I replied: "Err…nothing, I've just woken up." Not acknowledging the joke she typed: "You better phone work – your video, it's everywhere." I replied to her message: "Ok, will do."

I logged out of Facebook as quickly as I could. I leant back in my chair and put my fingers through my hair, keeping hold of the strands as I reached the top, then let out an almighty: "Fucking Hell!" I looked up at Karim, who'd already sensed something was wrong.

 "You remember that Dutch bird that took that video of me..."

"Yeah, the one who you told your bosses to fuck off to?" he said matter of factly.

"Yeah that one…Hold on, what did you say?"

"You told your bosses to fuck off on the video. You said it was well funny last night. Why, what's happened?"

"Everyone has seen it."

"*Everyone*?"

"Everyone in England"

He smiled and said: "Everyone in England? Come on Adam, you're exaggerating, we've only just got up."

"I know, I said that, but my chief reporter told me I have to phone work up immediately because all hell has broken loose"

We both looked at each other and said: "What time is it in England?" We realised it must have been 7pm back home, so everyone was five hours ahead of me and Karim.

"What you gonna do?" he asked.

"I better phone them. How much is that gonna cost?"

I got up and paced around the room for a while, pulling at my hair, wondering who was going to answer and what I was going to say about why I'd done the video. I couldn't for the life of me remember what exactly I'd said in it. All I remembered was making the Dutch laugh a lot, and that I found it all rather funny at the time. Oh yeah, and I also remembered finishing the video by sticking my two fingers up and saying 'Fuck off' to someone or something unknown.

As it was past 7pm only the person on the late shift on the Birmingham Mail would be working, so at least I wouldn't have to speak to any of my bosses. I felt a little sick, but I wasn't yet shit scared. Whatever I'd done I was on holiday so I wasn't going to take any shit off anyone. I'm not one to let people tear a strip off me at the best of times, so I'd be fucked if I was going to let anyone do it whilst I was on holiday and paying for the phone call.

I steeled myself and used the hotel phone to ring the office. The number rang out. I wanted to put it down but I heard the dreaded click.

"Hi, Newsdesk". It was Emma. I breathed a sigh of relief, as she would never bawl me out. The worst I'd get from her would be an air of disappointment, probably not even that.

"Hey Emma, it's Adam. What can I do for ya?"

Straight as a dye she said: "Oh, Adam. Nick is dealing with it all, I'll put you through."

As I waited to be put through I had mixed emotions. What did 'it all' mean? To me that suggested that this had become a big story, if one person in particular had been assigned to look after it. Again I was relieved because it was Nick I was going to speak to. Nick worked in the same Sutton office as me for several years and knew me inside out. He knew that I had problems with the management, knew that I could be a raging pisshead (he often had to wake me up) that I was unhappy leaving the Mail. He also knew that, despite everything, I was a talented hack.

He's a cracking reporter, better than me, but I did teach him the dark arts of journalism. How to get people to admit something they don't want to, the lengths you can go to winding up press officers and the necessity of lying to the newsdesk were just some of the lessons I taught him. The son of a Midland journo legend, Nick was great but a bit straight. Then again that's why he's probably married and lives in a nice house in Sutton Coldfield and I'm a perpetual bum.

I could hear the panic in his voice.

"Adam, what the fuck have you done?"

That one line filled me with dread. I must have done something bad if Nick was angry with me.

"Dunno? What have I done?"

"Do you mean you don't know?". I could tell he was surprised.

"I've just woken up, are you on about the video? I haven't seen it"

I'll never forget his reply as long as I live.

"Adam, you've been captured on video pissed out of your mind slumped on the pavement with the works laptop trying to send copy back to the paper. You've gone on about women, then you've admitted to cutting and pasting from the BBC, which is plagiarism if you've not forgotten, and then you've admitted smoking drugs and then to top it all off you have told the editor and everyone else at the paper to go fuck themselves."

There was silence. It was hard to take it all in. Smoking weed? That couldn't be right, I hadn't smoked in years. And telling everyone at the paper to fuck off? That didn't sound like me either.

"Adam? Are you there?"

"Hold on Nick, I'm paying for this call. Have you got a pen?"

"Yes Adam, I am a journalist."

"Take my American mobile number and phone me back, I'll be fucked if I'm paying for this. Oh yeah, and don't give anyone this number, or we'll fall out".

With that I put the phone down.

Karim looked at me and said: "Not good?"

"Not good." I repeated.

The phone rang.

"Alright Nick. So what happened then?"

"It's all over Hold the Front Page and the Press Gazette, Dyson is going fucking mad. You're so in the shit Adam"

That last line pricked me.

"I'm in the shit, Nick? I'm fucking leaving next week. What the fuck can they do to me?"

"Take your redundancy off you, you prat."

My heart sank, I hadn't thought of that. I certainly didn't feel as clever as I had a minute ago. I thought of Nicole, and having to tell her that she'd have to stay in the flat she hated so much. After a brief bit of reflection, though, I couldn't help but think 'Fuck it – it's only money'. If that was all these people could do to me then I could live with it.

"How bad is it Nick? How bad is the video?"

He told me the whole office had come to a standstill when the first person found it on the internet. There were people from other papers phoning up asking if I'd been sacked and Sly Bailey (the CEO of Trinity Mirror) had been on the phone. Apparently over 20,000 people had already seen it and, since someone had put it on Dyson's blog that morning, it had just gotten bigger and bigger.

"Steve said you have to take it off YouTube. Do you know the Dutch bloke? You have to get him to take it down."

I couldn't be bothered to explain that he was a she and said: "Don't you think it's a bit too late for that? Someone will have downloaded the video by now anyway, did you tell him the Internet doesn't work like that?"

"Just try to take it down"

He was certainly lending the whole situation a sense of drama, but what was getting on my nerves was that although we were friends he was describing the whole situation from the company's point of view.

I said: "Alright mate, I get the picture. Can I ask you one question? And this is as a mate, not as a colleague"

"Ok Adam, what is it?"

"Was it funny?"

There was silence. His voice lowered to a whisper, which put me at ease as he was obviously tearing a strip off me to impress someone else in the office. He said: "It's the funniest thing I've ever seen. People are pissing themselves. It's fucking hilarious, you're an idiot but it's hilarious"

A wave of relief swept over me because I was happy with that answer. If he'd said: "You've offended the Sikhs, Muslims, Blacks and the Irish" then I'd have shit myself. That everyone thought it was funny but that I was an idiot was ok. After all, most people probably think of me as a likable twat anyway.

"I suppose I'd better watch it then. Oh yeah, Nick, don't worry about me I'm fine, and don't give anyone that number."

Karim was staring at me. I must have looked like a mad man. I can't stand still when I'm on the phone so I must have been walking up and down the hotel room pulling my hair as I went. I reduced the situation into two sentences, saying: "20,000 people have seen it already. And I might lose my redundancy."

I felt hollow inside. I'd grasped this was a massive moment in my life. If I looked a complete idiot then who was ever going to hire me in journalism again? I was scared of telling the woman I loved I'd lost £5,000 being a drunken div too. Also, what had I said about women? How would she react to that? And what about my mates at the Mail who it looked as if I'd told to fuck off? I sat on the bed, despairing.

I couldn't have wished for a better friend then Karim at that moment. I'd have rather had him there than any of my close friends because all they would've done is take the piss out of me or wind me up. Karim isn't like that, he's a cool guy without a side to him and he was great. "We better watch this video Adam. I bet it isn't as bad as work are saying. They're bound to say it is bad aren't they?"

I got my laptop out and remembered I'd forgotten to ask how to find the video. I logged onto Facebook again. I had about 20 notifications. I looked at my status and noticed several comments. One name jumped out – Sam Holliday. Sam was the man who changed my life, the man who saved me from a life bumming from one call centre to another, the man who gave me my first job in journalism. He is the kindest and most charismatic man I've met in the media. This was man who'd said all those years ago at my interview for the Lichfield Mercury: "You're on £30,000 a year and I'm offering you £8,000, shall we end the interview now?" This was the man who'd hired me because I'd been honest enough to say that I hated myself for selling insurance and that I wanted to be a journalist. He was now editing a whole variety of papers, and I'll always seek his advice, his opinion and his approval.

I dreaded reading what he'd written. If he'd said 'You've let everyone in journalism down, you're finished,' or 'How can I help? I know you're in a lot of trouble now' then I'd have been sick to the pit of my stomach. I punched the air when I read what he actually had to say:

"Adam, here is the link to your video, it's hilarious – you are the new hero of British journalists. Legend." I followed the link. A video appeared on YouTube entitled 'Birmingham Mail – Obama Party'. It had 22,566 views. I grabbed Karim around the shoulder and we watched it together.

"It'll be ok Adam"

I grabbed his hand and said: "I hope so."

The video seemed to take an age to load but there I was, looking pissed. I said straight away: 'I can't believe I'm wearing that fucking jumper." We had to wait literally minutes for the video to load completely so we were left looking at a still of me in an awful jumper with a dazed expression on my face. At this stage, it didn't look good. We both watched in rapture as I opened my mouth. Imagine how weird it is watching yourself on video but having no idea what you're about to say.

The video came to life and I started talking:

"Basically my name is Steve Zacharanda, from Birmingham, also known as Adam Smith. Who is working for the Birmingham Mail. I jumped on a plane on Friday to volunteer for the Barack Obammer campaign."

After the initial shock of hearing how Brummie I sounded I was relieved. I realised by the way I was speaking that I thought I knew what I was doing at the time. Although I was slumped on the pavement, I was speaking very clearly because of the camera pointed at me. If I'd been truly caught off guard then I'd have been speaking way too fast so nobody could understand me. I was deliberately speaking slowly as I knew people would be watching the video.

"I've been working out the South Beach Miami baby office. We have the International Brigade of the Dutch, Swedish, German and the British."

Karim laughed and said with a smile: "No Belgium!"

We carried on watching.

"As a kind of an ill advised promise I decided to say to my paper back home that I would write about the American election"

Maartje: "So why did you want to be here?"

Me: "I wanted to be here because I am here for history. The trouble is the readers of the Birmingham Mail are gunna get my version of history. And I'm just a little bit pissed (I then pick up the remnants of a double rum and coke and drink it whilst looking at the camera).

Karim and I burst into laughter. "Great line Adam, great line!" Karim said and grabbed me harder. I couldn't help but laugh myself, but I still had a nagging doubt about what I was going to say about women and my colleagues.

Maartje: "Ha ha ha ha ha. So this is your copy? To Facebook now?"

Me: "Not Facebook! This is going to the Birmingham Mail in England. You're talking about 100,000 people in Birmingham will be reading this and it's their, it's their version of events in America as I see it."

Maartje: "So it's going to be online tomorrow?"

Me: "Online? It's not going online it is being printed in papers. I'm a proper hard news journalist"

Maartje: "So what do you think about what has happened with Obama today?"

Me: "I think it's brilliant because (there was a long pause here, then I looked directly into the camera) I've met so many women over here and its brilliant. I am a hard news journalist but as an Englishman who jumped on a plane to help Obama I thought I'd go to a swing state. I ain't gunna go to Oi-ho-oh am I? I can't even say it, I'll go to Miami because that's where the party is at and now I'm trying to file copy to my readers and um (another long pause) thank God for the BBC because I'm cutting and pasting it baby!"

At this point Karim didn't seem to have grasped how serious it was for a journalist to claim they'd cut and pasted some of their stories. As I'd basically just admitted to plagiarism, I explained that I was pretty much fucked. Karim swore for the first time: "Shit, Adam". Chastened, we carried on watching.

Maartje: "Obama all the way! The Dutch and the English in the swing state!"

Me: "Dahh, Dutch, dahh do (I looked up and the sky and adopted a mock Dutch accent). I have the deepesht respeckt for de Dutch nation, would you please schmoke hasish with me? I've been to Amsterdam 20 times, I love the P Esh Vee Eindhoven, I've been to the Van Gogh Museum."

I let out a gasp amid the laughter: "Jesus Christ, some Dutch guy said the bit about hasish to me in the Dam years ago". Karim said: "Man, you're funny. I'm not surprised so many people found it funny". "Cheers mate! You know what, I fucking hope I give Goggle-eye a mention because this is publicity gold dust. Pray that I mention Goggle-eye."

Maartje: "For a hard news journalist you do a lot of nice things."

Me: (looking earnestly at the camera) "Oh no I'm a bit of an idiot. Simply. Basically. I'm a hard news journalist, which my readers will see when they read my copy, which is cut and pasted from the BBC - ha ha ha. No, in fact I have come up with some award winning prose, in fact if I can just keep my battery on…I'm a bit drunk."

Maartje: "So what is your name again?"

Me: "My name is Adam Smith, also known as Steve Zacharanda, and I have just resigned from the Birmingham Mail, the Birmingham Post, The Birmingham Sunday Mercury to set up my own magazine called Goggle-eye (I look into the camera and stick two fingers up) Fuck you, I'm doing what I want to!".

Well, there was my Goggle-eye plug at least. We clicked on the second video, entitled 'Hard News Crying'. It went a little something like this:

Maartje: "Why are you crying?"

Me: "Because the world has changed in one night. Because of every European who has to put up with Anti-American sentiment but who has been over here and understands how wonderful and kind the American people are. And that he normal people of America didn't start the Iraq war, they didn't start the problems on Wall Street. The normal people from America, they believe anything ha ha ha, that's a joke. They really have got optimism and the great thing about America is that no matter what happens someone can reignite that optimism and hope and Barack Obama has done that"

Maartje: "So what is it in your heart? Sorry about the corny questions"

Me: "There are no corny questions when it comes to Adam Smith, Steve Zacharanda from Goggle-eye, who has just resigned from the Birmingham Mail. Errm, the fact that America is a place that's involved in optimism. America believes in optimism. Europe is so old, we are cynical. America is naive and they are naive enough to believe the optimism and you can never ever ever ever understand the beauty of being there when they believe it. Let's hope, God let's hope that Barack Obama does what JFK should have done because this could be the greatest country in the world and they could make a difference to everyone in the world. My name is Steve Zacharanda, aka Adam Smith, I've got to file some copy, I've come up with an award winning introduction but I'm gonna cut and paste the quotes off the BBC baby!"

Maartje: "Hallelujah!"

Maybe the videos weren't life destroying at all. They were funny. In all modesty, we could both instantly understand why the first one in particular had become a hit on YouTube hit. This is a quote from an old friend:

Former Birmingham Post journalist, who doesn't want to be named

No-one will forget that day when Adam's video went online. It was a horrible time to be working in the newsroom. The redundancy process had caused such bad feeling between journalists and between the workforce and the management who had lost so much respect because of how they handled the situation. A lot of people who decided to leave were working out their notice with people who were taking over their jobs. It was a depressing time to be in the office so when Adam's video came online it was the perfect tonic and at a stroke totally changed the atmosphere. Looking across the newsroom you could see people watching it in huddles and trying to suppress their laughter, when someone new came on shift it was just priceless watching their reaction. 'He's done what?!' Everyone who was leaving found it hilarious and the vast majority of those staying found it funny too. It became even more of a farce when news editors were telling us not to watch the video because it would piss the bosses off, who'd just sacked half of the people in the newsroom. Then we started to get calls from journalists around the world asking if Adam had lost his job.

I was massively relieved, of course, but still a little unnerved. However, I still hadn't grasped how all-encompassing the video and its immediate aftermath would become over the next few weeks of my life. The fear that Nick had instilled about drug taking, plagiarism, bragging about women and offending my colleagues had dissipated after seeing the video. Everything was said in jest. Surely people would see it as a joke, wouldn't they? At any rate, I knew that this video would be the first thing people would think about whenever I was mentioned in conversation.

Suddenly something occurred to me. I said out loud "Publicity Stunt!".

Karim said: "What?"
"It's a publicity stunt! Look. I told her to put it on YouTube, I knew what I was doing. It was all for publicity for Goggle-eye, so technically it was a publicity stunt"

Karim laughed at me and said: "You think you'll get away with that?"

"Mate, if I admit I was caught off guard I'll look a right prat but if I can convince people I meant it then I won't look so bad. It is technically the truth, because despite being pissed at that moment that's what I thought I was doing. "Come on, it's not like I didn't know what I was saying". I paused. A troubling thought had popped into my head. "Shit, I've pissed off some pretty powerful people with the video. A lot of people are going to hate me Karim."

Karim, as ever wise beyond his years, replied: "Adam, the people who like you will like you more because of the video and the people who hate you now will just hate you more. Don't worry about it. It's done now, so what's the point?"

I sat and thought about those words, and I liked what I heard. I wasn't universally hated; in fact the majority of people who know me like me, I think. At the start I'd just been thinking about people in the journalism game, but when I thought about all my mates I knew they'd find it hysterical. Nonetheless, I also knew I'd made some massive enemies with my three minutes of mirth. I'd got through life that far without having many, but now my editor Steve Dyson and the entire top brass of Trinity Midlands Media (not to mention Trinity Mirror in London) would be after my blood. I'd never get a job at one of their papers ever again and I suspected most other editors would steer clear of me as well. I comforted myself that if Goggle-eye was a success then it wouldn't matter.

My thoughts turned to my family. There was only my dad, my sister, two aunties and uncles and my mum, and that was it. My dad wouldn't be bothered by the video and neither would my sister, and since I couldn't envisage my mom or my aunties and uncles getting to see it as they aren't online I figured what they didn't know wouldn't hurt them. As it happened, my mum disowned me within three days.

Then it hit me again: my one weak spot. "What about Nicole?" I said, looking into Karim's eyes. Again he said the perfect thing at the perfect time. "She'll be cool Adam. Everything will be cool. She knows how much you love her, man. She knows, we all know".

The one person in the world I gave a shit about was Nicole. I knew if I did lose my redundancy cash it would have an adverse effect on her quality of life. I thought about her crying and how I'd promised to make everything ok. I needed the redundancy for her. If I'd been single I wouldn't have cared, but I had Nic and the dog to think of. I was the head of a family now, albeit a bit of a weird one. All the same, it was mine and the first I'd ever had. I figured the stuff about meeting women wouldn't piss her off unduly. She wasn't the most paranoid of women and she knew how much I loved her. I knew when I spoke to her next it would be a pivotal moment in our relationship, though. It's all very well having a boyfriend dedicated to his craft, but a whole different thing having a boyfriend who'd made a total idiot of himself in front of the whole world.

I decided I'd push the publicity stunt angle with her. It was for the good of Cheekie Media and Goggle-eye, surely she would get that? I wished I could have seen her that night, if nothing more than for a hug. It would be another four days before I could hold her and tell her everything would be ok. I couldn't even phone her straight away because she'd be on the way to working nights at a factory in Aston. I'd have to wait until the next morning until we spoke.

We watched the video again, and the second one where it looked like I was crying, and laughed. We agreed it wasn't as bad as I'd been told by Nick. In fact I was starting to like it, except perhaps for one part.

"Man, if only I hadn't said that plagiarism stuff it would have been perfect. It's a pretty big deal, Karim. Cutting and pasting. Everyone does it but nobody says they do"

Perceptive as ever, Karim said: "Well, perhaps it's about time someone did say it, everyone can see you were joking around. You were joking, weren't you?"

"Err, kind of. I cut and pasted a couple of Obama's quotes from the BBC and CNN, just to make sure they were correct. It's not plagiarism because I didn't take any of the journalist's words, just Obama's and he told the whole world!"

I comforted myself that Sam Holliday had lauded me on Facebook as I knew that meant something. Deep down I knew Karim was right as well. It was done, and there was no point wishing I hadn't done it. I had to come to terms with it, and quickly, or I'd regret it for the rest of my life. I could tell Karim had been woken too early as he was looking tired, so I suggested he went back to bed whilst I went downstairs for some coffee. I was also keen to start emailing and Facebooking people back home, to gauge their reaction and to ask them what I should or could do next. Then I remembered something.

"What's the date today Karim?"

"It's November 5, how could you not know that?"

"What's the day then?

"Wednesday."

"Shit! We have to move out of here today!"

I watched Karim's face fall.

"Don't worry, we're going to an even better hotel than this my friend. The Miami Gansevoort South, in the middle of South Beach"

"When till dude?"

"Till Friday morning my friend. We don't need to worry about where we're staying again!"

He grinned. He knew there was no chance of me leaving him high and dry. I was so glad he was with me, it was the least I could do to let him stay with me in comfort at a swanky hotel. I said toto myself as much as Karim: "I'm gonna go down to the reception and ask for my guided media tour. I don't want to piss Suzie off again. I didn't bother doing it at the Alexander Hotel, I've got to do everything by the book from now on".

I got dressed and wandered down to the reception, hoping not to see the manager, and as soon as I thought about his name I remembered putting my arm around Karim earlier that morning. I chuckled to myself; I couldn't have made it up if I'd tried.
Luckily he wasn't there, but the Latino manager who was hanging around reception. I explained that I needed a tour of the hotel for my travel feature. I got my mini notepad and pen out, put my 'absolutely fascinating' face on and followed the guy around the plush but yet to be finished Eden Roc Hotel.

It took about twenty minutes and surprisingly it was pretty interesting. It appears as I'd been told the Rat Pack really did hang out at the hotel, as well as countless other superstars of the 1950s, 60s and 70s. The manager happily showed me all the outdoor pools which I hadn't had time to have a dip in, the wonderful restaurants I hadn't had chance to eat in and the gym that I probably wouldn't have bothered going into anyway. However, one thing he didn't have to show me were the best rooms in the hotel, because I'd been in them thanks to square-necked Mark. I asked him how much they would have cost and he just smiled and said "Probably thousands of dollars". I shook his hand and told him that him that, because of the great service he, the manager and the wonderful black receptionist had given me I'd be writing thousands of dollars worth of publicity back in Europe. After the tour, we embraced as I thanked him and told him he was one cool motherfucker. He said the same about me. I left thinking I'd made a pretty good impression.

When I got upstairs Karim was on the computer, chuckling to himself. "Hey man, you wanna see the comments on your YouTube video! They're funny man! I think there's an argument between your boss and your colleagues. People are coming out for you, man". My heart fluttered a bit. I hadn't thought about the video for a while because I'd started to worry about paying for any phone bills I'd incurred during my stay at the Eden Roc instead.

I jumped on the computer and started reading the comments. I couldn't help but laugh. How could you not? Below is a fairly representative sample:

Globaltruth Give this man an enormous pay rise. This is the finest news journalism I have ever seen.

Moodudeuk OBAMA - propa bostin!

Officialdarkcompass I'm sure he was cutting and pasting from the BBC website.

FRANKPITCHFORD What a jerk --does this constitute hard news journalism --please sack him

TeddyRuxpinUK Hey Frank, why don't you take your finger from up your butt and get over yourself? This is a guy who took time off work and paid for his own travel (despite just being made redundant), yet still agreed to work for the company. He's given them more publicity than they could ever dream of.

FRANKPITCHFORD Still not journalism -- just self publicity - don't be abusive

TeddyRuxpinUK Oh get over yourself Frank. The man paid his own way there, worked as a favour and was having a joke. You know, the word for when you're being humorous.

FRANKPITCHFORD ok you win -- now get back to work

TeddyRuxpinUK Yes, you're right, I do win. Because I am normal and you are not.

Rascalsarchives love how people take a slovenly exploit and see the upside as "free publicity"--ignoring the IMMORALITY of it---The 1969 MANSON

MURDERS were great "free publicity" for sales of The Beatles "white album"--
so is THAT the upside of THAT tragedy??

Spleenteam I think you're getting just a bit carried away - bloody murder of
people and a pissed up Brummie journalist. Hardly in the same ball park. As
Ruxpin said, it's all a bit of a laugh after the election. Laugh or not, but get a life

Twist3dh4ck Hey, they've taken your story off the Birmingham Mail website...

Danvers21 "trying to make the world a better place." You did just that, by
showing the world an example of a typical, lazy, drunken, self-righteous hack
masquerading as a "proper journalist."

Seasick8 (Subsequently discovered that this was my mate Gurdo) he really is
the least "self-righteous hack" you will ever meet. It is a drunken laugh - why
are so many people losing their rag over it?!?!?!?

I've no idea who TeddyruxpinUK is but his words meant a lot and I owe him a
pint or two. I'd have been mortified if all the people at the Birmingham Mail who
I liked and respected thought like Frank Pitchford, whoever he was. However,
over and over again people who I worked with (many of whom didn't want to
give their name because they were also under threat of redundancy) backed
me.

I thought I better put out a comment and the YouTube comments section
seemed the best place for it. I decided immediately that I wasn't going to reply
to nasty or ill- informed comments; I'd just sit back and read them with a
detached, critical eye. I didn't realise how hard it would be over the next few
days seeing so many people, in and out of journalism, write amazingly weird
and sometimes libellous stuff about me. I mean, did my drunken antics really
deserve to be compared to the heinous crimes of 1960s mass murderer
Charles Manson?

However, just hours after seeing the video I still had no idea what was to come,
and that my rushed response would itself be cut and pasted and included in
dozens of articles about me. Here it is:

Right, the thing is, right I've just woke up.

And seen this video, which I don't really remember. I've been told to phone the
Birmingham Mail because I am in trouble.

I was off duty, I am on official holiday working at the South Beach Miami
Barack Obama campaign where I had just done a 18 hour shift trying to make
the world a better place.

Please check every BBC News Outlet and see if I have cut and pasted anything. I have not, it was a joke and should be taken in the spirit it was said.

Obviously 'Right, the thing is, right I've just woke up' is not very good English. However, this was an in joke for everyone in the Birmingham Mail newsroom, because I'm pretty sure Brummies are the only people to phone a journalist and start off a conversation: "Right, I'll tell you for something right, right....". I didn't want to go into too much detail but I thought the above sentences would clear up the plagiarism problem and serve to explain that I wasn't working for the paper at the time of the video. I wanted to get the correct spelling of Zacharanda out there too, as God knows the different ways people would spell it. Worse still, they might have reverted to just calling me boring old Adam Smith.

Looking back I wish I'd changed the last sentence slightly. To 'I have not, it was a joke and should be taken in the spirit it was said' I now realise I should have added 'which was rum and coke by the way'. It would have been a bit more jokey. I wish I'd put both the magazine's MySpace and my own MySpace addresses at the bottom as well, because it would have diverted loads of hits to them. Then again, there was some pretty rum stuff on both of them and they would have given my bosses more ammunition to throw at me.

After commenting I felt a bit more relaxed and I promised myself I wouldn't keep looking at the comments so that I could concentrate on moving to our new hotel. Not beforeD I'd checked my Facebook, though. That proved to be a relief because all my friends inside and outside of journalism had started posting good luck messages:

Steve Dinneen I'm speechless. Awesome. And not a bad start for Cheekie Media... Can I have the exclusive first interview?

Dale Martin I guess that's the last I'll see of the tenner you owe me..........

Lee Kenny The best bits:

An "ill-advised promise"
"I'm cutting and pasting it baby"
"I love the PSV Eindhoven"

Owen Strudwick Your a legend mate, your vids the funniest thing ive seen all year, least you got a plug in for your mag too.

Fiona Bartley So funny! You brought tears to my eyes watching that peice of footage - Classic! X

Caroline Crawford What a bloody Brummie...you could have at least pretended to have been a cockernay hack.....from The Sun!!

Jason Skarratt Brilliant.....you could see you were full of emotion about the election....or were you full of whisky????

Natalie Bardsley Fantastic...me and Rich are creeeaaaseddddddd...see you soon. xxx

Steve Zacharanda Thanks for your comments everyone, you have no idea what they mean. The first I heard about it was when I woke up and could not believe it was everywhere and the bosses knew. Thank fuck I actually did not cut and paste anything! I'd written it the day before :)
But to get an endorsement from the journalist great legend of Sam Holiday and the backing of miss top class Natalie Missenden is great, I was told by my bosses to remove the YouTube link. That is how much they know about the modern media. It's beyond my control.

Facebook status: Steve Zacharanda is a YouTube Sensation – oh dear, me and my big mouth.

Trouble in Paradise

My mood swung between happiness and despair. One minute I'd be thinking I was done for, then five minutes later that I'd pulled off the publicity stunt of the year. However, there's nothing like looking at an ocean to help me think. The sheer power and innate beauty of nature always puts problems in to perspective. As I stared out towards the Caribbean I thought about the cop during Halloween discussing being an official YouTube Sensation with 20,000 views. I'd already near enough doubled that. I said it out loud and I said it proud: "I am a YouTube Sensation".

Although I didn't know it at the time, I was in fact already in the running for the much vaunted title of YouTube Sensation of the 2008 American Presidential Election. My video was taking on a life of its own. At that very moment the link was zipping around the globe from one email to another and from one Facebook wall to another, not to mention Twitter, and I was powerless to stop it.

I had more important things to worry about though. My cash was running low and I didn't technically have the money to pay my phone bill at the hotel, never mind the money for a deposit at the Gansevoort down the road. Karim, proving his worth again happily agreed to put his credit card down for our new home, so we set about packing. "Hey man, I can't believe we got this penthouse suite man! It's awesome, I'll never forget it" he said as we took a last look round our room.

I handed in our keys at reception to the Latino manager. We shook hands and he didn't mention anything about the phone bill or any charges to the room. As we said our goodbyes he shook my hand again and added that I was 'a true gentleman' and 'a credit to travel journalists'. I couldn't help but agree with him and along with Karim headed for a taxi.

In November 2008 the Gansevoort South Beach Miami hotel was the coolest place to be. Celebrities hung out around the swimming pools, millionaires ate the finest foods and drank the finest wines at its restaurants and Miami's beautiful people would do anything to be seen at its rooftop bar. Since we'd won the election it was time to kick back and relax.

Karim and I strode into the reception and waited for one of the bright young things behind the counter to notice us. A cool looking Lebanese manager addressed us. Immediately I could tell he was showing off in front of the women in his team, but I was alright about that. Clapping his hands and snapping his heels together he said: "Hello boys, are you ready to party?

Because this is a 24 hour party hotel in a 24 hour party city. Welcome to Miami!"

I replied: "We've been partying in Miami for weeks mate, and last night we partied after helping Obama win the White House, so now we're ready for a bit of luxury my friend". I stuck out my hand. "My name's Adam Smith, I'm a travel journalist and I'm here to make this hotel famous across the world."

I could tell this had thrown him and that he was obviously a bit worried his welcoming gambit was not by the book, but I instantly liked him. As I handed him my passport I said: "So tell me more about these parties then my friend?"

He replied: "This is Miami's best hotel. The fact that you're guests here means that you can get into the best club in Miami every night. Upstairs you'll see how we party in Miami. It will take your breath away. You'll have never seen anything like it before"

Now I hate it when someone says that to me - how do they know what I've seen or not seen? Before I could say anything he was off again.

"We have all kinds of celebrities here as well"

I couldn't resist. "I am a celebrity, mate, and I'm in hiding from the world's press, so I'm going to write about what it's like to be a celebrity hiding out in Miami's coolest hotel. Karim tell him, am I a celebrity?" Quick as a flash he said: "He's an international YouTube Sensation". I smiled and mouthed the words 'International YouTube Sensation' to the receptionists. This revelation excited the manager and the gaggle of women behind him.

"Really? What did you do?"

"It's to do with Obama, after I've gone just type my name into YouTube and you'll see me. Now, where's our room?"

"Of course, I'll get your key. The lift to your room is just past the sharks"

"Sharks?" Karim and I said in unison. The Lebanese dude pointed behind us and blow me down there was a shark tank running the length of a wall, with menacing looking sharks circling inside it. I couldn't help but be impressed, and as a line "The lift to your room is just past the sharks on your left" ranks amongst the best I've ever heard from a hotel receptionist. After Karim gave them his credit card we set off to look at them. The mini-sharks were a nice touch, and I later used the manager's opening line as an introduction to a travel piece about Miami.

The decor of the hotel was impeccable. There were white floors, white walls and white ceilings with colourful furniture and tinted glass breaking up the ice cool interior. Our room itself was an avalanche of white and cream as well. There was a huge bathroom and a big room with two large beds, a television and a couple of couches. We had a balcony overlooking the ocean and an amazing complex of swimming pools and bars below. It was a man-made paradise.

I couldn't wait to have a sauna and then enjoy the steam room and a rum and coke on the rooftop bar without feeling guilty that I wasn't out volunteering for Obama. I wanted to head down to the office, though, because I had a feeling it would be closing soon and I wanted to take one last look around such a special place. Kale and Mark had also mentioned that they wanted to hit the beach with Barry the cardboard Obama. Karim decided he wanted to go into town to look at the shops before going in, so we agreed to meet at News Cafe for something to eat in an hour.

As we passed reception I'd totally forgotten that I told them about the video. "Here's the YouTube Sensation!" said the Lebanese guy. I can't deny I enjoyed the title. Sensation is a pretty good superlative. "You know it guys. When are you gonna give me a tour of the hotel? I need to write about how brilliant the staff are!" Everyone laughed and I strolled out without a care in the world. I was a YouTube Sensation, and the people of Miami seemed to love it. Perry Barr, my bedsit, Nicole, Steve Dyson and everyone else at the Birmingham Mail felt a million miles away.

As I was walking down the beach towards the office my phone rang. It was a Miami number so I answered.

"Hello, is that Adam Smith?"

"Yeah, who's speaking?"

"Hi. I'm the press officer for the Gansevoort South Beach Miami."

"Ahh, hello. Fantastic hotel. We were so impressed by the sharks and the room is magnificent. I've had the warmest of welcomes as well"

She said: "Thank you, but which paper are you going to write the travel review for if you've just resigned from the Birmingham Mail?"

Bang. I immediately felt sick. I'd fucked up again, because I hadn't thought of the consequences of blabbing about the YouTube stuff to the staff. Quickly I tried to regain my composure.

"I'm syndicated. I thought you were told that?" I said with more than a hint of arrogance.

"Err, well…"

"Look love. No-one from Birmingham could afford to stay at your hotel. It's a blue collar city, that's a fact, but I'm a syndicated travel writer. My pieces will be in papers across Britain, and magazines. In fact right now I'm the most famous journalist in Britain because of my YouTube video. Nobody has even heard of the Gansevoort in Britain, but by the time I leave a hell of a lot of very important people will have. You're going to get ten times more publicity because I've left the Birmingham Mail. I hope to God you don't think I'm some kind of con artist."

"Of course not Mr Smith"

"Good. So there's no problem then?"

"No, Mr Smith"

"Well, please leave details about when my tour is around the hotel. I really need to know as many details about the Gansevoort as possible because I'll be writing more than one article about your hotel"

"Of course. Goodbye, Mr Smith"

She put the phone down. I breathed a massive sigh of relief and foolishly thought they'd be delighted to have a 'celebrity journalist' in their hotel. I decided to ring my old mate Gurdip to see what had really happened that day. He was leaving the Birmingham Mail with me. In fact, his departure during the redundancy process was like the Robinho transfer of the previous transfer deadline day. He'd changed his mind at the last minute after seeing who was leaving and drove straight into Birmingham to head office to alter his form to say he wanted to go. He was part of the Goggle-eye family, always lent me money when I needed it, always defended me when I was being slated and always seemed to laugh at my jokes. If anyone would have found the video funny it would have been Gurdip.

The phone rang out before his Black Country twang burst onto the line.

"Hello?"

"Alright, mate"

"Is that you Adam?"

"Yep"

"Fucking hell mate! The whole world is looking for you. What have you done? Are you mad?"

I hadn't been expecting that response from him. I gave him my mobile number and asked him to phone me back. I started worrying immediately. If Gurdo hadn't seen the funny side then who would have done? Good as gold, he phoned back straight away.

"Do you know what has happened Adam?"

"Yep, I'm a YouTube Sensation"

"What, you know?"

"Yep"

"And you're not bothered?"

"Nope, it's a publicity stunt for Goggle-eye. Fuck the Mail, we're leaving next week anyway"

There was silence.

"Seriously, you're not bothered? You admitted cut and pasting! And what about the redundancy? There's no way they're gonna give you that now. You need that for Goggle-eye, and Nicole will kill you"

I'd forgotten about the money, but quickly put that out my mind.

"Gurdo, calm down. Three words. Was it funny?"

"Mate, it's the funniest thing I've ever seen"

"Well fuck 'em then"

Despite my bravado, his tone still worried me. He continued: "Nick phoned me up looking for your number in a panic and that put me in a panic. He told me you'd admitted plagiarism, admitted smoking weed and told Steve Dyson to fuck off and that you'd destroyed your career. I proper shit myself. Then I watched it in the Walsall office. We were gobsmacked. I can't believe you did it, but've I watched it again and again and it just gets funnier and funnier. Everyone has been looking to get hold of you. I still can't believe it's a good thing though, cos you mentioned cut and pasting"

The last line stirred me.

"Gurdo, trust me, I run a lads mag, and despite all the other shit the video is funny. If I hadn't mentioned Goggle-eye I'd be distraught but since I did this will put us on the map, man. The reason people are watching it is because it's funny. Trust me on this mate. Oh, and don't give my number to anyone either!"

"Well if you're ok with it Adam, then I suppose I am"

I could tell he was still worried.

"Hold on, how much is this call costing me?! I'll phone you tomorrow"

I consoled myself that Gurdo was a bit of a worrier anyway. He'd said it was hilarious and that was the main thing, but his attitude gnawed at me a bit. I wondered what his next phone call would have in store for me.

Gurdip Thandi, former Birmingham Mail colleague and friend

I was sitting at home settling down to watch TV with a couple of cans of lager when the call came. It was my colleague Nick McCarthy and he seemed excited, agitated, and panicky and was talking in hushed tones.

He needed a number for Adam in Miami because the idiot had only gone and got himself filmed, lying in the gutter pissed out of his head, telling his soon-to-be-former employers to fuck off, talking about smoking hash in Holland and, best of all, that he'd cut and pasted articles he'd sent to the Mail from the BBC baby…

"Have you got a number for him? He's in the shit. Someone told Steve Dyson about the video and he ain't happy…" Once Nick had finished hyper-ventilating, I gave him Adam's Miami number and we agreed that both of us will keep trying to get hold of him.

Nick's call had left me worried. If this video was that bad, what would happen to him? He was inviting me to work on his dream once we left the Mail and here he was putting it in jeopardy. So I took my first look at the video and sure enough, there he was looking every inch the tramp we know and occasionally love, dressed in a stupid stripy jumper, slurring his controversial words and putting on a, quite frankly, crap Dutch accent.

He eventually called me back. "Alright Gurdo!" was his cheery greeting and for a split second I realised why I loved his fat, stinking, sponging mass. I wanted to be sitting with him in a pub, me buying all the drinks and laughing about what had happened. But, at the same time, I also had Nick's words ringing in my ears. Dyson was fuming; Adam needed his redundancy cash for Goggle Eye/Cheekie Media; things weren't looking good and he needed to know.

So I told him. "Adam, you are in the shit man! What happens if they just sack you with no redundancy? How will you do Goggle Eye without that cash? Why did you say you cut and pasted stuff off the BBC when I know you didn't?! Why? Why? Why the fuck?! WHY??!!!" I ended the call telling him to take care.

I watched the video again and discovered there was a part two and my worries and concerns started to drift away. They were funny. Bloody hilarious in fact and so I watched them again. I picked up on things I missed on that initial nervous first viewing. His Brummie accent, the sappy look on his face as he announced he was "just a little bit pissed", the revelation that he is "a bit of an idiot", his claim that he was a hard news journalist, "BBC BAYBEE", *that jumper, that Dutch accent.*

Every second of both videos was golden. Comments were already appearing on YouTube. Some celebrating Adam's "work", others damning him, some psychotic Republicans telling him to get out of their country. But this was just the tip of the iceberg.

I met Karim in News Cafe on Ocean Drive, Versace's favourite breakfast haunt, and we ordered a monster breakfast for some protein after the huge amount of alcohol we'd consumed the night before. We both had our Obama t-shirts on and all of the staff made a comment about the night before - everyone seemed happy our man had won. Though it must have been 4pm everyone was eating breakfast. It appeared even by South Beach standards the night before had been a heavy one.

The sun was shining and there was a gentle breeze coming off the sea. After grabbing several newspapers, which were becoming collectors' items as each minute passed, we began talking about the new world under Obama. It began to sink in what we had taken part in. We'd helped Barack Obama become President of the United States of America, and Karim couldn't help be overcome by youthful optimism. He said: "This is the first day of the 21st century, Adam. All the George Bush stuff, all the wars and lies will be forgotten. A line will be drawn under everything because Obama won. The world is going to be a better place because of Obama. Everything has changed".

The headlines in all the papers screamed victory, and as we leafed through them we soaked up the details of Obama's huge margin of victory. The Democrats had won both the Senate and the Congress and Obama was in the perfect position to drive through change. There was also a story about a foiled White Supremacist plot to kill Obama. I decided not to remark on the chances of our hero being gunned down before he was sworn in.

The two English girls from Nottingham, who'd had taken their photo with Barry the day before, saw us and came over for a chat. They had the same 'morning after the night before' look as us and said they'd also partied the night away with happy Americans. They'd been in South Beach when revellers had poured on to the streets. Part of me wished I'd been on Ocean Drive when the news came through but I wouldn't have traded my night for anything. It felt great that we could speak as volunteers and not just voters or supporters. We bid the Nottingham girls goodbye and hurried to the office to see all our comrades.

As we were walking the short distance to the office I heard someone shouting. "Adam! Adam! Stop! Stop!". I turned to where the familiar voice was coming from and there was Maartje, the Dutch journalist who'd made my video. I could tell she was worried. I wondered what I'd done wrong now.

"Adam, Adam, are you ok? Do you know your video has gone crazy? Are you ok? I haven't got you in any trouble have I?" I planned on keeping her guessing for a while. I said with sad eyes: "I've lost everything. I can't believe you put it on YouTube."

"You told me to! I had no idea this would happen. It's already had over 20,000 views. People have been saying horrible things on the internet about me, that I tricked you!"

I couldn't keep up the pretence anymore, especially as I'd read some of the comments about her and had a quiet giggle to myself as everyone presumed she was a man. I gave her a big smile said: "We're YouTube Sensations baby! I'm not sure when you put it up on the web but someone put it on my boss' blog within hours and all hell has broken loose back home. I was leaving my job anyway. Don't worry about it. I might lose my redundancy, and my missus will kill me, but on the upside I think I'm an official YouTube Sensation"

She didn't beat around the bush: "Can we do another video?"

From one journalist to another I had to admire her balls. Her video of me being pissed and talking shite was zipping around the world and now she wanted me to do another whilst hung-over. Obviously, I said yes. I couldn't help myself, and I thought it would give me the chance to tell everyone again that I hadn't been plagiarising the BBC. I told her to come to the office in ten minutes and for another interview. As she walked off I remembered that Nick had asked me to find 'the bloke' who put it on the internet and demand it be removed. I chuckled to myself. I'd just arranged a follow up instead.

After the Tesco jumper fiasco I didn't want to make the same mistake twice. Obviously there was only one t-shirt to wear this time – my sky blue 'Brummies for Obama' number. I'd left it in the office the night before. As we walked in the first thing I spotted was a table full of different t-shirts with the slogan 'Yes We Did' emblazoned across them. I grabbed Karim and showed him. We both laughed out loud and said 'Yes, we did!' together. Ericka was the sharpest political merchandise operator in the whole of America. Wherever her t-shirt sweatshop was she must have been on the phone as the states started turning blue the night before. She was the only person in the office and we both gave her a hug. Ericka had a youthful glow about her. She was happy. A lot of her local Democratic candidates had lost but she knew she'd been involved in one of the most amazing political campaigns of her life. I think the campaign and all the young people who'd gotten involved must have taken years off her.

Ericka said to nobody in particular "It's all over now guys, we'll all have to find something else to do before we do it all again in four years time. I wonder how hard it'll be to settle back to our normal lives again after this campaign". Karim piped up: "Adam won't be able to, he did a drunken video telling his bosses to f-off at the party last night and now it's everywhere on the internet. He's a YouTube Sensation". After thinking about the revelation for a second she said in all seriousness "A video on the internet of Adam? And people understood what he was talking about? Well, I'll be darned."

The office looked different without anyone in it. The phones weren't ringing and the printers weren't spewing out endless lists of voters to harass. It was still full of all the campaign paraphernalia, but that would soon be packed away until the next election. There was still plenty of other evidence of the campaign though; half eaten pizzas, bottles of Dr Pepper and open boxes of Pringles were strewn across the desks and mobile phones were on every table and chair. This was the morning after the night before, and seeing the office this was was kind of bittersweet. I sat down, trying to remember the hustle and bustle of previous days, and I imagined what it would have been like if we'd lost. I was overcome by a feeling of melancholy and said to Karim:

"Do you think we'll see anyone ever again?"

"Who?"

"Everyone. You, Mark, Kale, Claire, Jelvis, Eric, that fit mother and daughter with the Hummer, the lawyers, the guy with the beard, Ophelia and all the Danish dudes? I wonder if we'll ever be together again".

"Of course we will. And if not, no-one will ever be able to take away from us what we did and what we experienced. I live in London anyway so you'll certainly see me again".

Our reflective moment was interrupted by "Yes we did, I love that! You guys are the best man. Obama all the way!". Maartje was standing at the door, and as usual she cut an impressive figure, I thought South Beach just seemed too safe for her. She seemed born to be walking out of a war-torn village with a child tucked under arm as gunfire ricocheted above her head. She had a young blonde haired girl with her who she introduced as Alex, no doubt one of the CousCous family. It must have been a strange sight, just me and Karim sitting in an empty office that had been a hive of activity for the last few weeks.

"Can we interview you now Adam, or should I call you Steve?"

"Call me whatever you want. Yeah, go ahead". In the corner of my eye I saw Ericka smile and shake her head as she continued to pack election stuff away.

Maartje prodded Alex, who also sounded Dutch, and she nervously said 'So, who are you?'. Ever the professional, Maartje jumped in and started the interview herself. "So, what happened? Adam Smith, the day after!"

"Hello. I had a bit of a surprise when I woke up this morning and discovered I was a YouTube Sensation on CousCous Global. Errr…I think I've lost my job because it appears I've resigned live on air. Erm, I don't remember much about it but one thing I have to point out - I **was not** cut and pasting from the BBC. Please check every single piece of copy written by the BBC, it's my own work baby, it's Obama baby, it's Birmingham baby!"

The camera pans back as I held my hands aloft awaiting the next question.

 "Do you still have your job?"

"No. I think I've lost it. Basically, I'm a bit scared to phone work, I've been told words like 'outrageous', 'bringing the company into disrepute', which if I have I'm really sorry because the Birmingham Mail is a fantastic organisation, staffed by people who really care and I, along with 65 others have got to leave next week, due to job cuts at the Birmingham Mail"

"Because of the American economy?"

"Because of the American economy and because of lots of other things but thank God for Barack Obama because my friend Karim (the camera panned to Karim, who produced a fey wave) over there told me something today. He said: "Steve, Adam, Goggle-eye, whatever my name is, today is the first day of the 21st Century". Is that ok?"

I laughed and then shook Maartje's hand. I could tell Maartje was happy. Every journalist knows that if you break a story it's your duty to get a follow up, and she got hers. Of all videos I did the 'Adam Smith :The Day After' is my favourite because I'm not drunk, I seem happy, I'm wearing my Brummies for Obama t-shirt, I'm funny and I'm in my favourite place in the world, the Miami South Beach Barack Obama office. If you listen carefully in the background you can even hear one of the phones going off, playing Ode to Joy. Just like the previous night's video, though, as soon as Maartje said goodbye I totally forgot about it until I saw it online the next day.

We switched Fox News on and laughed as the presenters seemed to be trying their hardest to be kind about 'their new President' Barack Obama. They'd lost this battle, but you could see in their eyes that they were chomping at the bit to attack everything he stood for in the coming weeks, months and years. Over at CNBC they looked just as bad but you could tell that was because, like us, they were all hung over after celebrating into the early hours. Film clips of people celebrating across America seemed to be on a continuous loop as the news began to register that Obama had won, and had won big. CNN were already talking about a 'post-racial' America, which seemed as bizarre as it did stupid. The argument seemed to be that America had voted for a black man so their society could no longer harbour racism, when in fact Obama's victory would be the catalyst for more.

My phone rang. It was Suzie. I thought she was calling about the election so I picked up the phone expecting a pleasant conversation:

"Hey Suzie, what a great day to be an American!"

"ADAM! HOW COULD YOU DO THIS TO ME AGAIN! You are un-bel-iev-able! UNBELIEVABLE"

Immediately I panicked and ran outside of the office into street to talk to her.

"What,what,what? What have I done wrong Suzie?"

"You left the Eden Roc without paying your phone bill! How could you do that after everything happened?"

Bugger, she had me there. Nevertheless, I mounted a valiant rear guard action using the truth.

"I left the Eden Roc with the words 'You are the perfect gentleman Adam' ringing in my ears Suzie. I had the tour with the manager and he said I was a credit to the travel journalism industry"

"Perhaps you did but you didn't pay the phone bill – it's $60!"

"Look, calm down Suzie, I'm telling you I left there with their blessing. They didn't say a bloody thing about the phone bill. I'll go up and pay them now, the bloody amateurs. I've been a travel journalist for years and I've never experienced anything like this. I'm not being funny but I reckon the PR woman for the hotel is a complete idiot because after speaking to the manager about the last incident I got the impression she totally blew the situation out of proportion".

Suzie was silent. I was encouraged by that. Then, for the second time in a week she took me apart. Her anger was personal, which hurt me, and also made me ashamed of myself. This time I held the phone away from my ear but I could still hear phrases like:

"Well I've dealt with hundreds of journalists and no-one has ever been like you…"

And: "We were friends but you've brought so much trouble to my door…";

And: "You even came into my house!"

And: "After everything I've done for you…"

And: "I believed everything you said!"

The coup de grace: "I should have known. How many travel journalists don't have credit cards?!"

There are only a handful of people who I've ever let speak to me like that, but I thought I'd just let her carry on until she ran out of steam. However, she upped the stakes considerably. "And what about the Gansevoort? You've been there less than three hours and I've had a complaint from the PR executive. You have to move out straight away". This was trouble because I hadn't spotted this one coming. One hotel complaining about me was bad form but two was a complete and utter disaster. In Suzie's words, it was 'unforgivable'.

I butted in with "What the fuck? I only spoke to her an hour ago and she was fine."

"You've resigned from the Birmingham Mail, so she wants to know why she's giving you a free room when you don't work for a paper anymore"

Ah, well that was a good point. However, feeling the adrenaline rush through me because I know I was speaking for a roof over my head, again, I said firmly: "I'm syn-di-cate-d! You know that. And yeah, she's right, I have resigned from the Birmingham Mail and at this very moment I'm the biggest story in British, if not world journalism. I got over-emotional at Obama's victory and became a YouTube sensation. I bet you if I release a statement about where I'm staying I'll get more coverage in British papers about the Gansevoort, which by the way no-one has heard of in England, than any travel journalist you have in Miami in the next ten years. I don't know what the problem is. I'm a walking PR goldmine at the moment, can't you see that? And as I said I'm bloody syndicated, you know that Suzie".

I think Suzie could have had Olivier, Brando and Mother Teresa all in front of her begging for forgiveness on my behalf and it wouldn't have done any good. She was one hell of a pissed off woman. Not acknowledging anything I'd said, she tore into me again. "I'm getting my ass chewed for this Adam. You need to pay your bills. What bullshit did you tell the receptionists at the Gansevoort so you didn't have to give a credit card there? I really don't know how you do it, you can't check into anywhere in America without a credit card, but somehow you manage to".

Feeling inordinately pleased with myself I said: "Karim put it on his credit card".

In retrospect, this perhaps wasn't the best move.

"KARIM! Who the hell is Karim? On second thoughts, I don't even want to know. You are unbelievable. My boss has been told all about this by the hotel managers. You've made me look like a complete joke"

This made me feel even worse, so I jumped in with an offer that hopefully she couldn't refuse. "Well, tell your boss to phone me. Or give me her number and I'll phone her and explain everything. Let me do it for you Suzie. I'm sorry. I never wanted to leave a bad taste in your mouth after everything we've been through. I never looked at you as a contact or a press officer, I thought we were friends. I'm sorry". I decided to leave out the fact I'd put myself through hell to come up with a way out of her impossible 'Don't say you're an Obama volunteer' puzzle.

Suzie gave me the number of her boss and told me to phone within 30 minutes. I was so stressed out I instantly needed a cigarette and a pint of cider. This was a disaster, I didn't want to leave the Gansevoort hotel, not that I had the money to go anywhere else, and I certainly didn't want to traipse around hostels with Karim looking for somewhere to sleep. I really hated myself. Over the last few days it seemed everything I'd touched had turned to shite. I really wanted a hug. Perhaps all the problems with Suzie would stand me in good stead when Nicole blew her top about me losing over £5,000 because of a drunken video.

Karim poked his head out of the office and said "Bad news?". I snapped at him, which I immediately recognised was unlike me. "Of course! I answered my phone didn't I? It's hardly going to be good news is it?". I'd now reached breaking point. Consumed with guilt, anger, confusion and fear I decided to walk to the Irish bar on Collins Avenue to buy a Strongbow. Hair of the dog, call it what you want, but I needed to be on my own with a pint of cider to gather my thoughts. It may be a bit immature, but for me it's a tried and tested method of thinking things through. A pint can last ten minutes or half an hour but if you have a problem to solve it concentrates the mind and the closer the cider gets to running out the more important it becomes to come up with a solution. Of course, there's always the danger you'll end up spending all day and night in the pub getting totally pissed.

Looking back, I hadn't grasped how big this video thing was going to be. Telling your bosses to fuck off on YouTube was apparently something very out of the ordinary and a gesture that people would either love or hate. Nick, Gurdip, Karim and Maartje, Steve Dyson, Teddyruxpin, the receptionists and the PR woman at the hotel had all obviously taken something different from seeing exactly the same video. I think my first impressions were right, but as that first day continued I just was too hungover, exhausted and emotional to understand what it would mean for my life. I was across an ocean from my life. I was in Miami. What mattered to me was what I was doing now; to expend a lot of energy worrying about facing my boss would have been a total waste of time. To me, the problems with Suzie totally dwarfed the YouTube situation.

When I got to the Irish pub I discovered the Villa had already played in the UEFA cup. I'd totally forgotten about them playing, which is something I've never done. The funny thing is, I was told the Villa team turned out to have been shown my video before the game. Anyway, after two pints I'd summoned up enough Dutch courage to contemplate phoning Suzie's boss. I also decided I'd better send out an email to various friends asking if they could pay off the phone bill at the Eden Roc. That way I could begin to smooth over my problems with the Miami Tourist Convention.

On the walk back to the office I phoned Suzie's boss. My Strongbow inspired plan was simple. I'd say I was sorry, beg for forgiveness and dangle the carrot of several travel reviews, each of which would be different and would contain overblown praise for her clients. I comforted myself with the knowledge that arguing as a journalist is always better than arguing as an individual.

My stomach churned as the phone rang out.

"Hello?" Her voice sounded calm and clear.

"Hello, my name is Adam Smith, I'm a travel journalist from England, writing several pieces about Miami life. I have phoned to apologise to you personally"

"Hello, Adam"

Then there was silence. She was waiting to hear what I had to say. I realised she might represent the calm yin to Suzie's angry yang.

"The thing is, right…I've been a travel journalist for ten years and this is the first time anything like this has ever happened to me. I've let you down, Suzie down and most of all I've let myself down. I'm not a bad person, but I've just emerged from an extremely hurtful relationship breakdown and the pain of this, I realise now, has obviously effected my decision making whilst in Miami. Also I had no idea how losing one's credit cards a few days before a trip could lead to so much trouble"

(Can I just point out that I've never used the term 'one' in my life but being in trouble with an American professional I thought it might help, somehow)

I continued. "Suzie has been amazing to me, and I feel very guilty that someone so professional could be in trouble because of my actions. She is a first class travel professional. I have to say there have been some misunderstandings which lead to unfortunate conclusions being made, but one thing is true – I've never demanded an upgrade on my hotel room and I've never refused to pay an incidentals bill. That is the truth. I just want to tell you that I've been severely embarrassed by what has occurred, but as Suzie rightly pointed out I am responsible for the actions of those I trust. I would like to extend a personal apology to you and your wonderful organisation".

There was silence, before she said in a measured voice: "Thank you. However, I have to say this has never happened to us before and now that you've resigned from your job as a journalist we're in a difficult position regarding yourself".

I sensed an opportunity and replied: "Look, I'm a syndicated travel journalist so it doesn't matter whether I work for the Birmingham Mail or not. In truth it doesn't have a readership that could afford to come to Maimi anyway. The fact is, whatever I write about my trip to Miami will be published in papers across Great Britain. Concerning the resignation video, well it was entirely planned - as we speak I'm the most famous journalist in Britain, and we all know journalists write about journalists. People will be writing about the fact that I'm hiding out in Miami, which will be great publicity for your city. As I've said before, no-one has heard of the Gansevoort in Britain so it's priceless PR. But because of the guilt and shame I feel about my own personal conduct in Miami I can give you a gold plated promise that I'll write several different articles about Miami, all of which will include longer profiles about the businesses that you represent than if none of this had happened. I mean, how often does the hotel get a mention in travel features? Not very often, and I won't even mention that the Eden Roc is not finished and its staff obviously trained by monkeys.

I paused for dramatic effect, and then added: "From a PR point of view it really doesn't make sense to end our relationship now, because you'd lose all of the travel pieces I'm going to write. Again, I apologise but I promise I'll get you coverage to die for!"

Sharp as a tack she said: "So you're saying if you have to move out of the hotel you'll fail to write anything about Miami and our clients that have already helped you?"

"Err, no, I'm not saying that (I was), what I'm saying is that I'd have to sleep on the streets if I'm told to leave the Gansevoort and that experience would obviously colour anything I write about Miami. I promise you, in fact I give you my word that I'll bring a lot of great coverage to the table if we just stick to the current arrangement. It's the least I can do, because you guys have been fantastic. What better type of travel journalist is there than one who's indebted to you?"

Which, though I say it myself, was a pretty decent argument to foist on a PR woman in the hope she'd let me stay in one of the best hotels in the world for free. Again there were a few seconds of silence before she said "And you won't be coming to Miami again in the near future?"

I figured I'd clinched the deal now. "God, no. The only time you'll hear from me again is when you get an avalanche of cuttings through the post, all about your wonderful clients".

"I don't know what to say Mr Smith, I really don't. I suppose I look forward to seeing your coverage about our city then".

I breathed a massive sigh of relief and said with as much emotion as I could muster: "Thank you so much. I won't let you down, I promise". Brilliantly, she replied: "You already have Mr Smith, you already have. I just hope you won't let it happen again", then put phone down on me.

I literally jumped for joy. I'd saved the day. OK it was my own incompetence I was making up for, but I'd done it. All I had to do now was to get someone to pay the $60 phone bill and I was home free. On my approach to the office I noticed Karim was outside talking to a couple of great looking women clasping 'Yes we did' t-shirts.

"Where've you been?" he asked. "Putting out fires my friend! Don't worry, we can stay in the Gansevoort hotel tonight, it's sorted." He looked confused. "I know, we've just checked in Adam." "Keep up mate, since then we've been thrown out and let back in. Don't worry about it though, we're cool now, that's the main thing".

One of the girls said: "You guys are staying at the Gansevoort South Beach? Wow!" I thought I'd leave Karim to bask in the glory as I had to hover over Facebook instant messenger to ask unsuspecting friends to lend me some money. First though I thought I'd better phone the Eden Roc to say that I was about to pay the phone bill. I couldn't get through to the reception and ended up speaking to someone in a call centre who had no idea who I was. They didn't have my details, didn't think I owed any money, and I didn't have any of the information they needed, for example the booking reference. After lots of confusion I just gave up. For all they knew I could have had a credit card waiting to pay the bill.

Shortly afterwards I recalled that it was my laissez faire approach to paying bills that had got me into this mess in the first place, so I phoned back. After even more confusion and repetition I managed to get the woman to put a note on her computer stating that if anyone phoned up wanting to pay a bill off for me they should take the money, give me a special reference and email the Miami hotel's manager with it. It was like pulling teeth. Life is so complicated in America, especially if you have a Brummie accent and no credit card.

I logged on to Facebook and waited to see a friendly name under the 'online friends' section. It didn't take long. Steve Dinneen, a Scottish journalist who I'd met on a press trip to Colorado the year before, messaged me on Facebook.

"You're a fucking legend! Can I interview you? You're video is everywhere!"

"Alright mate, thanks pal. Shit, I'm in trouble over here - could you pay off a £30 phone bill for me before I get chucked out of my hotel?"

"I'll pay it mate. Give me the details"

"You're a lifesaver, so stressed about this shit. I've got half of the Miami Tourist Board wanting to kill me. Anyway, what's the deal with the video, is it causing a stir?"

"Are you for real Adam? It's everywhere now. Most people think it's hilarious but a few bloggers have said you've destroyed the reputation of British journalism"

"WHAT? Seriously? People have said I've destroyed British journalism?"

"Yep. Can I interview you?"

"You work for a Scottish paper, what the fuck would you want to talk about me for?"

"The story's gone national mate. You've gone national. Have you any links to Scotland?"

"My granddad was Scottish and I've a soft spot for Ayr United"

"That'll do!"

"Cheers for paying the bill, bud. I can stay in my hotel safely tonight"

"It's a pleasure. You're a fucking hero amongst journalists, don't let anyone tell you any different. Everyone who's had redundancy hanging over them loves ya".

Steve had lifted a massive weight off my mind. As he was going to pay the phone bill I didn't have to worry about a thing. I shouted over to Karim: "It appears I've destroyed British journalism!" Still engrossed in conversation with his two new fans, he obviously hadn't heard me because he just replied over his shoulder: "That's cool man."

Ericka was doing a brisk trade selling 'Yes we did' t-shirts. The atmosphere had obviously changed. Anyone who came into the office was welcomed with open arms and we all had time to chat to them, unlike in the last few days when stress levels had gone through the roof. Every so often someone would come into the office and pick something up - a printer, scanner or chair - and shout across to Ericka "Can I have this back now?", and she'd smile and motion them to take it.

The place was being dismantled before my eyes, like the famous scene in Brewster's Millions. I didn't want to leave the place yet, I wanted to see some of the old faces, so I was delighted when Mark and Kale walked in, both wearing shorts and shades.

Kale said: "Hey man. Where've you been? We were supposed to meet you on the beach so we could introduce the new President to all the women"

"Sorry guys, you wouldn't believe the day I've had. You know that Dutch bird filmed me telling my boss to fuck off, well she put it on YouTube, someone put it on my boss's blog and now it's already had 20,000 views and some people are saying I've destroyed the reputation of British journalism. Oh, and we've nearly been thrown out of our new hotel"

Mark raised an eyebrow and said: "Shit, what time did you get up for all that to happen? We've only just got up, man"

"So have I mate, so have I. New President but same old shit for me"

Kale asked: "Where's Karim, we've got some good news for you two?"

He and Mark took us around the corner and began to speak into hushed tones. Mark took the lead: "Listen, we can't tell everyone this, but a guy who's been coming into the office for weeks and saw how much work we were doing has offered us the use of his yacht for the day. There aren't enough spaces for everyone in the office, that's why we can't tell everyone. Jelvis and Claire are coming, and we've all decided that we want you two to come along. What do you say?"

Karim and I looked at each other and smiled. I was over the moon Mark and Kale had picked me, as it made me feel a little less like a shit volunteer. We both said at the same time "Of course!" and shook their hands, before Karim hesitated and said "Hey, when is it? Tomorrow?"

Kale and Mark both said together: "Nah, Friday." From happiness to misery in seconds. Karim and I spoke in unison again:

"We go home on Friday!"

"What time?"

"In the morning"

"What about changing your flight?" Kale said.

Karim said he'd think about it. I said: "Mate, my missus would kill me! I've already got to tell her I've probably lost over £5,000 because of my video, so telling her I'm going to stay for an extra day because I'm gonna swan around the Caribbean on a yacht probably wouldn't be the best idea". Mark said: "Ahh well, perhaps next time." Karim and I both mumble in agreement, but we knew deep down there wouldn't be one.

We lounged about outside the office in the sun for a while, talking about anything and everything. We were emotionally drained and too tired to think about going out on the town again.

"What's in store for you two then?" I asked Mark and Kale.

"Ahh, next week, we are gonna drive back to where we came from - California with Eli"

"California? How long's that gonna take?"

"A few weeks. We might stop off at New Orleans on the way, we're in no real rush and then we might go back to school"

I was so jealous. I really envied Kale and Mark for being able to go on such an adventure.

"What about you Adam? You going back to the kitten and getting her a new flat?" Kale said in a mock English accent.

"I've got to set up my media company and relaunch my magazine, which is gonna be tough because of the credit crunch, but it's got to be a success cos I need to provide for the kitten and Nathan!"

Mark looked at me strangely. I'd forgotten he'd had not been in the car when Nicole had phoned the day before.

Kale said: "His girlfriend and her dog"

"What about you, Karim?"

"Ahh, I'm going to finish my law degree, then who knows what I'm gonna do"

I said: "Mate, whatever you do, you will be a success. The shit you've got up to already is amazing!"

After grabbing something to eat we agreed to get the whole gang together the next night for a farewell meal, meeting at the office. Mark and Kale came and had a look around our hotel and were amazed. It felt great to be in the

Gansevoort, in a room that I could never have afforded to pay for in a million years.

Every time we walked into the hotel reception something seemed to be happening, whether it be a drop-dead gorgeous model checking in or a group of familiar looking men in tracksuits checking out. Karim and I were the only ones who seemed really impressed by the shark tank. Every time we walked past it we ended up taking photos, especially when there was a diver in there. I suppose that was the height of uncoolness but we were too happy to care.

I checked my flight details after finally finding the all important piece of paper. I was flying back on Friday morning. I remembered the Going Places bloke had asked me if I wanted to move back my return date after the foul up with the flight out. I'd told him to keep the day the same because I wanted to see Nicole on the Saturday night, as she worked nights on Sunday. I hadn't changed my mind, despite the chance of sunning myself on a yacht with Jelvis in the Caribbean. I just couldn't wait to be in my girlfriend's bed, in her arms.

I knew it was time to phone her. I thought about going down the old 'I've got some good news and some bad news' route, but decided against it because, after all, I was 32-years-of-age. I knew it had to be fast because I couldn't spend much time on the phone. I'd put $10 credit on my mobile just to hear her voice. I decided to give her the optimistic spin. There was no point getting her down. She was prone to depression and after her phone call the day before I knew the last thing she needed was me saying I'd ballsed everything up.

The first time she didn't answer, nor the second. However, it was third time lucky.

"Hello?"

"Hello Nic, it's Adam."

"Oh, hi Adam! I'm so glad you phoned me. I'm sorry about yesterday, I hope I didn't worry you too much. I spoke to you last night but you sounded tipsy."

When I heard her speak, my knees went weak. Just the soft way she spoke made me love her more than before she answered. At that moment in time she could have said "Adam, I need a kidney", and I'd probably have cut the thing out myself and sent it by DHL.

I said: "It's ok babe, I'm just glad I could talk to you. I've got some good news. I'm a YouTube Sensation! Do you remember I was telling you about needing a big publicity stunt to relaunch Goggle-eye and Cheekie Media? Well I've done it! I went on Dutch TV and pretended to resign live from the Birmingham Mail and told my bosses to fuck off and it's become a hit, thousands of people have seen it already. I might lose my redundancy but the free publicity for Goggle-eye is going to make it all worthwhile baby! God's been looking down on me, baby!"

I waited for her response. She wasn't stupid; that was one of the many reasons I loved her.

"You might lose your redundancy?"

"There's a chance, but I doubt they'll take it that far. I'm in the union babes, it'll be ok".

I've no idea what she thought at that moment - perhaps she knew that, despite my bravado, I was phoning for some love - but I'll never forget what she said: "Adam, I don't care about any of that, I just want you back home with me. I love you."

I can't describe what it meant for Nicole to say that. She just wasn't the type of person to say 'I love you' for the sake of it.

I continued: "As a thank you for all the work I've done I've been given the chance to sail around the Caribbean with Jelvis on Friday, but don't worry, I've turned it down because I can't wait to see you on Saturday. I love you so much Nicole. Thank you for loving me. Everything is gonna be ok. Give the dog a kiss for me"

"Bye Adam, take care, love you".

That short conversation was the most important of the whole holiday. She had the power to ruin my day or to make it. When she said "I don't care about any of that" it gave me so much strength. No matter what unfolded concerning the video, the woman I loved, loved me and supported me, so what could possibly happen that would have any real adverse effect? As far as I was concerned, nothing – after all, the love of a good woman can make a man face any battle. I didn't give a shit what the head of a multi-million pound media conglomerate thought of me so long as she was by my side.

I shouted over to Karim and gave him a big hug.

"She's cool! She's cool"

"Man, I'm so happy for you Adam!"

There was only one thing for it.

"Let's go to one of the coolest bars in Miami. Let's go upstairs!"

The bar was near enough empty, but that was fine with us because we had the run of the place and also the undivided attention of the beautiful barmaid, who was happy to indulge us and listen to how we'd changed the world. The bar overlooked the sea, and had amazing swimming pools throughout its length and outdoor beds to lounge on. Again, we were uncool enough to get our photos taken. We only went up for one drink but of course ended up staying for several. It was great listening to the stories of Karim's life and telling him some of my outlandish tales. After talking through everything with him - the video, the future and Nicole - I felt I had the night before again. I was totally content. Nicole, the magnificent city we were in, the uplifting house music, Obama's victory and the fact that my video had made thousands of people laugh all came together to fill me with happiness. As the night wore on more people came in, some we chatted to and some we didn't. None of them had a hair out of place and at times it felt like we were in the middle of a photo shoot.

When we got back to our room we put the news on, sat back for an hour and watched as world leaders came on one by one to congratulate Mr Obama. The news anchors talked of history in the making, and the most amazing political campaign ever, and how racism had ceased to be in the land where slaves had worn shackles just a century and a half before. After we turned it off I had an idea that wouldn't go away.

"You know what I'm gonna do Karim?"

"No, what're you going to do Adam?"

"I'm gonna try to come back over here to Washington, for the inauguration in January. I'm going to take Nicole with me and propose. What a story that'd be!"

Karim's voice in the darkness said: "No way, are you going to stay at that girl with the Hummer's house? I'd come then!"

The story's not quitting baby!

Thursday, November 7

On Thursday, the Guardian's Media Monkey decided to get in on the act and write an online story. They included my exploits, and an obligatory link to the video, in their daily email and my first comments about the story on the website. By now almost every journalist in Britain knew about the pissed Brummie who'd told his bosses to fuck off whilst covering the election.

The Guardian - Media Monkey

Steve Zacharanda: One man who didn't feel as great as Obama the morning after ...

It probably seemed like a good idea at the time. You are a local news journalist from Birmingham and a big Barack Obama fan and you want to do your bit to help make history. So you fly to Miami, join the campaign, and offer to write a story for the readers of the Birmingham Mail back home!

Except this reporter, identifying himself as "Steve Zacharanda, also known as Adam Smith" celebrated with a few drinks, by the looks of it. And was then caught on camera filing his story and "cutting and pasting from the BBC". "I'm a bit of an idiot, basically," says Smith/Zacharanda. "It's been brilliant. I've met so many women ... Actually I've just come up with some award winning prose. If I can just keep my battery ..."

Monkey can't help but feel his parting shot, which we won't repeat here, wasn't entirely sensible. "Steve Zacaranda" has since posted a comment under the YouTube clip. "Right, the thing is, right I've just woke up. And seen this video, which I don't really remember. I've been told to phone the Birmingham Mail because I am in trouble." He adds: "I was off duty, I am on official holiday working at the South Beach Miami Barack Obama campaign where I had just done a 18-hour shift trying to make the world a better place. Please check every BBC News outlet and see if I have cut and pasted anything. I have not, it was a joke and should be taken in the spirit it was said." We're sure his bosses will agree. But has he really resigned? Steve/Adam – drop Monkey a line!

Within moments of waking up I logged onto my computer and opened my emails. There was one name I was dreading, Ian Murray of the Southampton Echo (he of the Colorado press trip). He'd said he'd print my Obama stuff and I prayed to God he hadn't stayed true to his word; I didn't want him and his paper to get dragged into my shit storm. Luckily he'd been on holiday so didn't get my emails until it was too late anyway. There was an email from Tom Watson that buoyed me up a bit. It simply said 'I love you. I'm your London PR man". I thought about dropping Media Monkey a line but instead put another comment up on YouTube, this time mentioning the Gansevoort.

I signed into my works email. This meant that people from work could see I was online and instant message me. I didn't want to be on too long in case one of the bosses saw my name. Within seconds an instant message came through from Nick.

"Twat"

"Sweetcorn!" (I had intended to explain why I called him this, but it's probably best I don't)

"You phoned work yet?"

"Yeah".

"What did they say?"

"I spoke to you".

"Me? You mean you haven't phoned since?"

"I'm on fucking holiday mate. How often to do you phone to speak to Steve Dyson when you're on holiday? And I've just woken up, don't forget I'm five hours behind here".

"Neil (the father of the NUJ chapel) has been in the office with Steve Dyson about you. Hold on, he's telling me something. You've been suspended".

"Suspended? I'm leaving next week! Tell Neil I'm sorry if he's getting any shit about this".

"Kevin Maguire has backed you. Dyson has gone mad. I think he phoned Sly Bailey to tell her to remove it because Kevin works for Trinity Mirror".

"Kevin Maguire? What, THE Kevin Maguire? Whaddya mean, backed me?"

"There's a debate about you in the media, about whether you're a complete twat or not. They should just have asked me, I could have saved everyone the time and said you were a complete twat from the start. However, Kevin Maguire reckons you're 'a decent journalist'".

"Cheers mate. I'm off, anyway"

"Hold on, don't go yet!"

"Watch me, I've got a five star hotel to explore sucker!"

"Neil said to get in touch with Chris Morley"

"Will do, bash out a nib for me!"

This was the moment it dawned on me that my video really was big news. Before, and despite milking my Youtube Sensation status for all it was worth, I'd just figured a few thousand people had seen it and that everyone I knew would take a position. As Karim had said, the people who liked me would like me more and the people who didn't would ridicule me, and though different people had told me it had gone big I still only looked at it through the prism of Midlands journalism. Kevin Maguire, however, is the associate editor of the Mirror. and one of the most high profile journalists in Britain; as well as landing big exclusives with comparative ease, he was a regular in the newsrooms of the BBC and Sky reviewing newspapers. For him to comment on the situation meant it was a national talking point.

I logged onto his blog, and there it was – a picture of me in that Tesco jumper. Kevin had indeed written something along the lines of 'I know the journalist in question and he's a fantastic one. You decide whether this is his finest or final moment in journalism', followed by a link to my YouTube Video.

Sitting in a hotel room thousands of miles from home, Kevin's brief blog meant the world to me. I was pretty certain not many Birmingham Mail journalists had received lavish praise from one of the best hacks in the business. I'd met Kevin a few times socially, through Tom Watson, and we'd got on really well. I'd bought a few Great Barr Observers to show him when we shared a curry in the Black Country a few years before, and Tom had told a slightly convoluted story about a time when I tried to get the 17-year-old sister of a hit-and-run victim to have her photo taken for a story in the Birmingham Mail. Several photographers had tried and failed to convince her, and we needed the shot for the front page, so it was left to me. Knowing she was from Kingstanding, just by where I grew up, I took a different approach. I said "Look, how many times do you get turned away from off licenses when you wanna buy alcohol?", and she replied "Loads, and it's only a few months till my 18th birthday too". I came up with a proposition. "Well, have this photo taken and in the story or in the caption I'll put that you're 18-years-old, so you can take the paper to the off-license to prove you're 18". She agreed and we got the front page - Bob's your uncle, everyone's happy. I remember Kevin laughing and saying that I was one of the old school.

Perhaps that's why he put his neck on the line and called me 'fantastic', or maybe Tom Watson called in a favour as my London PR man, but whatever the reason I owe him a pint. The powers that be finally removed the blog a few hours later, so it must have caused ructions in Canary Wharf.

I watched the video again, and again, and the more I watched it the more I liked it. I read some of the latest comments:

Consoletech Wow, respect to you man. You show them how Midlanders do it! :) Me = Tammie

Sandyway I cannot believe they have sacked the poor guy. Unbelievable :-(

Patrick Holly: Hey Adam, was it in Amsterdam when that guy asked you to 'schmoke hasish' because he had the deepest respect for the English nation? It was one hell of a night.

Bumbleclark Well Adam you're certainly brightening up a dull night post-Obama night shift here at the BBC! Your video is doing the rounds and we LOVE it. Hope you've still got a job...!

Smawson Has he still got his job?

EvilUmpire "A proper news journalist" ... wasted!

GREENTAMBOURINE This is fantastic from start to finish... the dangers of trying to file after a few snifters.

Not1yourmom We would have gladly hosted him in Ohio, even if he couldn't say our state's name.

PjBukem 'No, I'm a bit of an idiot.' Too right. How does a moron like this get a job as a journo. Goes to show what a state the British media is in. Goggle-eye magazine and cheeky media must be a pile of turd. Why would I want to know what an idiot thinks of the world.

Rachellarvell whoever made that last comment is a real n*b. pj bukem - n*b

SneydGreener Ay-up Adam, I hope you don't lead my daughter astray and try and recruit her for your new mag !!!! All the best in your new venture, Sam's Dad!!

Prowl777 I went to University in Salford with this guy. He shagged a woman I fancied. Boo!

BhamDanny What a star. Made me proud to be a brummie. Note to self never ever get interviewed when blathered. Still Adam, what a geezer, fair play mate that was quality!We need to have you imortalised on the Broad Street hall of fame!

Superfly1st Quality, a real bloke whose had a "Tot" and feels free to speak his mind in a World where we are too afraid to even say, "Boo" to a goose.Good lad..

TysonSavage fair play Adam - going over to work on Obama's campaign was a legend move good job! And the video is priceless ya drunk! Dont mind the nob ends with no sense of humour! As jesus said "let he who has not been a drunken ass cast the first pint" Mark 2:22

FingersMark: Ha ha, Villa team watched this before the Prague game. Spurred them on!

Job or not, this is funny, British, humour. May we brush arms in the queue for a balti pie in the Lower Holte stand soon. Up the Carew.

It seemed the majority of viewers were on my side, and every so often I'd read a comment from someone I knew, and they were usually amongst the funniest. It was open season and I was getting the chance to find out what people really thought about me. We go through life knowing what people want us to think they think of us, but rarely do you get the chance to find out exactly how they really feel. Courtesy of those anonymous and not so anonymous comments I was getting a bloody good idea of what kind of impression I'd made on people throughout my 32 years on this planet.

Of course, there were also thousands of people making snap judgements on everything about me from watching two three-minute videos of me talking shite, and the Comments section of any website is a world where dark and nasty elements hang out to spew out vitriol and bile. Read the comments under most songs on YouTube and sooner or later an argument will descend into racism. I'd still decided to keep to my promise and not respond though, because I'd just descend to the morons' level, and this applied even when I spotted glaring mistakes about me written as fact.

However, I wanted to see what journalists were writing about me so I logged on to Holdthefrontpage.co.uk.

Reporter 'resigns' and tells the world about it on YouTube

by HoldtheFrontPage Staff

A regional press hack covering the presidential election in America appears to have found a novel way to resign.

Adam Smith was writing for the Birmingham Post and Mail and sister weekly the Sunday Mercury while taking in the campaign build-up.

But now a four-minute video has been posted on YouTube which shows Mr Smith clearly worse for wear and announcing his resignation from the Trinity Mirror papers.

He chats to the camera about his time in Miami, the delights of the local female population and his award-winning prose.

At the end, he says: "My name is Adam Smith.....who has just resigned from the Birmingham Mail, Birmingham Post and Birmingham Sunday Mercury to set up my own magazine."

After an audible obscenity, he then adds: "I'm doing what I want to do."

Trinity Mirror declined to comment on this story.

The video can be seen below:

The following comments have been placed under the video by "Steve Zacharanda" - a name Adam also calls himself during the video: "Right, the thing is, right I've just woke up. And seen this video, which I don't really remember.

"I've been told to phone the Birmingham Mail because I am in trouble. I was off duty, I am on official holiday working at the South Beach Miami Barack Obama campaign where I had just done a 18 hour shift trying to make the world a better place.

"Please check every BBC News outlet and see if I have cut and pasted anything. I have not, it was a joke and should be taken in the spirit it was said."

Comments

Chris Gaynor I hardly think this gives a good image of British journalism do you? What was the point of it being posted. This just reveals how social and video networks can have a dark side too. Don't post videos of what you do in your free time otherwise you'll be in trouble...

Cameron Orson I admire the guy's attitude. Laughs in the face of authority.

Pygmalion Duh!

Revenge is sweet! Whilst not exactly professional behaviour I don't think anyone can not feel a tad of satisfaction. Trinity Mirror have treated their staff pretty shabbily when it comes to recent upheavals and if this causes a bit of embarrassment then game on!

E Considering how Trinity Mirror are treating the staff at the moment and many are in the process of being made redundant I can't blame him at all for making the comments. Only wish more of us had the guts to tell newspaper bosses what we think of them...

Greg Kettle Her Majesty's Press at its finest. Top man!

Mhmedia Classic :-)) I haven't laughed so much in ages. He may regret when he comes back to these shores, but not for long. It's good to see someone who's not afraid to speak out! Now, where can I get a copy of that magazine?

K Arrogant, unfunny, drunk, embarrassing fool. He should think himself lucky he has a job at all, and on the strength of his attitude here if he starts his own mag it will be rubbish. He gives Brit journalism a bad name.

Mister Hack "thet theye" - ah, maybe we shouldn't have sacked those subs after all.

Double D Fair play to this bloke, this is very funny. Nice to see someone who has a big enough pair to get back at an organisation with an extensive track record of dumping on staff. Good luck with the new magazine, TM was just a bad memory! And as for those saying this is not a good image of British journalism - have you read 'Flat Earth News'?! For all the hard news print hacks digging for the real stories, we salute you!

Laffin! Robin Jones? Wasn't he the large, bearded ginger lad who folk used to fear kept a Klashnikov under his desk? Scary. Yep, he'd have done something like this in his time.

M DO IT! Start your own mag! If this video carries on getting hits like these you're off to a flyer before you've even started! Good lad!

Derek Weekes Adam Smith should be on the couch when Jonathan Ross returns: maybe get his own chat show?

I found out subsequently that it was the most read story of 2008 on Hold the Front Page. I read it and read it again, and particularly liked the opening; as a fan of punchy introductions I admired its snap and brevity. I couldn't really argue with the whole tone of the article either, and I laughed out loud when I realised that the journalist who wrote it had obviously cut and pasted the statement I'd written on YouTube.

The comments below also made me chuckle as it demonstrated how I'd certainly stirred up emotions in a lot of journalists. It did give me one sobering thought though - I didn't see why I'd be painted as the villain of British journalism when Trinity Mirror were ripping the heart out of titles left, right and centre and sacking thousands of journalists across the country.

I thought I'd better put another statement on the YouTube comments section to let people I knew (or didn't know) how I was getting along. I also wanted to fulfil my promise about getting the Gansevoort Miami some coverage. Within hours

The Guardian's Media Monkey had picked it up and put another slant on the story, one that was perfect for me, Cheekie Media and Goggle-eye:

Media Monkey – The Guardian website – Thursday, November 6, 5.29pm.

Another round for Steve Zacharanda

More now on the Birmingham Mail reporter who flew to Miami to campaign for Barack Obama and was filmed and ended up on YouTube while filing his copy being, how you say … a little well-oiled. Adam Smith - AKA Steve Zacharanda - is "technically" still employed, he says, and is enjoying a drink by the pool at his Miami hotel.

Better make it a double. "Hello everyone. Thanks for the kind comments, it has meant a lot to get the backing of so many people I respect," he writes on YouTube, and even manages to shoehorn in a plug for his new media venture. "I'm currently in hiding at the Gansevoort South hotel in Miami tryin [sic] to come to terms [with] what's happened whilst sipping rum and coke at the pool. I guess I'm going to have to face the music when I get back. Adam Smith, aka Steve Zacharanda. Technically, still a Birmingham Mail reporter. But definitely editor and founder of Goggle-eye magazine and Cheeky Media." Could it all just be part of a viral marketing campaign so cunning you can afford to relax by the pool with a rum and coke?

The viral marketing angle was perfect and I was soon getting messages from people saying that commentators in the PR industry were now agreeing it was just a brilliant publicity stunt. I certainly wasn't going to argue. Whatever anyone says about that video, there was a reason I referred to myself as Steve Zacharanda. I was desperate to get the name recognised inside and outside the British media.

My mind was still racing with possibilities as I saw more stories on the web springing up about me. One minute I was daydreaming about having my own chat show, and the next thinking I'd never be let near a newspaper again. Different people from my past would keep on popping into my head. "I wonder what my old teacher Mr Garrett will think when he sees it?", or "I wish I could have seen Armadeep Bassey's face when he first saw it," or "I bloody hope no-one shows it to my mum".

However, on the other side of the Atlantic a rearguard action to stick up for me had begun and a plan was already being hatched to save the redundancy I'd all but given up on.

A Titan Enters the Fray

Chris Morley was the industrial correspondent and father of the Birmingham Post and Mail NUJ chapel when I started at the paper, but courtesy of his legendary negotiating skills he'd risen to the top of the tree and by then was head of the union across the whole country.

My previous employers hadn't recognised the NUJ but as soon as I'd joined the Mail I signed up, and it proved to be money well spent considering the amount of scrapes I'd gotten into over the years. Again, the fact that Chris Morley had gotten involved made me realise afresh that the video stuff must be big news. I hadn't really thought of troubling the union because I'd brought the whole situation on myself. I was leaning towards milking the story for all its worth, getting loads of publicity and sacrificing the £5,500 redundancy, as I couldn't see how even Chris could save my money.

I wasn't looking forward to speaking to him. I like him and I hoped I hadn't disappointed him. I also had a nagging worry that I hadn't paid my subs for a while, due to my habit of not ever looking at my bank statements, but I kept that to myself. Karim was out buying an Apple Mac and time was running out to ring because of the time difference, so I decided to use the hotel phone and bollocks to the cost.

"Hello?"

"Hey Chris, it's Adam"

"Bloody hell Adam, I wondered when you'd phone"

The tone of his voice suggested that of someone trying to suppress a laugh in church.

"I can't speak for long cos I'm on the hotel phone. Neil said to phone you, I take it you've been putting out some fires on my behalf?"

"Yeah kind of, they've suspended you. I take it you're not too distraught about what's happened then?"

"Ah fuck em, it's done now, there's not a lot I can do is there? Sorry you've been dragged into this. I don't suppose there's a lot the union can do is there? Let them keep their money. I finish next week anyway and I've got someone to invest in my business."

The money comment must have pricked Chris slightly because his tone suddenly became a lot more serious.

"Don't be bloody stupid Adam. You can't just give up and let them have your redundancy without a fight!"

"You reckon? Have you seen the video?"

"Look, you were on holiday. I think you should fight this, and look at it this way - imagine being able to say that you did what you did and still got the redundancy"

"Well, you know I'll take your advice. I suppose it would look great for the union if you could get me the redundancy too"

"They are expecting a meeting with you on Monday and I'm going to come down for it. Can you do one thing for me, though?"

"What?"

"Don't give any interviews or say anything to anyone, can you do that?"

"Umm, I'll try but I don't want to say nothing for weeks and then they take the money off me. I could do with all the publicity I can get for Goggle-eye"

"Five thousand pound is a hell of a lot of money Adam, remember that. We're on your side"

"OK then Chris, see you on Monday. Oh, one thing"

"What?"

"Did you find it funny?"

"Bloody brilliant Adam, bloody brilliant."

That short phone call cost over £20, but Chris had given me a lot to think about. As I mentioned I'd all but given up on the redundancy money, and as the day wore on on I was erring towards the 'Fuck 'em – let's be a star' approach. His confidence gave me hope I could get the £5,000, though, and as for not doing any interviews even though I'd promised Steve the exclusive I was sure he'd be fine if he knew my redundancy was at stake. Even though I've never been good with money and would normally have wasted the cash within a month or two, I had Nicole and the dog to think of I so I changed my mind and decided to at least try to get my redundancy. This meant there was a chance of my short-lived fame dying a death as I waited for a decision from Trinity Mirror, only for them to shaft me anyway, but for my future with Nicole it was a risk worth taking. I thought I could use the cash to come back to America and propose to her. As uncertain as everything was, I was glad of one thing though: Chris Morley was on my side.

Facebook status: Steve Zacharanda is humbled by the reaction of everyone's unbelievable comments, it means more than I can describe, I can't believe the villa watched it before the Prague game!

Saying Goodbyes

When I got to the office everyone was crowded around a computer laughing. I thought it was my antics they were laughing at. Perhaps that is what it's like to be a celebrity, you always think everyone is talking about you, but in any case they weren't. They were laughing at a sketch on a television show chronicling the new epidemic of 'Obama withdrawal'. Millions of people across the country were left wandering around aimlessly and staring into space after the election, with nothing to do after months of frenetic campaigning. It was a spoof but so true. The campaign that started in people's living rooms and relied on donations of $5 or $10 had mushroomed to include millions of people, many of whom who had never campaigned before, and now it was over.

I thought about what Nate said about how all the networks of people had to remain together for the country to change. That would be a battle I could not fight. Karim, Mark, Kale, Jelvis, Claire, Nate, a couple of lawyers from the North Beach Office and the woman that Kale had been avoiding since I'd got there all went for a meal. I was counting the pennies, which is never a good situation, but Jelvis said he'd cover some of my bill which meant I could enjoy the proceedings.

With all the stress of the campaign behind us we could all laugh, joke and get to know one another a little bit better. I was enthralled by Willard Morgan, who predicted that if I'd got 20,000 views within two days it would just grow and grow. I wanted him to put up the video of him going into Jerry's Diner on Halloween when I was his MC but he'd had problems getting it online. I promised every time I talked about my time in Miami I'd mention him, which by and large I always have. He told me about the mysteries of New Mexico, the beauty of Montana and his life in Greenwich Village. I promised one day to get him a gig in Birmingham and in London. I knew he'd be a star in the UK. I mean he was the Jewish Elvis for fuck's sake.

I enjoyed speaking to the New York lawyer too. He was in his forties and ran his own practice somewhere but he'd been running the North Beach office like a military operation for weeks. I'd seen him about throughout the campaign and it always seemed like he could get something done, but to see him let his hair down and hold court telling great stories was a joy. By contrast, the meal that Kale's ex-bird made of dividing up the bill, which included her spelling out to everyone that Jelvis had paid for my main course, made me realise that Kale had got off lightly. She would have bullied the cool out of him.

After the meal some of us headed to the office, where we sat in the dark having a drink and a smoke. It was a beautiful moment, and reminded me of the last episode of Cheers when Sam and the gang crack out the cigars and discuss the meaning of life, with every character contributing their own individual take on the world as they see it.

Jelvis then invited us to his penthouse. It was in one of the landmark hotels on South Beach, the one with the globe spinning on top of it. His pad was perfect; there were jump suits slung over chairs and guitars resting against the walls. As it happened there was a rooftop bar underneath the Globe and Mark, Karim, Kale, Claire and Willard decided to have one last drink together, which naturally turned into many underneath a beautiful Miami sky. Willard brought his ukulele with him and gave an impromptu concert to his select band of friends, and also anyone within earshot. It was just perfect, absolutely perfect. None of us knew when, or if, we'd ever be together again.

I couldn't help but speculate on what Barack Obama would think of it all. His unlikely quest for power had brought together the Jewish Elvis, a Belgian Moroccan, two friends from California, a Miami native and a penniless bloke from Birmingham. We all promised to return to Miami in 2012 for the next election. Perhaps we will, perhaps life will get in the way for a few of us. At that moment though, with Jelvis playing a medley of ukulele-friendly pop music hits, I thought going to help Barack Obama and making friends with such wonderful people was one of the greatest achievements of my life. As we said goodbye each of us gave one another a proper hug and a look in the eye, and Kale and Mark agreed to drop Karim and I to the airport the next day before they set sail on their yacht.

When we got back to the hotel I noticed I didn't have enough money to go upstairs to Miami's swinging hotspot. Having realised Karim might have to foot the bill for some of the phone calls I'd made, I didn't want to take the piss by asking him to buy more rum and cokes either. I e-mailed a few friends to ask them to put some money in his account, but it was 5am in the morning in the UK so I knew it would probably be a lost cause. Karim reckoned that buying his Apple Mac might have maxed out his card and it might default when the bill came for drinks and phone calls anyway.

When he fell asleep I popped to reception to ask if that was the case. They reckoned it was impossible because they'd already taken enough to cover a few hundred dollars incidentals when we'd checked in. It's fascinating the things you learn when you can't sleep.

It's a shame lack of money affected the last few days. A few hundred more pounds would have improved the situation no end, but as I'm used to being skint and living on my wits it certainly didn't ruin anything. However, it was obviously meant to be. When I got back to Birmingham I popped into the Sutton Coldfield branch of HSBC to withdraw £3.50, and out of curiosity asked how much was in the savings account I'd transferred my wages into. The answer came back: £400. I withdrew it there and then. Someone somewhere had made a mistake - either it hadn't flashed up the pending payments to America, or the idiot on the phone had done her sums wrong and there was in fact money in my account.

My emails were really hotting up now. The 'Adam Smith – The Day After Video' had gone online that afternoon and was already getting lots of hits. It seemed to have gone down a storm, as an email I'd received from an old colleague called John pointed out.

We worked and drank together throughout my time at the Sutton Observer. I sat next to him and was in awe of his brain and his sinewy prose, as well as being relieved that he rarely complained about having me shouting down the phone inches from him. One week we read Stan Collymore's autobiography, then next Graham Greene's The End of the Affair between us, turning the page when we'd both read the last sentence. I might also add that we produced some top class news and features for the paper whilst doing it.

He's one of the cleverest men I've ever met, and he's not afraid to call me a complete idiot, so his email out of the blue was food for thought:

You, sir, may very well be beautiful; if not perfect.
Can't begin to tell you how proud I am, as if this is what it's always been building to.
You are now a genuine 21st Century star, in a C21 way.
I think what I like best is that despite the booze, you're still pretty knowing and being ironic. Not enough people have clocked that. The other thing is, you have completely eclipsed the Mail. As big as it pretends it is, the individual has outweighed the many. You were talkin cobblers, but it's they that were left looking foolish. And they are.

I've read the comments you've since added to the tube, and I'm sure you know it's taking on a life of its own; it's all over Google, including Hold the Front Page, Press Gazette and Guardian blogs. It was been emailed around PA before I even told Danielle (his girlfriend) about it. And in the time it took to watch it in the flat, and drive to Danielle's mom and dad to show then, there were thousands more hits.

If you're cute about it kid, you could really use this as a springboard to something, whether that's Goggle-eye or something else. You could control it and make it bigger.

I really wanna write about it, Ad; for a proper paper, and interview you - you probably do yourself. I reckon given the Obama thing, the f-you, the job issue in the current climate, it's just so of its time. Throw in the Zacharanda and the Collymore biog read, and it's a special thing - for even a broadsheet.

Awwww, i wish you hadn't said you were kiddin about cutting and pasting. And I wish journalists weren't saying you resigned on air (although, Englishman in New York, er, Miami, dealin with redundancy is still sh*t hot).

Just wanted to say that something often said about mates is 'legend'. The fact is, you're the only person I can think of who is actually living up to theirs.

Zacharanda 1, Psv Eindhoven 0

My brief reply read as follows:

Hey mate! Thank you so much that email means a lot, I'm flying back today, thanks for getting it. Steve Zacharanda will have his own radio show.....................

Dude, don't let the trail go cold. You have to form a narrative by continuing to have vids posted. You gotta use the Dutch again. Whatever happens with the mail, upload it. If you can, call the desk and get them to film it, then upload it. Then call the British press. Then get them to put links on their websites. You can change your life if you strike now. Don't wait.

I just watched 'the day after' (part 3 from couscous global).
Dude, you can honestly be as big as you want to be. I'm serious. So many people are emailing Danielle to tell her they think you're a genius. Just the sheer cult of personality, the knowingness, the amount of hits, and the genuinely beautiful sentiments about that nation; it's such a special thing. I honestly think there's grounds for a documentary.

Anyway, just wanted to say that 'genius' is being banded about. you may have known it all along. You say 'today is the first day of the 21st century', but it's the first day of the rest of your life. You being yourself is entertaining thousands Ad; How many people can say that.

How many people can say that, indeed. I admit, I'm not a humble bloke. I think I'm one talented mo-fo, but conversely no-one on this planet thinks I'm a twat more than me. I suppose I'm a self-deprecating big head. I knew John was right though, and that if handled properly these videos could be the making of me. The fact that thousands of people saw a video of me performing to the camera and found it hilarious was not lost on me. I'd been shocked by how lucid I was, and was impressed by the lack of erms and errrs, given all three videos were off the top of my head and recorded in one take. I'd spent my whole life trying to make people laugh, either in person or in print, so why shouldn't I turn my attention to some kind of live entertainment career?

The possibility of the trail going cold was something I was acutely aware of, so I was already thinking of more publicity stunts. I even thought about the potential PR mileage of proposing to Nicole in Washington as Obama was sworn in. I'd promised no interviews, and I wasn't placing comments anymore, but what about a few more YouTube videos, none of which would make mention of the Mail? I suppose looking back that was a stupid idea, especially as Chris had obviously meant 'Don't do anything, anywhere, about anything until Monday', but I couldn't stop thinking about John's phrase: 'You can change your life if you strike now. Don't wait'. Obviously my responsibilities to Nicole and the dog precluded me from doing anything too outrageous, but I totally understood John's narrative argument, and it was playing on my mind.

Friday, November 8

The Times was the first of the big British papers to put my story in the news section of their website. Before that I'd mostly been featured on media websites, or the media sections of other websites. However, when Times Online plastered my story on the front of their website the whole world seemed to sit up and take notice. My comments on YouTube and in the video in the office had given them the chances to flesh out a story worthy of a broadsheet.

The Times Online Article

British journalist covering Barack Obama caught on camera in drunk, plagiarism rant

Adam Smith, of Birmingham Mail, is YouTube sensation after drunken 'F*ck you' resignation and admitting to copying BBC

Kaya Burgess, David Byers

Sometimes, you wake up following a drunken night out and realise you have sent an inappropriate text to an ex-girlfriend or your boss.

And sometimes you realise you have drunkenly admitted to plagiarism to camera, and spectacularly resigned from your job, shouting "F**k you' to your boss.

This is what happened to *Birmingham Mail* reporter Adam Smith on Wednesday morning, as footage appeared on YouTube of him writing a report on the US election, slumped on a Miami pavement, and barely able to speak.

Mr Smith, who also calls himself Steve Zacharanda in the hit video which was viewed almost 20,000 times in 48 hours, had taken a week's holiday to go to Miami to volunteer for the Barack Obama election campaign.

After the victory, and very much the worse for wear and drink, Smith was caught flopped against a set of railings, a laptop on his lap, filing an article about Mr Obama's victory for the *Mail.*

The maker of the video, a Dutch amateur journalist from *Couscous Global,* had stumbled across Smith by the roadside, and asked him what he was doing.

"I jumped on a plane on Friday to volunteer for the Barack Obama campaign," Mr Smith explained in a strong, if rather slurred, Brummie accent. "As an ill-advised promise, I've decided to say to my paper back home that I'd write about the American election.

"I wanted to be here because I'm here for history. The trouble is, the readers of the *Birmingham Mail* are going to get my version of history. And I'm just a little bit pissed..."

With a laugh and a clap of the hands, he added: "And thank god for the BBC, because I'm cutting and pasting, oh, baby!"

Not wanting to seem too unprofessional, he added: "I'm a proper news journalist."

To pile further misery on his ignominy, Mr Smith ended the video by announcing: "My name is Adam Smith, also known as Steve Zacharanda, who has just resigned from the *Birmingham Mail*, the *Birmingham Post* and the *Birmingham Sunday Mercury*, to set up my own magazine...F**k you, I'm doing what I want."

Mr Smith's employment status remains unclear today within a company which is undergoing significant restructuring.

Steve Dyson, editor of the *Birmingham Mail*, said: "This is an internal matter, so we cannot discuss it."

Asked about the company's attitude towards plagiarism, he added: "Whilst we cannot discuss internal matters, plagiarism will not be tolerated in any form by BTM Media Limited - although we do not believe that any has been taking place."

In a further comment left the next morning by Mr Smith on the YouTube page, he appeared to have sobered up significantly.

"Right, the thing is, right I've just woke up. And seen this video, which I don't really remember. I've been told to phone the *Birmingham Mail* because I am in trouble.

"I was off duty, I am on official holiday working at the South Beach Miami Barack Obama campaign where I had just done a 18-hour shift trying to make the world a better place. Please check every BBC News outlet and see if I have cut and pasted anything. I have not, it was a joke and should be taken in the spirit it was said."

In a follow-up video, filmed in the Obama campaign office, a more sober Mr Smith said he did not have a job anymore, and was "scared to speak to work" after phrases like "outrageous" and "bringing the company into disrepute" had been banded about.

He said: "The *Birmingham Mail* is a fantastic organisation, staffed by people who really care."

Gurdip Thandi.

By now it had all kicked off. Adam, the Perry Barr tramp, was news. He tipped me off, saying he'd made the Guardian. That seemed like an achievement in itself. But it wasn't just the Guardian. He'd made The Times! Soon enough, he was everywhere. More of the British press caught up with it, The Stirrer blogged about it, American radio stations broadcast snippets of it, and it was only going to get bigger.

Fucking hell, this was amazing. I phoned Adam and told him what was going on. Thousands and thousands of people were viewing it each day but the reaction was incredible. And very funny. Strangely enough, it didn't make the Birmingham Mail!

A friend from the Express and Star text me about it, various colleagues from the Post & Mail contacted me about it, people who didn't even work in the media asked me about it. I felt a sudden surge of pride that people were connecting him with me. They knew we were good buddies, they knew he constantly tapped me up for cash and they knew I'd kept in touch during his successful campaign to get Obama elected. In my own little way, I was in the eye of the storm and my ego loved it.

Caught Short Again

Karim and I got up early as we had plenty of packing to do before we left. I'd mislaid several items I desperately wanted to find, namely my Iceberg sunglasses, my MP3 player, some money and my house keys. I also had to be at reception at 10am for a tour of the hotel. Karim decided to come along, and we enjoyed an interesting half hour learning exactly why the Gansevoort was Miami's premier hotel.

I'd kept hold of about $40 because I knew it'd be a long 24 hours waiting around at airports and train stations before I got back home. As usual leaving the hotel room was a mad rush, as I frantically checked underneath beds and cushions to see if I'd left anything. Mark phoned to say they were ready and waiting to take us to the airport, so I quickly changed my shorts, crammed everything into my case and bade farewell to one of the best suites I'd ever stayed in.

Karim's credit card went through without any trouble and I cursed myself for worrying so much about it over the last 24 hours. Kale and Mark were positively blooming - their skin seemed shiny and their eyes were bright. They were recovering from six weeks on the campaign trail and looked better than ever. Then they reminded us why they were so bushy tailed.

"Come on guys, we've got a Caribbean cruise to go on!"

Karim and I looked at each other, both thinking the same thing: we had a nightmare journey ahead of us, and they had a day on the ocean.

We jumped in the truck and headed out of Miami. It was pretty emotional. I had no idea when I'd see Collins Avenue again, so I was over the moon when we got on the causeway and our holiday song 'Whatever You Like' came on the stereo. We all starting singing and Mark, who was in the front seat, took out his camera to record a video of me. Forgetting everything that had happened over the last few days, I started to perform for the camera again, only this time I was wearing my John Taylor Hospice t-shirt for the world to see.

"This is Steve Zacharanda, aka Adam Smith, just about to leave Miami to our Miami song 'We can do whatever we want'."

The song was turned up and like a rapper I started gesticulating to the camera.

"To the haters out there, where were you in the election? Where you when Barack Obama got elected? To the haters out there, who was here?"

We've got Karim here, he's Belgian Moroccan (The camera panned to Karim).

We've got Mark from Californ-i-a (and then Mark).

We've got Kale (and then Kale).

And we'e talking about two of the finest political operators on the East Coast of America. Let's talk about what happened. Who did I almost meet?"

Karim chipped in: "Barack Obama!"

"Yeah Barack Obama, but I got there late and missed him.Who else?"

Karim: "Jay Z!"

"Yep, Jay Z but I missed as that as well. Who else? Alicia Silverstone!"

Karim: "Really?"

"Yep got there late then too. And Matt Damon, I missed him too. But you know what I did see? I saw Barack Obama become the first black president of America. And ok, I got a bit emotional and some Dutch journalist interviewed me, but at the moment 34,000 people have seen that. And, what can I say. Fucking hell – I'm famous. Get ready for the Steve Zacharanda Radio Show!"

We all had a bit of a giggle after the video finished, and the talk turned to if and when we'd see each other again. The promise to come back in 2012 was solemnly reaffirmed. We all knew that we might not live up to it, but we all meant it at the time because in three weeks we'd all become friends, and nobody could ever take that away from us..

As we got to the airport John's words went through my mind again and again: 'Keep on making more videos'. I thought about the previous video and decided I might have come across as a bit cocky, so I came up with another video we could do at the airport. I asked Kale and Mark and they agreed.

We unloaded our stuff at the airport and then Mark handed me the camera. I pointed it at the two Americans. Speaking in a cod-Dutch accent I said: "Yah, for sure, this is the Dutch TV, a`nd we are talking to some crazy crazy Americano guys who met Birmingham's Steve Zacharanda. So did you understand a word he said?"

This was Kale's chance to shine. "I'll tell you one thing. Steve Zacharanda is a huge prick. He's very high maintenance, and was very hard to deal with. But the things I did understand he said were gems."

"So Mark, the crazy Californ-i-a-an?"

Mark picked up the baton. "Once you understand what he's talking about he's actually a pretty good story teller. But he is a huge prick."

"So Kale I understand he had some lovely words for his girlfriend, what did he sound like?"

"He called her kitten a lot. He said I love you a lot (and at this point Kale assumed a mock English accent), he said 'You know what, when I get back kitten we're going to move into a flat and everything is going to be grand. I promise. I love you so much kitten. You do love me don't ya? Don't ya?'"

Struggling to suppress laughter, and with my Dutch accent growing yet shakier, I said: "This is Dutch TV saying goodbye from America. Thanks guys, and good luck with your country man, it's doing very well with this new Indian, I mean black, president".

We all broke about in laughter and Mark promised to get both videos up on YouTube by the end of the weekend. We gave each other proper and meaningful men hugs, then said goodbye. I've never seen them since.

Karim and I then shook hands and said good luck as we headed to our airline queues. For the first time in a long time I felt alone, so I rang Nicole, and it felt great to say I was coming home. It felt even better to think that I actually had a home to go back to.

After getting through customs I decided to go to look for Karim. However, first I thought about my stomach. I queued up at Burger King and ordered a Triple Whopper. When it came to paying I remembered I'd left my money in my shorts, which were in my case, which I wouldn't see again for about 20 hours. I couldn't find Karim in departures so forlornly waited for my flight to Philadelphia. Tonya, who had sent that email to the Miami press contacts weeks before, was going to meet me in Philly but thanks to my money problems all my plans had gone to pot.

I slept all the way to Philadelphia and had four hours to kill in the airport before my flight back to Manchester. I'd wanted to get the train to the centre of Philadelphia so I could run up the world famous Rocky stairs and maybe do another video. However, I had no money to phone Tonya so I had to sit on Facebook and wait for her to come on instant messenger. I had loads of messages about the video which all seemed positive.

There was one name in particular that I was delighted to see had cropped up a few times. The first time I saw a comment that compared me to Hunter S. Thompson my heart nearly burst with pride. I'd taken *Fear and Loathing on the Campaign Trail* - one of the greatest political books ever written - with me to America, and I'd already thought how sad it was that this tormented genius hadn't lived to see Barack Obama elected. The funny thing is, I know a lot of hacks would have been offended (or even distraught) to have been compared to the drug-addled Gonzo journalist, but not me.

A few comments comparing me to him outweighed the thousands from Fox News fans slating me. After I've been featured on that august channel the comments on the YouTube video started to get nasty. Here are a few fairly representative examples:

DukeofTruth Why do limey bastards and euro weenies have to stick their noses into our political process?

YoYoSweetiePie Woohoo, everybody in the world thinks AmeriKKKa is going to throw them keg parties now that Obama is prez-elect!

C'mon world citizens, let's all get liquoured up. it's the kind of "hope" that will numb us to the things to come. we're going to need it.

We already have some socialism in ameriKKKa. it's called welfare, public school. . . hey, world, just wait until we have a civilian security force. Scary, huh?

Deucemcjo Oh Yeah, I would LOVE to triple my taxes and have a 10 hour wait at a hospital because its clogged with every jackass with a headache.

Live in Your garbage if You want. No thanks, I'll live in the best nation in the World. I've lived on your garbage continent, and I love America 100,000 times more.

Europe is jealous because it doesn't pull the weight it used to even 15 years ago.

What made for true hilarity, though, was the sheer number of Brummies who were sticking up for me against the rabid right wingers. Perhaps their wry Brummie ridicule was lost on my Rush Limbaugh loving correspondents, but it certainly cheered me up. I also noticed that over 80,000 people had now seen the video, a jump of over 50,000 from the night before. I sat there dumbfounded. 34,000 had seemed a massive amount of people, but 50,000 in one day was mind-blowing. What must they all have thought?

It didn't take long for me to realise why my video had seen so much traffic. I saw a reference to the Huffington Post in one of the comments, and realised that I must have made it onto the biggest political website in the world. I visited Huffpo and there I was on the front page, bold as brass. My head joined my heart in swelling with pride. Here's the story:

Drunk British Reporter Video: Adam Smith, Birmingham Mail Obama Reporter, Caught On Tape Admitting Plagiarism

A British reporter covering the 2008 Presidential election for the *Birmingham Mail* was caught on tape in a drunk rant, admitting plagiarism and acknowledging that he was writing his story while "pissed" drunk.

Adam Smith, also known as Steve Zacharanda, came to Miami last week to cover the election because, as he put it, "I ain't going to go to Ohio, am I? I go to Miami, because that's where the party is."

Smith said, "I wanted to be here because I'm here for history. The trouble is, the readers of the *Birmingham Mail* are going to get my version of history. And I'm just a little bit pissed."

He then said, "Thank God for the BBC, because I'm cutting and pasting, baby!"

Smith ended his rant with a "fuck you" resignation from the *Birmingham Mail*, saying, "My name is Adam Smith, also known as Steve Zacharanda, who has just resigned from the *Birmingham Mail*, the *Birmingham Post* and the *Birmingham Sunday Mercury*, to set up my own magazine...Fuck you, I'm doing what I want."

The Times reports that Smith's employment status is now very much up in the air:

Steve Dyson, editor of the Birmingham Mail, said: "This is an internal matter, so we cannot discuss it."

Asked about the company's attitude towards plagarism, he added: "Whilst we cannot discuss internal matters, plagiarism will not be tolerated in any form by BTM Media Limited - although we do not believe that any has been taking place."

In a further comment left the next morning by Mr Smith on the YouTube page, he appeared to have sobered up significantly.

"Right, the thing is, right I've just woke up. And seen this video, which I don't really remember. I've been told to phone the Birmingham Mail because I am in trouble.

"I was off duty, I am on official holiday working at the South Beach Miami Barack Obama campaign where I had just done a 18-hour shift trying to make the world a better place. Please check every BBC News outlet and see if I have cut and pasted anything. I have not, it was a joke and should be taken in the spirit it was said."

Here is a selection of the best comments:

RoiseBond007 Drinking in Britain is getting beyond a joke.
The pubs are open too many hours in the day, too much barfing in the streets, too many fights, too many problems at sporting events, too much much time and money spent on sobering these idiots up, too many lost days of work (too many lies - "I have a touch of flu/cold/stomach pains and on and on ....!"), too many black out drinkers, TOO MANY ALCHOLICS IN DENIAL, broken homes, spousal abuse, dole money spent on beer .... It's impossible to count the costs to the NHS and the taxpayer. Are all of the Parliamentarians in the pub or are they trying to solve this CHRONIC problem??
It's just not funny any more.
YOU BRITS MAKE ME EFFING ASHAMED and when travelling abroad, I avoid you at all costs.
A "reporter?" - strike a light ......fire the idiot please - he's a disgrace.

Differenteye One can look at this so many different ways. Really, it is hilariously funny, especially if he didn't plagiarize. The only person potentially hurt by his actions was himself. I'm thinking that this is a guy with dreams and ambitions who has wished he could make the leap and go after them. Obama has validated that hope even acknowledging the audacity of it.
Smith volunteered to work with the campaign and they won. In a state of elation, euphoria and inebriation, out it all came.

Wow. I bet a lot of us wish we could do that. That is, know what it is we really want and darn well just go and do it.
I bet he is still in shock.
I wish him all of the best however things turn out. One thing for sure is... this guy just totally changed his life in one moment.
Wow. If, and I mean 'if", he has a drinking problem I hope he addresses it so it doesn't sabotage his dream.
I wish for all of us one of those exquisite moments, when we feel so ALIVE. It's not like we get a lot of practice for these big moments. They just happen. They don't look perfect.
Yes, Adam Smith, reclaim your own name and go do whatever it is you want to do. You have, in a foggy way, made the way clear. If you do it with integrity, you won't go too far wrong.

XavierCugat Steve Dunleavy's retiring from the New York Post. This guy would be the perfect replacement.

Zeedubya I loved it! He was celebrating like the rest of us. He's probably a really good journalist and a really good chap.

Navy26Yrs We need this guy to tend bar at my Obama party in January.

Devadasi I think this guy is wonderful....even if he is a bit high....he's having the time of his life and celebrating like all the rest of us in praise of Obama and our better angels. A great story about a European contingency canvassing for Obama in Miami---gotta love it!

HatingTheGame Love the Brits. Really do.

KataVideo A print reporter? Who cares?

Gluvox12 What was he on when he bought that sweater?

Seasick8 Er...he wasn't sent to cover the election. he went to do some volunteer work for the Obama campaign. he paid his own way out there and then offered to send copy for his employers - which he did. you make me sick and I wouldn't hire you as a journalist if you missed these obvious points...

Now, I know I'd said I wouldn't comment on blogs, but this was the Huffington Post. I added my own comment on the Sunday after I got back. I couldn't help but be delighted. I had to laugh as well because like the Times the story quoted BTM media; in fact it was BPM media and the company had just spent thousands on rebranding. Now all across the world it was being referred to by the wrong name.

I noticed a comment from my friend Tonya and replied to say that I was in the airport and needed her to get in touch. I wonder how many other people featured in the Huffington Post have used the comments section to get some dinner?

Facebook status: Steve Zacharanda is in Philly airport with $2 to his name and has got no idea what to expect in the next 24 hours..... 80,000 views and counting.

As I waited for Tonya I checked the YouTube video again – it was becoming a bit of an obsession. The hits had leapt by tens of thousands within hours and had now broken the 100,000 mark, but my blood ran cold when I read the latest comments. Someone from work had gone on there to slate me:

Everthoughtofbusking: Thanks, Adam. And yes, that's barbed with sarcasm. Workmates here in Bham are NOT impressed. While you bask in the 'glory(?)' of studentile pranks, some of us work as professional journalists on a paper we respect. You are pretending you resigned on air to the world. A big fib and you know it. You volunteered for VR two months ago (desperate to leave after previous antics got you in hot water). Funny thing is, do you think you will get a penny of the £10k you boasted you were due to get??

Pretty nasty don't you think? I can think of about two, or maybe three, people who might have written it, but it mattered not. A couple of minutes later I looked again and Everthoughtofbusking had been shouted down. What's more, they'd hidden the comment to save themselves from more abuse from other colleagues that shared my low opinion of the management:

TeddyRuxpinUK: Sense of humour bypass - I think we all know who this is...

TeddyRuxpinUK: You only have to look at the colleagues who have come out in support of him to see how well liked he is and how funny they found it.

MattBod: You really are a wanker. He was only having a laugh.

Tokiohotelkidd: mmmm... no guessing who this is. Arsehole.

Instead of rowing with each other in the newsroom, my colleagues were using the internet and the anonymity of false names to tear strips out of each other.

I'm guessing that the people at Media Monkey used the EverThoughtofBusking comment to come up with their final story about me. Perhaps someone was briefing against me back home, but being a journalist myself I asuumed they were just keeping an eye on the comments below the YouTube story. After all, the 'five figure' £10,000 redundancy had only been mentioned on that forum:

Media Monkey – Steve Zacharanda – Parting Shot?

So did Adam Smith, AKA Steve Zacharanda, really resign in his drunken YouTube rant after Barack Obama's US election win? Monkey only asks after hearing that Smith was in fact one of 65 staff to take voluntary redundancy in a restructure of the Trinity Mirror's midlands operation. However, Smith's bosses are understood to be less than impressed with his video appearance, not least his claim - which he has since retracted - that he was cutting and pasting copy off the BBC website. What a shame that there won't also be a camera in the office when he is called in for a disciplinary hearing next week. Let's hope Smith hasn't already spent his five-figure redundancy payout because now Monkey hears he might not be getting it.

Anyway, eventually Tonya and I got it together and she came to the airport. It was so lovely to see a friendly face, and one that would buy me dinner, because by now I was feeling very faint. She was so enthusiastic about the video and everything that had gone on. I was glad I could see her in person to say sorry about pissing off Suzie, who was a contact of hers. She took it in good grace, despite getting an e-mail slating me a few days later and then explaining I was blacklisted from all Miami hotels. Just seeing someone who's a friend but lives across the world is always a real buzz. She did some videos on my camera before we separated, but like so many others they didn't work when I got home. She also gave me one hell of a hug when I left. I must have looked like I needed one.

I walked past customs and thought back to when that smart Latino immigration officer had held my destiny in his hands. What an amazing three weeks I'd had. I wondered if he'd read the Huffington Post, and what he'd say if he saw me. As I waited for the plane I felt I'd been through a 12 round fight. A flood of emotion hit me all at once. I knew I had to face a load of shite when I got back, both at work and from the landlord that I hadn't bothered paying before I left. I thought about Nicole and felt lucky, but then about all the women I'd met in Miami. I'd had so many opportunities to pull, but I was glad that I'd stayed faithful. At that moment I couldn't have handled the guilt.

When I clambered onto the aeroplane it didn't take me long to realise that American Airlines charge for earphones. I didn't have any money. I was sitting next to a lovely bloke from Wigan, or Bolton, or Burnley (somewhere up North anyway), and he agreed to go along with my plan to get free headphones. I tucked in one side of my collar and flattened my hair down to achieve the appearance of someone an air hostess short of a cabin crew. When I caught the attention of the air hostess I called out to her whilst stretching my hand to the ceiling, like a child wanting to answer a teacher's question.

"Air hostess, air hostess?"

"Yes sir, how may I help you?"

She was about fifty with blonde hair and had obviously seen better days. She didn't seem too enthusiastic about facing the prospect of a return journey across the Atlantic.

"I've got a problem"

"What kind of problem sir?"

"A big one"

"I'm sure it's nothing we can't sort out."

"I need some earphones"

"Of course sir, I can get you some straight away. They cost $9.99"

"That's the problem. I've left all my money in my shorts, and they're in my case"

"We can take credit card sir"

"Haven't got one"

"Well, I don't think we can give them out for free." She turned her head to the side in a patronising manner and said: "What about your parents?"

I thought 'The cheeky bitch! 'm 32-years-old!', then I remembered I was trying to act a bit soft and my hair was in a slapped down parting. I concluded that my ruse must have been working.

"My parents? They're waiting for me at the airport"

"Well, I'm sure you'll be fine"

With that she did an about turn and walked off. Well, I wasn't having any of that.

I bellowed: "AIR HOSTESS!", then did the terribly British thing of apologising to everyone who turned around to look at me. She stood deathly still and then slowly turned round. She looked at me like Medusa on her period, and I was almost struck dumb by death stare. She walked up to me, coming so close I could see the individual trowel marks in her layer cake orange make up. Pronouncing every syllable like words were soon to become extinct she said: "What is it sir?"

"I need some earphones"

She sighed heavily.

"You haven't got the money for earphones, sir"

"I'm scared"

That threw her.

"Scared?"

"Yep, scared"

"Scared of what sir?"

"Scared of going a bit mad in a weird way"

I now could see the passengers the other side of me taking a keen interest in the conversation, and thought that that could only be a good thing because it would increase the pressure on her.

"I'm sure you're exaggerating, just relax and go to sleep"

"I can't, I won't, I've got ADHD with added hyperactivity. If I can't have something to occupy me, like for instance an in-flight entertainment system where I can watch movies and listen to music, I will crack up completely. I'll probably be defecating myself by the time we get over Greenland. I need earphones. Please give me some earphones"

She just stared at me. There wasn't a flicker of emotion on her face and I couldn't help think she was playing the hardball card at bit much over a $9.99 pair of earphones. Even for American Airlines this was a bit much. As she wasn't budging I played my ace in the hole. "Look, please give me the earphones, if not for me then for him, I talk none stop and I'll drive him mad for nine hours if I don't get earphones".

I looked at my Northern mate, who in turn was looking at me as if I was stark raving bonkers, and he clicked into life and said: "Please God give him the earphones, he's obviously insane". Then someone in a Stoke accent piped up: "Yeah go on duck, give him the bloody earphones or you'll have a bloody riot on your hands".

She didn't say a word, but instead walked down to the middle of the plane and disappeared. For one moment I thought she might be complaining about me and images of me being carted off the plane and charged with air-rage shot through my mind, but a couple of minutes later she came back with a pair of earphones and just threw them on my lap as she walked past.

Job done, and expertly executed if I do say so myself. It's winning the little battles that makes life worth living. Funnily enough I ended up bending the poor Northern bloke's ear anyway, and I forgot to fix my hair and collar afterwards.

Facebook status: Steve Zacharanda is back in England after faking ADHD to get free earphones cos he didnt have £5 'i'll go mad in a weird way'.

Back on Home Soil

Inevitably the weather was horrible in England. Within seconds of stepping off the plane Miami seemed a million miles away. I checked the Sun to see if I'd made it into Britain's biggest paper, which I hadn't, so I bought the Guardian as well and waited for the train back to Manchester. I had to take all my clothes out of my case and dump them on the station floor in order to find my return train tickets from three weeks before.

On the way to Manchester I sat opposite an old guy. I didn't take much notice until he started talking to me. He was blind, and was struggling with his mobile phone. I helped him out and suddenly felt lucky to be alive. This old guy had so much dignity it was inspiring. I felt tired after my journey, but I couldn't imagine having done it without one of my five senses.

I managed to charge my English phone as I was waiting for the train to Brum. I was scared to turn it on; I knew a whole heap of trouble would be in store for me in the form of texts and voice mails. It flashed to life. A couple of seconds passed before the message tone went (the first few bars of Spandau Ballet's True), then it didn't stop going off. There must have been about 200 messages backing up. After making a couple of strange noises it vibrated a bit and died a death. My battered old Nokia had buckled under the pressure of my newfound fame. I never did get to see those messages, but a year later I managed to hear my voice mails. There were over 50, including;

Alex: "Adam, you crazy fuck, I'm in Thailand and I've just turned on the news and there you are! You crazy fuck. I haven't laughed so much for years!"

Eamonn: "Ha ha ha I've just seen your video. Get in touch I'm now your manager. You've got to open an ice cream shop in Kingstanding in the morning. All the ice cream you can eat mate!"

Steve Brown: "Hello Adam? My name is Steve Brown and I am the boss of Trinity Mirror Midlands, it is important that you get in touch with me as soon as possible regarding what has happened in America. This is important for you and your future. Phone me".

By the time I heard the last message both he and I had left the company.

I checked Facebook and liked what I saw – there were more supportive messages from friends. On the train to Birmingham I also had a chance to see where the story had gone. I was amazed to discover that it was now totally global; there were mentions of me in papers and on radio stations and websites in Australia, Sri Lanka, Russia, Holland, France, Germany, Switzerland and of course countless news sources across America.

One of the reports mentioned that there was a Steve Zacharanda Appreciation Society on Facebook. I couldn't help but look and realised a guy that had been on work experience in my office a couple of years before had set it up. There were quite a few messages from friends and strangers saying how funny the video was, but a fair share of haters too, as this little Facebook exchange shows:

Phillip Brewer: Saw your drunken vid. You complete and utter cunt. hard nosed journalist? No! Your a twat!

Steve Zacharanda Ha ha ha ha ha and you know it baby. Where were you when Barack Obama was elected? Stop hating and start loving.

Phillip Brewer: You're a Brummie Cunt!

Phillip Brewer: And your now on block you drunken dickhead. I lol how you got the sack for being a cunt hahahahahahahahahahahahahaha!!!!!

Not very nice is it? He blocked me from replying so I couldn't even pass comment on his bad grammar and spelling, which always is a red rag to any dickhead on the internet. I've no idea who Phillip Brewer is, and whether he set up his account just to call me a cunt or if he regularly abuses Brummies in the news. However, I did feel a bit stymied by not being able to message him back, so I posted his abusive messages on the wall of The Steve Zacharanda Appreciation Society and asked if my new found fans would unleash a barrage of abuse against the prick. His account was taken down a few hours later. There were upsides to being a Z list celebrity.

Paul Hayfied, founder of the Facebook group The Steve Zacharanda Appreciation Society.

I'd worked with Adam whilst doing work experience in 2006 and he was this crazy journalist who didn't give a fuck and would often wake up drunk at work after a night on the beer. So when I saw the video I sent the link to all my friends but that was getting tiresome, so I decided to set up The Appreciation Society on Facebook and it just mushroomed with hundreds of people joining. He was getting a bit of grief in some blogs and in the papers so I thought it would be a great way to support him. Everyone who knew him seemed to back him and when I found out that he was leaving the paper anyway it all kind of made sense.

A warm feeling came over me when I saw the tower blocks of Birmingham as I approached New Street station. I was within touching distance of home. I shot more videos of myself in the taxi from New Street to Nicole's block of flats, remembering as ever John's advice. Even if they were just for my own amusement I wanted to show my return to Birmingham too, but I looked a right state. I don't think I've ever been happier to see the flats of Newtown than I was that day.

I put my key in the door and turned it. Perhaps Nic would be in, perhaps she wouldn't. Perhaps she'd seen the video and perhaps she hadn't. I just hoped she still loved me. I could hear the dog; as I walked in he started jumping up and down and spinning round in excitement. I looked into the bedroom and saw Nicole on her knees sorting something out on the floor. She smiled the most amazing smile when she saw me and ran across the room towards me. Her little steps made her look like a geisha girl. She hugged me with so much force I thought I was going to fall over.

I held her close and smelt her hair and adrenaline surged through my body. The dog was yelping with delight and jumping between our legs. We both said 'I love you' at the same time. It was one of the happiest moments of my life. Too many times I'd come back some far flung part of the world to an empty room.

That night there was a school reunion organised and part of me wanted to go. After all, I'd have been the centre of attention, which is nice at any kind of reunion. However, Nic didn't want to go and I didn't want to leave her. I was dead skint so I popped down my local pub - The Crown and Cushion in Perry Barr - to borrow some money from the gaffer.

Facebook status: Steve Zacharanda is going down the pub for a pint of Strongbow, he really deserves it this time.

The Crown and Cushion is an acquired taste. Run by West Indians, who hire the toughest women to man the bar, it can often scare the life out of new patrons but I love it. I love the ska that's continually playing, the food, the fearsome bartenders and the argumentative regulars. I couldn't wait to have my first pint on British soil. Wherever I go in the world I always go the Crown when I get back. It feels like home, and there's no way I could ever get too big for my boots in there.

Denton, who'd told me not to bother going when I'd told him how much money I had the night before I went, grabbed me. "I was having a shit reading the paper when I saw your face staring back at me. Brilliant, absolutely brilliant".

Everyone seemed impressed that a local boy had put Perry Barr on the map, sort of. Another regular said "My uncle from Washington phoned up and said did I know the Brit journalist who was in the Washington Post and who'd told his bosses to fuck off? I said 'Know him? The bugger owes me a tenner!'".

After a few pints I headed back to Nicole's, looking forward to a lazy weekend thinking about what to do next. The signs were encouraging because Stuart, who'd wanted to invest into the business, liked the video and therefore was happy to take on a bigger part of Cheekie Media. It turned out Nic had seen them the night before and found them funny as well. She didn't even mention the 'meeting loads of women' remark, which came as a relief, but she couldn't understand why it had become a global story. In fact, it was about to get bigger still.

An instant message from Pietro popped up on Facebook:

"I'm watching you now on Good Morning America!"

"What, THE Good Morning America, or the local Florida news?"

"THE Good Morning America – you've gone national, baby!"

"I don't believe it. Really?"

I was dumbfounded. Appearing in a few newspapers of high repute was one thing, but being featured on Good Morning America blew my mind. Nicole couldn't believe it either, which was handy because it all fed into my argument that being a YouTube Sensation was great for me and the business whether I lost the redundancy or not.

My happiness quickly subsided when I opened my hotmail and there was an irate email from Suzie Sponder, who though thousands of miles away could still make me feel like shite for letting her down. It appeared that an article on an Australian website had mentioned me staying in the Gansevoort, which had been picked up by Google alerts, which in turn was picked up by the marketing woman at the Gansevoort who then forwarded it to Suzie, who sent me this email:

Adam

Not only have you made a complete ass of yourself, you've basically ruined the trust and my reputation with my boss and two very key PR agencies.

If the hotel does not get a proper review/credit in a legitimate story I will be held accountable.

I don't see how any news agency will pick up your story after this so I guess I'll have to answer to this.

I helped you out in the good spirit of the cause and you promised me coverage for the hotels in the Birmingham Mail and other Trinity outlets as well as your blog but I never expected you to return the favour like this.

Thanks for this.

Suzie Sponder

Director, Media Relations - Europe & Asia

The email cut me to the quick, again. I'd made her look bad at work after she'd treated me with such kindness. However, as a former music PR woman I thought she might have appreciated a publicity stunt when she saw one. In any case, her email had put me on a downer. My mental state was fragile because of the exhaustion so Suzie's appraisal of me hurt more than normal. However, Nicole and the dog gradually brought me out of it, and I'm glad to say that nearly a year later I came good on my promise. I emailed Suzie the links to the travel features I wrote in seven different titles, which combined had a much bigger reach than the Birmingham Mail, and again apologised for my behaviour. She replied in good spirit, saying that although I'd been a pain in the arse I'd at least given her some good memories and a chuckle or two.

Meanwhile, a friend of my mum's from church had almost choked on her cornflakes when she'd seen my boozed up fizzog in The Times. She'd decided to tell my mom straight away, ostensibly because 'she didn't want her finding out from someone on the street', although I suspect she just wanted the joy of telling her herself. How very Christian of her. I'd still assumed that, despite how big the story had gotten, the chances of my mom finding out were pretty slim because not that many of her friends are avid Times readers. Now, though, the cat was out of the bag. Mum had stormed up to Perry Barr post office and bought a copy of The Times for the first time in her life.

Needless to say she didn't understand it was a perfect piece of brand recognition and a publicity stunt any new magazine would be proud of. Nope, she saw it as evidence that she was right every time she'd called me a drunk for the last fifteen years. When I did finally speak to her that Christmas she addressed me as if I'd murdered someone, saying (amongst other things) "I've never felt so embarrassed", "You've let the whole family down", "Even your dad thinks your an idiot", "You've let your country down", and "Sometimes I wish to God I'd never had you, the worry you've caused me".

However, I knew about her reaction to it even prior to this because everyone she'd met from the vicar to the candlestick maker she'd told about me and the video (which to this day she hasn't actually seen), normally adding that she'd disowned me, again. As a friend's dad said to me: "I wouldn't even have known about it if your mom hadn't told me".

Richard Lines, an old friend from Boys Brigade

My mom, who goes to the same church as Adam's mom, had been told by the same woman who had told his mom. She said 'Adam's been all over the TV for being drunk.' I thought she must have got it wrong until my dad got the laptop and showed me. There he was drunk on camera with a stupid look on his face, and then he started speaking in his Brummie accent. I don't think I've laughed as much in all my life, I looked at the amount of people who had watched the clip and it was in the hundreds of thousands, I hoped Adam knew what he was doing but figured he was probably somewhere have a pint laughing about all the trouble he had caused. I just hoped he, or I for that matter, didn't bump into his mom anytime soon.

The Saturday after my return she set about scaring the rest of the family half to death about me. An answerphone message to my auntie and uncle in Wales darkly urged them to buy The Times because 'a very grave thing has happened to Adam in America'. My auntie went to the newsagent thinking I'd been kidnapped or murdered so she was mightily relieved to see me alive and well.

I thought I'd forewarned my dad about the situation with an email I sent the day before I left America. However, his computer had broken and he only found out when one of his wife's work colleagues asked if the drunken Brummie journalist that had been on Sky News was his son. He'd also had a hysterical phone call from my mom about my actions, but then he was used to that. When I did speak to him a week later he said he thought with my luck I'd probably get a job with Obama in America.

At the end of my first day back at home I'd grasped that everyone I knew from every different part of my life either knew, or would know about the video. I was just happy to be in Nicole's bed and away from the outside world.

Facebook status: Steve Zacharanda is chuckling to himself to sleep knowing he will have passed the quarter of million mark when he wakes up....

The 'unguided missile' defence

Monday, November 9

The jetlag had kicked in by Monday morning and I really didn't feel like going to the Birmingham Mail for 'an investigation'. I didn't have much choice though, so I met up with Chris Morley and my union representative Neil Elkes. I was more pleased than ever to have them on my side.

Birmingham Mail employee, who doesn't want to be named:

We all knew Adam was coming in to have his disciplinary and a lot of us wanted to say hello. However, it was obvious the boss did not want him to see us. In fact we knew he was in building when the cry came from the office 'he's got into the building, he's free in the building, don't let him in the newsroom' and then security guards blocked the entrance so he couldn't come in.

I was totally unaware that there was a problem with me wandering around the building, but I did think it was a bit odd that a security guard hurriedly ran down the stairs and asked me to accompany him to the meeting. Chris, me and some bird from Human Resources sat there waiting for Steve Dyson. My stomach turned when he entered the room. When I got up to shake his hand he smiled, which I thought must be a good sign. Of course I didn't know that five minutes before he'd been freaking out because I'd got past security.

I was determined to be very aggressive in the meeting, to let them know that if they didn't give me my money I'd go off like what Chris would have described as 'an unguided missile', telling every media outlet I could that Trinity Mirror was killing the paper. Perhaps I'd been buoyed by the sheer number of good wishes I'd received from everyone, or perhaps hubris had taken hold of me.

However, when we got down to business I was blindsided by Steve Dyson's adroit handling of the situation. He hid almost all of the anger that everyone had told me he felt towards me. He started asking me how my health was and told me he had a duty of care for me as an employee, which I hadn't expected at all. Slowly but surely though, the questions started coming, and I had to keep what Chris had told me at the forefront of my mind – to let him do as much of the talking as possible. I think we both knew I could easily hang myself with my own words.

I thought it was only fair to offer Steve, as an editor, the first person piece though. I told him the whole world wanted to know what was happening, and suggested we do a jokey video with him clipping me round the ear and so on. The Mail's website would certainly have gotten an increased amount of traffic. I didn't want to say it at the time, but I was the biggest international story the Birmingham Mail had had for years and I felt that they should bloody well take advantage of my goodwill instead of burying their heads in the sand and letting the rest of the media laugh at them. Steve didn't see it that way though. He said The Mail didn't do gimmicks and that he had shareholders to think of.

Within a couple of minutes I realised that he'd had his minions tracking every move I'd made since the video because every website I'd commented on (which thankfully wasn't many, although probably too many for Chris's liking) he knew about. He started banging on about The Steve Zacharanda Appreciation Society on Facebook. I laughed, thinking about all of his employees that had commented on there to piss on the argument I'd let my fellow journalists down.

He had all the comments I'd written since the article printed out in front of him, and to my horror he knew about the videos that Kale and Mark had recorded on the way to the airport, Mark having them posted on YouTube the day before with 'Birmingham Mail' in the titles. I was even asked 'is that you doing the Dutch accent' in the video with Kale and Mark. He seemed to be concentrating more on the videos after election night, probably because I'd repeated the assertion that I'd resigned live on air when Chris and I were obviously arguing that I hadn't. For the first time I began to think taking John's advice about making more videos might not have been such a good idea after all.

The bint from Human Resources was pissing me off too. A few weeks before I'd seen her jump with delight when 65 people had applied for voluntary redundancy and that still rankled with me, particularly now she was sitting in front of me asking questions.
When I mentioned all the abuse I'd got from people after the video I was sure to pronounce the word 'cunt' with as much venom as I could. It had the desired effect, and she shivered as if someone had thrown cold water over her. Chris and Steve also recoiled because there was a woman in the room, and I had to apologise.

As usual in boring meetings I started to daydream, but I snapped out of it when for some bizarre reason Dyson started going on about the song I was singing in the video as I was leaving Miami (TI's *Whatever You Like*). He said it reflected badly on the Mail. I thought he might have been joking, but he was deadly serious about that particular song. When Chris and I conferred in a break I had to tell him it was not only my holiday song but also one of the most popular in America, and could have been heard blaring out of every radio station and club in Miami. I've been in some weird situations but being in a minuted meeting explaining how popular badboy rapper TI is in America is as strange as it gets.

In the break I was close to storming out, but as usual Chris calmed me down. He kept on saying they haven't got a leg to stand on. Back in the meeting it felt they had a caterpillar's worth of legs to stand on. I mean, they had enough evidence to show I'd brought the company into disrepute. I couldn't help but think this would have already have been done and dusted if I hadn't got a big media profile and so been in a position to do the company damage. My stance was that I'd shown them up once, and I could do it again, but if they paid me my money I'd keep my mouth shut. We were all journalists and knew the story wasn't dead yet. If they sacked me that day then it would start up again and they would have no control over it because I would be free to say what I wanted.

I'm sure everyone knew the deal really, but no-one wanted to say so explicitly so Chris and I continuously mentioned all the media outlets that wanted to interview me, the implication being that I was under a lot of pressure and so might go off like the aforementioned missile.

I was just so glad to have Chris fighting my corner. I marvelled at his love of arguing over the detail, over single words, over the slightest thing. The bosses knew everything had to be done to the letter of the law because he'd come down on them like a tonne of bricks otherwise. As I mentioned, without him and my deep respect for his abilities I would have stormed out ten times over.

The bottom line was that I was suspended without pay, and I wouldn't find out about my redundancy for over a week, until the last day of my official employment in 8 days time. I was convinced they'd stitched me up because I'd have to keep quiet for long enough for the story to be almost dead. I knew within 48 hours all the requests for interviews and the interest in me would have died down. This was my only chance to get national exposure for the magazine and I was about to give it away for not even a guarantee of five grand.

These are the official notes of the meeting:

Notes of an Investigation Meeting with Adam Smith

Present: Adam Smith, Chris Morley, Steve Dyson and Helen James.

SD Confirmed it was a formal meeting in line with company policies. Asked if Adam had received our letter?

AS Replied that he had not received the letter. He had received our email.

HJ Confirmed that the letter was sent to Aston Lane Perry Barr address.

AS Confirmed that he no longer lived at Aston Lane Perry Barr, that was about 5 addresses back.

SD Stated that we needed an address at which we could contact Adam.

AS Gave a contact address, his mother's house.

Wilnecote Grove, Perry Barr, Birmingham.

SD Then asked if we could have a contact telephone number for Adam.

AS Responded that he currently had his American mobile with him, he no longer had a UK mobile. Adam gave us a contact number, his girlfriend's mobile. Her name is Nicole if we need to ring this number.

SD Confirmed that Adam was suspended on full pay, to allow our investigations.

CM Asked SD to confirm that was a neutral act?

SD/HJ Yes.

SD The first question that I have for you Adam is, are you OK healthwise?

AS Yes, I don't know what I would have done without my girlfriend, she has been amazing.

SD I am your employer your boss and I am concerned for you.

AS I just needed a hug and someone to tell me that they loved me and I got that on my return.

SD Seriously Adam, just calm down and if you need any help then let me know. I do have a duty of care to you, I would like to give you my mobile number, and you can call me if you need to.

AS Writes down Steve's mobile number.

SD What has happened has caused a number of problems for us. I want to investigate and need to ask you some very direct questions. With regard to the first video on U Tube I can see that you did not set that up and that you also denied the comments on plagiarism.

But I have to ask you did you plagiarise the BBC?

AS I denied this at the first opportunity that I had. I didn't plagiarise the BBC, go through my copy.

SD I've gone through your copy, but I must ask you did you plagiarise?

AS Plagiarism – no. If anything I checked my notes against the BBC write up of Obama's speech to ensure I was accurate.

SD About the interview, what happened?

AS I was trying to make the Dutch woman behind the camera laugh, she was beautiful.

CM She never said where she was from did she?

AS No. I was working from 6am US time to 2am when the video taken – his speech really affected me – the elation - the emotions.

The next day I woke up happy as Larry, as I couldn't remember a thing.

SD On the video it appears that you have resigned from the Birmingham Mail?

CM Be specific, which video, where?

HJ The U Tube first video.

SD It is incorrect that you resigned on air, which is how it appears.

AS It was just a woman with a digital camera.

SD I want to check that you have not resigned?

AS No I have not resigned.

CM You would have received a letter of resignation. You have not put in a letter of resignation have you Adam?

AS No.

SD You applied for voluntary redundancy, and you are still in consultation till 18th November.

CM It was actually others interpretation, not what Adam was saying.

SD We tried to contact you, why didn't you try to contact us?

AS I did call in, I called in to the Newsdesk, Emma put me through to Nick. I called 5411 Newsdesk. I was told to speak to Nick about this.

SD It has passed now but it would have been helpful if you had been put through to the Management team.

AS I was told to phone the Newsdesk and I did. I got Emma's message on Facebook.

SD We were trying to get in touch with you via your mobile.

AS I have not used my UK mobile, just my American one while I was over there.

SD I need to know how to get in touch with you direct.

CM It is clear that Adam was on holiday at the time this happened.

AS I phoned the first chance that I had, I was 5 hours behind.

SD There are two things that I want to talk to you about. Firstly, the Appreciation Society on Facebook.

AS When I returned to the UK I had about 20 messages from people calling me the C word. It felt awful. I was just so pleased to get some support. Paul Hayfield sat next to me on work experience for 4 weeks, about 5 years ago. He set up the appreciation society. When I arrive home I was very tired and very emotional. It was just beautiful to get such support.

SD So it was not something that you initiated. The second video uploaded on U Tube is entitled Birmingham Mail.

AS Me leaving for the airport is it?

CM Have you got a download of the video's?

SD Yes, Chris we have got them, But I don't think there is any merit in us all watching them together now.

AS The Dutch woman found me again and I did another interview. I could have given interviews to Radio WM, Radio 5, Talk Sport, so many people, but I haven't.

SD What about The Huffington Post, you are quoted on there as 'the worst thing that can happen to me is that I loose my £5k redundancy money".

AS I have only responded to one Blogg and that is the Huffington Post. I have had a lot of people worried about me, what are you doing to do, people worrying that I might top myself.

SD I want you to understand the consequences of the publicity, the snowball effect that this had had. If I have been asked to comment I have given the same comment each time, 'This is an internal matter, and we will not tolerate plagiarism". I have given this quote to 8 Newsagencies and other organisations. It is a funny story and so has been picked up globally.

AS I apologise, I am embarrassed. Any publicity is good publicity and the traffic on our website has gone up.

SD No Adam, this isn't the sort of publicity that the organisation would want. Is there anything else about the questions that I have asked?

AS I apologise.

SD Proposed that we adjourn to allow Adam to talk to Chris and SD & HJ to have a short discussion.

CM Stated that he thought that it would be more helpful to view the videos.

HJ Responded that they were loaded onto laptop.

SD It is the fourth video with the Birmingham Mail on.

HJ I have the 3 video's on the laptop, but not the final one of Steve leaving for the airport.

SD I will bring it up.

SD Accesses the U Tube site, article entitled Steve Zacharanda leaves Miami.

Explains that it is not a healthy thing to keep linking it to the Birmingham Mail. The clip shows Adam on his way to the airport.

Unfortunately the laptop does not have flash player installed and so it is not possible to view the video, just the site where it is posted and the surrounding text.

SD It is possible for people to place their own interpretations on things. The Times On Line article placed a certain interpretation on it.

CM We will have to discuss this with Adam, who these people were in the taxi.

SD I think the Times On Line did you a massive favour in their reporting. U Tube says drunk British Reporter caught on camera.

CM That is an example of poor Journalism, what Adam said on video was not the whole picture. Have you been approached?

SD Anyone who has approached me has been given this comment. I have laid out the facts, Adam was on holiday, rather than leave people to make their own interpretations.

AS I saw the Times On Line thing, I was on Good Morning USA, I knew that I had to get quotes out there, otherwise the phone would just keep ringing, people would just try to keep contacting me.

CM Since you have returned to the UK you have not spoken to anyone have you?

AS No.

SD 284,000 people have viewed the website, and people have commented on it, I am bringing your attention to it, so that you can understand what has happened.

CM Comment is free and people will comment.

SD In the video in the taxi it shows Adam singing the Rap song, 'We will do what we want'.

AS That is a Private Eye video that someone loaded up.

SD It maybe someone else's video on the way to the airport, but you singing 'We will do what we want' does not look very good. To some people it looks as if you are taking the Michael, and that is not what I would want to see.

ALL agree to adjourn.

Adjournment – 11.40 am.

Reconvene 11.51 am

CM There is something that maybe relevant, 'we will do what we want' is a very big song over in the USA at the moment.

AS It came on the Radio while I was in the taxi, it was just coincidence. You know you always have a holiday song whenever you go away, well that was it. TI.

CM The video was made by 2 people from the democratic party using a hand held digital camera.

AS I will get in touch straight away and ask them to take off the Birmingham Mail.

SD As I confirmed you are suspended on full pay. I don't want you to come into work at this time, or to work upon company systems. Therefore I have deactivated your Raz card during your suspension.

AS So I can't get my email?

HJ You have a personal email don't you?

AS Yes.

SD We will need to conduct a disciplinary hearing into this. When are you available?

CM The first day that I can do is next Monday.

SD That is our first day over at the Fort Dunlop site. How about Tuesday 18th November at 10am?

AS At the Fort Dunlop site? I can't get there by public transport.

SD I will arrange for a taxi to come and collect you. I will need an address to get you from.

AS My girlfriend's address is Thornton Tower, Newtown Birmingham.

SD Confirmed that a taxi would collect Adam from that address at 9.30am on the morning of Tuesday 18th November.

In the meantime I would like you to treat this issue with confidentiality.

CM I will also impress this on Adam.

SD There is a potential that any further actions may also bring the company into disrepute, so I would like to ask you to abide by what we have discussed. Any further linkage of your activities and your trip to the USA with our business, will be looked at seriously.

AS So I can talk about me.

SD Of course you can, you are a human being, but don't talk about the Birmingham Mail.

AS I need to send letters out to people to thank them for their support.

SD No. The videos are currently being played around the world. Any further actions could lead to further unwarranted publicity. I am asking you to think very carefully about confidentiality. These are internal matters.

CM I personally feel that it is best to say as little as possible.

SD It can trigger other links, other discussion and interpretation.

CM The time to thank people would be after all this has concluded.

SD You are still employed by us and still paid by us, and we will follow the correct processes. Has anyone else got anything to add?

HJ No.

AS No.

CM No. I am obviously disappointed that I have to wait a week to have this all concluded. It has been quite stressful.

SD I am concerned that it has been a stressful time for you, but your representative is not available until then.

CM Will you send copies of all the videos to Adam?

HJ Yes.

AS To my personal email: adamsbigapple@hotmail.com

HJ Hotmail is not good with large attachments if I send the video clips through.

SD We will send the links through to each of the 5 video clips. I have also viewed additional external correspondence as mentioned earlier in the meeting.

AS What can I say about all this, when people ask me, I need to know what I am able to say?

SD CM Adam can say that he has been suspended on full pay, as this is a neutral act. He should also say that he is unable to discuss this further as it is an internal matter.

CM Is this what the company will say?

SD Yes.

HJ Actions; To provide all with notes of the meeting and re advise SD of Adam's address

All pretty bizarre, I'm sure you'll agree – especially with five grand on the line! I lied to Nicole and said t it had gone brilliantly and that the next meeting would be just a formality. I could tell she was getting worried about me not getting the money. She was working nights to make ends meet and it was near enough killing her. I wanted the money as quickly as possible so she could give up work and get back to full health. We'd been so close after I got back that she agreed for me to stay for a while, which was perfect. I wanted to avoid my landlord Mr Mensah at all costs, because I owed him rent and knew I'd get a lecture about how he'd been let down 'by a man of letters and a trade'. I hadn't even bothered phoning him to tell him I was going to America. I told myself I'd pay him that when my wages came in a couple of week's time. And though that made me feel bad, I was as happy as could be at Nicole's and I didn't want to leave her side at any cost.

Waiting for decision day

Facebook status: Steve Zacharanda is suspended on full pay whilst an official investigation is completed, that's all he can say whilst running scared from mom on the warpath.

Ellie Piovesana Off work AND getting paid? You're living the dream Adam! CALL ME!

It appears being suspended from a job in the media was pretty en vogue. I was in rarefied company because Jonathan Ross, Russell Brand and Jon Gaunt were all suspended too. The difference between them and was that they were already financially set up for life and could afford what had happened to them. I, on the other hand, had my balls well and truly in a vice.

I was in limbo as I sweated on my redundancy. If I'd been single and living on my own I wouldn't have been able to stop myself either phoning up a radio show, commenting on a blog, or e-mailing my story to various papers. However, living with Nicole meant that every time I saw her I knew I had to keep quiet to protect the cash. We'd been so happy since I'd gotten back and there was no way I was going to risk losing that, not for any amount of publicity.

I read more of the stories written about me across the world, which took what seemed like days. I was amazed by how many people had made so many mistakes about me based on the videos. People had written that I was in Chicago, that my fare had been paid for by the Birmingham Mail, and that I was a music reviewer. Reading all the comments underneath the YouTube video was probably funniest though.

I also found out that I'd been nominated for Brummie of the Year on the website 'Birmingham: It's Not Shit'. I was up there with local DJs and it was nice to see people voting for me because they reckoned I was the person 'who' put the city on the map this year'. I didn't win, in fact I came third in the end, but I didn't stand a chance anyway as Kerrang DJ Johnny Doom's many fans made him the clear winner. Just to have been nominated was a great honour anyway.

I contacted Maartje from CousCous Global. She'd been getting a hell of a lot of grief from people assuming she'd stitched me up, and bizarrely everyone still seemed to assume that she was a he. She was as amazed as me by the reaction and had kept track of where the story had gone more diligently than myself. She told me I was temporarily massive in Holland, Germany and Switzerland. She'd waited a week to write a blog about the situation, but my jaw dropped to the ground when I saw 'Adam told me to put it on YouTube'. Trinity Mirror were seemingly seeking out everything written about me and I knew this admission, whether true or not, would be the smoking gun that would give them grounds to take my redundancy. I e-mailed her and to her eternal credit she changed her blog within a couple of hours.

CousCous Global Editors blog: Tuesday, November 12
"The drunk journalist case"

We have a Hit Vid for the last 5 days. Must admit that I did not know what it was when I first read this word.
Anyway we are all over the Internet in at least 3 continents now. USA, Europe and Australia. Bloggers report us on what sites we are….just heard that we are now on the biggest news site in Switzerland…in German….
Numerous sites are "cutting and pasting us, baby". But we are proud of it.:)

Must say that I did not sleep for a night about this all.
Was I the "trashy amateur journalist who should be shot" as some of the comments were on the Internet?
And how come that I am putting hard- work-movies on the net about young people in China, Africa, Holland or USA but that this accidental video gets all the attention?
Only a month ago I received an Emmy Award nomination for my last tv- series of Couscous & Cola, but nobody wrote about that in Switzerland or Australia.
But 3 minutes of drunken journalists babbling together about Obama, BBC and the Grasshopper and off we go…..OK, the guy appears to resigns on line...that too...:)
We had a quit interesting 5 days but I did not feel like reacting on line, just wanted to follow what was happening on the Internet . But now a short first reaction.

Here it is:
I am not a guy.
I am not an amateur journalist, although I like the term.
I like Steve/Adam he is the best sport and a very funny likable guy and no, I did not knew him before I filmed him.
Yes, I did run in to him by accident the next morning and very happy I did, otherwise I would feel guilty.
Yes I would have liked other movies to explode like this one, but you guys don't even look at "Hardnews crying" (part 2) and I think that one from Steve is really brilliant.
No, I do not feel sorry I did this. Nor is Steve/Adam. We both thought "it was a bit scary, very funny and a textbook lesson in the new media". Just quoting….
So now watch the other movies from our site…..they are lots of fun!

She also told me that she was considering doing a documentary about what happened to me after I'd become a YouTube sensation. That was pretty exciting, but it also gave me some food for thought about how the next few months would pan out. I was still hoping that Cheekie Media would be a success.

On the Friday I decided to go to the Queen's Head, near work, for a drink with a few people who were leaving that day; we'd dubbed ourselves 'The Departed'. I worried all day before I went into the pub because I wasn't totally sure how people would react. For all I knew there might have been a sizable minority of people who thought I'd let them down with my antics.

I needn't have worried. After opening the door gingerly I walked into the bar and saw the old school of the Mail (Tom, Jim, Paul, John and Alf) amongst some of the young bucks. Between them all I reckon there was about 200 years of journalistic experience staring back at me. Tom Reid started slowly clapping and then the rest joined in. These old hacks had seen it all, including the gradual decline of the paper they loved, and they were on my side. It meant a hell of a lot to me. Jim Levack, who had been my News Editor and had kept me in job all those years back, ran over to me and gave me a massive hug, telling me that I was his kids' new hero. He carried on repeating all the lines I used, and everyone came over to shake my hand and say well done for sticking one to the bosses. Everyone seemed to think that I'd be getting my redundancy too, which was a nice surprise. In fact they seemed to know a lot more about the situation than me.

It was a great drinking session but a very sad one too. All those great journalists were walking out of the door to pastures new, most of them lost to journalism forever, with all their knowledge and talent going with them. The Departed left a massive hole in the Birmingham Mail, but the sad thing is that the same brain drain had happened in countless papers across the country. That's why so many journalists enjoyed my video I think, because those of our ilk were in the midst of been culled and my actions spoke for all of them somehow.

As the days went by I realised it wasn't just fellow journalists who wanted to talk about the video. Every time I went to the pub or to the shops people wanted to ask me questions and for me to tell them the story. I can't deny I loved the attention, but Nicole's eyes inevitably rolled skywards when someone else asked me to regale them with the tale she'd heard a hundred times. However, I loved hearing the stories of people, about where they'd been and what it meant to them.

Bill Kirkland, an old contact who I hadn't seen for several years.

I was in Goa on my laptop when a friend sent me a link to the video. I hadn't seen Adam since his days on the Great Barr Observer when I was part of a community group and he was a journalist. Within minutes I was laughing that much I had drawn a crowd of about 30 Indian guys who wanted to know about him.

Loads of people had heard it on the radio, as I'd been discussed on TalkSport, Heart FM, BRMB, Kerrang, Radio 5 and a few more. Another pleasant surprise was that journalists were now getting in touch from far and wide to see if they could contribute to Goggle-eye. It was very humbling, especially as I didn't even know if I'd have the resources to resurrect the magazine.

The Final Reckoning

Tuesday, November 18

I looked across at Chris upbraiding the Human Resources woman and couldn't help but think that he was bloody enjoying it. What better union man can you ask for than someone who enjoys arguing about whether he should be paying for parking whilst he attends a disciplinary meeting?

The next hour would decide whether I would get my redundancy money or not. If the answer was no there was a good chance Nicole would go to pieces and never look at me the same way again. I'd have blown the chance of us moving out by being a drunken idiot. If the answer was yes and I'd won it meant I'd become a YouTube sensation, pulled off a publicity coup, made the world laugh and still got my redundancy. I could then use it to move into a new home with my girlfriend and maybe take her to Barack Obama's inauguration where I could propose, and in doing so get more publicity and help turn Goggle-eye into a reality.

I was in the lap of the Trinity Mirror gods. My story had died a death in the media over the last week as I'd known it would. If I was double crossed on the deal that never spoke its name my last throw of the dice would be a press release to every radio station, paper and website I could think of within an hour of the meeting. I'd missed my chance of interviews with the world's media to talk up my new venture though, and I knew it.

The meeting was with Marc Reeves, then editor of the Birmingham Post. In the company he was known as the 'axe-man' because of how many people he'd sacked at his previous paper. He didn't even bother with the niceties that Steve Dyson had allowed me, so it didn't look good on the face of it. However, I couldn't help but feel that the decision had already been made and that if I kept my mouth shut they'd give me the cash. After all, for all they knew this missile was still armed and *very* unguided.

Again I let Chris do most of the talking, because he's brilliant. He was picking up on points that had totally escaped me. I had the best in the business fighting for me and I think the bosses at the Mail knew that. I wasn't exactly over the moon that I had to answer even more questions, many of which were exactly the same as Steve had asked, and we even had to watch all of the videos again. The funny thing was that we were watching them on YouTube, so we were adding to the all important hits total.

As I looked through the glass panels at old colleagues I felt really uncomfortable and couldn't help but think 'How has it come to this?'. I'd loved working for the Birmingham Mail, despite its general crap-ness, because I'm a Brummie through and through. As I was waiting for the decision I couldn't help but feel a bit morose; I'd probably never get to work on a daily paper in my local city ever again. The paper had moved into its shiny, new and cheap offices in Fort Dunlop that week and I thought it resembled a call centre. I wondered how long I'd have lasted if I'd stayed.

I tried not to seem too eager to listen to the verdict, in fact I adopted the stance of a bored teenager being quizzed and lectured by toothless cops. The one thing t I had to use all my strength to avoid launching into a tirade about was when Marc said to me: "What you did was an affront to everyone who works for the Birmingham Mail, the Birmingham Post and the Sunday Mercury. And worse still, it's an affront to every hard-working employee who had to make the hard decision to take redundancy". What a crock of shite. I would have been mortified if I'd made things tougher for people threatened with losing their jobs, but I knew that wasn't remotely true. I can't remember whether I pointed that out, but I do know my mind was swirling with fury because of what had happened to my paper.

After about an hour we were told to wait whilst Marc made the big decision. Chris made a point of getting an extra ten minutes because he had to go down to the car park to put more money in the metre. I couldn't help but laugh, despite my stomach turning over at the thought of telling Nicole I'd lost the money we were relying on to move out.

Notes of a Disciplinary Meeting with Adam Smith

Present: Adam Smith, Chris Morley, Marc Reeves and Helen James

This is not intended to be an exact transcript of the meeting but a record of the main points discussed.

MR Thank you for attending this meeting today, I think you know why we are here, to discuss the allegations regarding the clips featuring interviews with you, posted on You Tube and your subsequent comments, that this may have brought the company into disrepute.

HJ Provided further copies of the letter, investigation meeting notes and disciplinary policy to both Adam and Chris.

CM I do have a comment on the invitation letter. The second paragraph from the end causes me concern, it sounds as if you have prejudged.

HJ I included that paragraph because I wanted Adam to realise that this was potentially serious with serious consequences.

CM May would have been better than will.

HJ OK.

MR If technology permits I would like to play the clips. The first clip that I would like to play is the initial one from You Tube.

AS That one has had 330,000 viewings.

Clip 1 is played.

HJ Are there any points that you want to make about the clip?

AS No, I think that everyone has spoken enough about it.

MR I will now play Clip 2.

MR In terms of sequence?

AS They were both put on the website at the same time.

MR I am now going to play the 3rd clip.

The clip is filmed at the Barack Obama office the next day. 'I think I lost my job'. 'I was not cut and pasting from the BBC'. 'I am basically scared to speak to work now'.

'The Birmingham Mail is a fantastic organisation, staffed by people who care'. 'I am leaving along with 65 others'.

MR What is the significance of the alias that you use?

AS It is just an alias that I have got. There are 3 Adam Smith's in Journalism, one who reports on boxing, one in The Times. It is a name from when I was at school that is where it comes from.

MR I would like to play the next clip. Clip 3. This was posted on You Tube along with the heading, Who is Steve Zacharanda?

AS This is a holiday video, the Birmingham Mail is not mentioned.

Clip 3. This features two men that Adam worked with while in America. Adam is behind the camera, doing the interviewing. Adam is asking, 'what is this Steve Zacaranda like?'.

Some of his actions are described, such as he talked to his girlfriend a lot.

AS I was having a laugh on camera.

MR I would like to play Clip 4.

This clip shows Adam in a taxi about to leave Miami, singing what he describes as the Miami song, 'I will do what I want.'

AS The other people in the taxi were volunteers from the Miami South Beach office, there were my two bosses while I was there.

MR We could also trawl through all the other publicity that this generated, such as the Independent, The Times. But let us just concentrate on the content of the clips first. The first key issues raised are; You state that you have resigned from your job; You clearly link yourself with the Birmingham Mail; and you claim to be cutting and pasting information from the BBC.

AS Can I just say that the first clip was taken after two weeks out there when I had been working extremely hard. I was tired, extremely emotional. Barack Obama's speech had affected me greatly. I got drunk and I got caught out. I went from being the journalist when I am used to hunting people to being the hunted. Everyone was trying to get hold of me. It was on Fox News. The far right saw me as the face of the Obama campaign and I got a lot of hatred from that.

I haven't turned my phone on again since then. I have had so many people making comments about me. It is a tale of the modern media, when something catches fire.

MR There is a Facebook Group set up, and you have put a comment on that?

CM This group was not set up by Adam and this is covered in the investigation meeting notes. What do you want to discuss Marc?

MR I want to establish if there has been anymore activity?

AS No more activity. I have not even answered my phone, because I know that as soon as you do you are technically giving an interview. I have had loads of requests for interviews. (Adam names a number of radio stations including Kerrang etc.)

HJ How are people contacting you?

AS You can be contacted thru Facebook. People are leaving me messages thru that. You can type in messages without being a friend. I have had a lot of abuse from there.

MR So you have not said anything else?

AS We did agree what I could say at the last meeting, but to be honest I have not even said that.

MR Is there anything more that you would like to say?

AS Yes, it is very stressful right now.

CM Are you going to ask any further questions?

MR No I think that I have an understanding of the issue.

CM I would like to mention the context in which this happened, it was not pre planned. Adam decided at short notice to get on a plane with not much money. When covering big elections when the winning post comes you are euphoric. Adam had been working on the campaign from 6am to 2pm. He had a drink, and this mixed with the emotion is a heady mixture.

There is an argument that he is on holiday and therefore normal company rules do not apply. A very attractive young lady comers along with a camera and he tries to impress her. The woman never introduced herself as part of the couscous community. She did a good job of getting Adam to talk. At the time of the initial video Adam was sat by the roadside minding his own business.

AS I did not write anything while I was drunk.

CM You can see that Adam was referencing something on the screen. It was a joke, with hindsight not a very funny one. It was absolutely clear from the following day that Adam regretted it. Straight away you can see from the comments on the Huffington Post that no plagiarism has taken place. It is now accepted by Steve Dyson that no plagiarism took place.

I understand that the company was concerned at the F*** you message at the end of the video.

AS No, I was saying that to the world, not to the company. That is the amazing thing really that people have taken what they want from it and the number of different messages that they have taken.

CM Adam is a good journalist, if an unconventional one. He just wanted to get across that he was going to do things in his own way.

AS I have had a lot of questioning from friends and family about whether I can do it my own way.

CM People have read into it different things. One of the issues is Adam's resignation on air.

AS If you looked at the wording I said that I had resigned form the Birmingham Mail, I did not say now.

CM The statements that Adam made were not accurate, but he was not looking to be accurate.

AS I would have never dreamt that someone Dutch would be interested in a Birmingham paper. The first opportunity that I had I apologised.

CM We are coming on to that. The woman from Couscous sees that it attracts interest and goes out and looks for Adam again. Do you think that there is anything important on the third clip?

MR No, I don't think so.

AS At the height of the abuse that I received it was horrible. I tried to get the name Birmingham Mail taken down from You Tube, but I could not contact the two guys that posted it as they were driving across America.

HJ So what did you do?

AS I left a message on the message board.

CM Things take on their own momentum. Steve Dyson was concerned about the 5th clip, with Adam singing 'we will do what we want' But that is just a metaphor bearing in mind what Adam is going through now.

HJ All that I documented in the investigation meeting notes.

CM Adam was doing this in his own time. It is not up to the company to police staff in their own time. This has arisen because of a sequence of events that could not have been predicted.The company did try to get in touch with Adam.

HJ Yes, this is documented in the investigation meeting notes.

AS I called the Newsdesk number which I had been asked to call.

CM Adam has received no payment or commission for this. He has been responsible since his return to the UK. We are dealing with someone whose last day with the company is today.

HJ We are very aware of that.

CM Adam has acted with contrition. You have not yet mentioned the fact that Adam has a previous disciplinary on file.

HJ Yes I think that alcohol was involved in the last disciplinary?

AS I had no money to spend on alcohol. I was using my money for the lap dancer to try to get dances for Mike Tyson.

MR Well I need to adjourn to consider my verdict.

Adjournment 11.05am.

Reconvene 11.50am.

CM I need to put more money on the car as I did not realise it would take quite so long.

Adjournment. Reconvene 11.59am

MR I have considered the material facts of the case, your defence and any mitigating circumstances and the consequences.

The main video and the second video contain material that does put the company into a bad light – By association with the statement that a person identifying himself as a Mail reporter, saying that he is filing copy while he is drunk. Adam also states that he is plagiarising material from the BBC, and also as it gives the very clear impression that he is telling the company to F*** off.

The third video in the Obama office makes some attempt to repair the damage.

In your defence, or mitigation you say that different standards of behaviour are acceptable in a person's own time. That may be the case when engaged in activities completely unrelated to work, but in this case by actually offering to file copy for the company, and of course identifying yourself as a Mail reporter, then it is implicitly accepted that you were representing the company, and you should have conducted yourself as such.

The mitigation around being carried away by a mix of excitement, alcohol and the attention of a woman are noted, but do not absolve you of the responsibility that you should exercise in this situation, when as I said you were implicitly representing the company.

On the consequences, it is noted that you did not instigate or in any way make the video, and that you say that some of your words have been misinterpreted. However the impact and the consequences are clear. The subsequent media interest and comment has brought attention to the Mail, other Titles and the company, all of it unwelcome.

It is my finding therefore that your actions did bring the company into disrepute, and the allegations are therefore upheld.

As to the sanction I have noted and considered your apology, and your adherence to the agreement to avoid commenting to outside parties. I have also noted the current disciplinary case on file, in which you received a verbal warning for your conduct.

Under the Capability and Disciplinary procedure I have considered whether the offense amounts to Gross Misconduct, which would clearly result in a very severe sanction. The consequences of your behaviour have lead to considerable harm to the company at a very sensitive time for the Editorial department in particular. Other colleagues have taken difficult personal decisions, either to leave or to stay with the company and your lack of consideration and thoughtlessness amount to a serious insult to them also.

However you have shown a willingness to apologise and to set the record straight. There was clearly no malice on your part.

I propose to issue you with a Final Written Warning, with a further sanction that further reflects the seriousness of the offense.

As you know a proportion of your redundancy payment is at the discretion of the company, and we can in some circumstances reduce this to statutory redundancy pay.

However, I have decided not to take this route, and instead take the view that your suspension which started on 6th November should be without pay.

As for your redundancy payment and notice pay this shall remain at the agreed level. A new compromise agreement will be drawn up for you, stressing again the need for complete confidentiality on these matters. A payment will be made to you 21 days after we have received the signed copy.

HJ I will be drawing up a compromise agreement for you, not issuing you with the standard agreement.

CM Please send through to me also.

HJ All that remains is to wish you well for your future, as today is your last day of employment.

AS Thank you.

CLOSE

Dear Adam,

Final Written Warning

I am writing to confirm the outcome of the disciplinary meeting you attended on Tuesday 18th November, in which we discussed the allegation that you had brought the company into disrepute by the video clips hosted on You Tube and the subsequent publicity. You chose to be accompanied by Chris Morley, northern regional organiser of the NUJ. Also present was Helen James, Regional HR Manager.

I opened by reminding you of the reason for the hearing. I played the clips from You Tube as evidence, and you presented your explanation of the incident. Chris also made a statement on your behalf presenting the mitigating cirucumstances as you saw them.

As I explained at the meeting, I upheld the allegation that you had brought the company into disrepute with your conduct, given the content of the first video and the impact of the subsequent publicity.

I also rejected your defence that you were not representing the company and therefore not subject to the same standards of conduct that we expect staff to adhere to. As I noted, you have volunteered to file company to the Mail and the Post, and by this implicitly accepted that you were respresenting the company.

I also noted that you did not instigate the video, and that you say that some of your words have been misinterpreted. However the impact and the consequences are clear. The subsequent media interest and comment has brought attention to the Mail, other titles and the company, all of it unwelcome.

Under the Capability and Disciplinary procedure, and in the light of the current disciplinary case on file, I have decided to issue you with a final written warning. As a penalty, your suspension which started on 6th November will be without pay.

Your redundancy payment and notice pay shall remain at the agreed level. A new compromise agreement will be drawn up for you, stressing again the need for complete confidentiality on these matters. A payment will be made to you 21 days after we have received the signed copy.

Finally, if you wish to appeal against this decision you must do so in writing explaining clearly your reason for appeal. You must lodge any appeal in writing with Alan Thorburn Human Resources Director, within 7 days of receipt of this letter.

Yours sincerely

Marc Reeves

Editor

Chris and I kept a straight face until we got to the car park, but when we were out of sight we jumped in the air and hugged one another.

"We bloody did it Adam! We bloody did it! What a bloody result, I can't believe it!"

"Thanks Chris, thanks so much m…hold on - I thought you knew we'd win?!"

He looked at me as if I was mad and I hugged him again. Chris had been playing me as much as he'd been playing the company. He knew I'd been on the verge of telling them to shove their money, but he also knew that as long as there was a chance of me getting the cash he had to keep on trying. It was a great feeling and we were delighted to get out of Funlop with the job done.

I figured that the redundancy decision was made at Canary Wharf but the decision to fine me my wages, like some errant footballer, was made by the management in Birmingham. Not getting my wages in a week's time would mean that I'd be skint for the foreseeable future, putting more pressure on Nicole, but getting the redundancy was what mattered.

When I got home Nicole was in bed. I tried to creep in without her hearing but as usual the dog was excited to see me. She opened her eyes gradually as she rested her head on my chest and asked in a whisper: "Did you get to keep your redundancy?". "Course I did bab, it was just a formality", I whispered, trying not to betray how worried I'd been about missing out on the money. She smiled and nuzzled her head into my chest, whilst at the same time the dog wriggled under my other arm. I felt like a true king. The two things I loved most on this earth were nestled under each arm and we were all happy.

Finally for the first time in about a month I could totally relax without anything to worry about. I'd won. I'd helped get Barack Obama elected. I'd become a YouTube sensation and kept my redundancy. After years of drifting I even had my own little family in Nicole and the dog. What was more, I was on the brink of launching a brand new Birmingham media company and resurrecting

Britain's funniest lad's magazine. My unbelievable Obama adventure was over and I was officially the happiest man in the world.

THE END

August 2009 – The Man Who Lost Everything

I looked at myself in the mirror. I was how I'd always wanted to look, about two stone thinner than normal. My cheek bones were pronounced and a fat face no longer stared back at me. My eyes told a different story though. They betrayed a catalogue of dreams dashed, epic professional failure and a broken heart.

I hadn't slept properly for weeks and I hadn't eaten for days. My stomach constantly turned over and bile was never far from my throat. I'd spent hours dry heaving over the toilet as Nathan nuzzled my ribs worried out of his canine mind.

The business had collapsed. The entire West Midlands media establishment had seen Cheekie Media and Goggle-eye crash and burn. That had just hurt my ego though; it was my heart that was the problem.

I knew she'd been having an affair. It's the small things you notice, like her hiding her mobile phone, and the fact she couldn't lie to save her life didn't help either. She'd even brought him back to the flat and told me to leave so they could spend time alone. I couldn't kick off because I had no money and was living in her flat. She had all the power and wielded it ruthlessly.

For weeks I'd seen her skin crawl when I touched her, and she'd evaded every kiss, but In the end it was only when I read the e-mails that I couldn't ignore it anymore. I hadn't wanted to read them, but I was putting about £1,500 down on a house for us and friends were now constantly telling me she was having an affair. I wanted proof.

I wish I hadn't gone against a lifelong policy of not snooping and looked at those emails. Something in me died when I read the 'I love yous' in capitals, their plans for a future, her dismissal of me as if I was a disease that needed curing. The songs I'd sent her professing my love had been forwarded to him with the same meaning.

I knew all those e-mails were sent as she was sat opposite me in the office. How they must have laughed at me. I cursed myself for being the kind of weakling prick I normally despised. It was all there in black and white on my Blackberry. I couldn't even speak to her, because she was staying at his house and her phone was off.

I knew I'd forgive her in the end, but did she want forgiving? I looked back at the mirror and Nathan pawed at me. He'd been a great friend, so maybe he knew what was going on. Maybe he knew the master he loved was being taken apart by the woman who'd reared him.

It had been a week since I read the e-mails, but that night the dog was my only company. The only conversation I'd had was with the Samaritans. I'd lied and said I was thinking of kill myself to get through to someone. I just needed some human contact at 4am. Nic hadn't come back; she'd talked casually of suicide and of ending it all, so I lay in bed praying that she was being held by him and not hanging from a noose in a hotel. Loving someone with mental illness is exhausting and you find yourself in a world where logic isn't wanted.

I could have forgiven her anything, because most affairs are only temporary, but my business had collapsed and he was a financial advisor who set up savings accounts for her, so I didn't stand a chance. It had all started all so well. The launch of Cheekie Media and the free spending that came with the redundancy meant she hadn't gone without for months.

I hadn't gone to Obama's inauguration to propose as I'd planned, because in the end it would have cost too much. Instead I paid her ex-boyfriend off with £500. It's the alarm bells you see - my brain just doesn't have any. I should have just taken her to Spain or somewhere, anywhere to show her I cared, but I didn't; I had a business to set up. I neglected her in the short run to provide in the long run.

The six months after I got back from America were wonderful nonetheless. I was working hard trying to make my business a success and I believed I was with someone for life – what could have been better? We talked of marriage, we talked of children (in fact we even adopted one in some Brazilian rainforest) and we talked of epic futures criss-crossing the globe. I'd wake up and she'd nuzzle into me and tell me she loved me, then I'd look to my left and Nathan would start wagging his tail. Every day I wanted to succeed, despite knowing deep down that the business wasn't cutting it.

As the months passed the money dried up and the business struggled more and more. I fought off the inevitable for too long, as my pride wouldn't let me call it a day until I'd lost everything. My business partner Stuart was feeling the strain too. I could see his problems mounting and I felt guilty for getting him involved. To his eternal credit he never let it get personal though, and we remain friends to this day.

Every 25th of the month I felt sick because that was the day I would have been paid if I'd stayed at the Mail. After the novelty of being my own boss wore off I missed being a journalist. I missed the power more than anything. I now had to arse lick customers instead of arguing with people. It just wasn't me.

Also, I would have been on a good wage if I'd stayed at the Mail, and I'd have been able to give Nic and Nathan a good life. Instead I was begging, borrowing and blagging everyday of my life to ensure the electric meter was topped up and there was food on the table. I had to promise success in the future instead of delivering financially every day.

Whenever I thought about what would have happened if I'd stayed at the Mail I thought about Miami though. I thought about my videos. If I'd left silently I would have been gutted, but I'll never regret being a YouTube Sensation – in a way it defined me.

I was scared I'd never be a journalist again though. Who would employ a bloke who told his bosses to fuck off in front of so many people? No-one, that's who! The videos took the edge off the fact I'd given up the one thing I was ever good at – being a local, hard news hack.

Fortunately I became a regular on Radio WM, thanks to Danny Kelly taking a chance on me, and so via the Goggle-eye website, Radio WM and my own show on Scratch Radio my profile was great - but it wasn't translating into cash. Nic used to come with me to every show, and everyone had loved her; now she couldn't even be bothered to tune in, let alone leave the house with me.

I wasn't perfect I'll admit that. She had OCD and I was messy, too messy, horribly messy, but I got better. Perhaps those early pant scattering days had done for me in the long run, or perhaps when the money ran out she'd always have gone anyway. We were so close as a couple, but it was a struggle not to get dragged into her depression. It was relentless. The previous month she'd packed all her belongings up. I asked "What for?" and she calmly explained that she was going to give them all away and kill herself next Tuesday. She said she'd planned to steal my credit card to pay for the hotel. I thought 'Christ, she must be insane if she thinks there's any money on my credit card'.

Maybe my mum was right, and I'd moved in too quickly, but if I hadn't chased half way across the world to help Mr Obama I wouldn't have been homeless and forced to move in with Nic. Then again, I paid my way, and we were deeply in love when I got back.

She had no luck with work. She couldn't get a job to save her life, or a loan or anything. In the end we had to stop her coming to the office because of the black cloud of depression she brought with her, but still I loved her, and still I believed everything would be ok.

Eventually I got her a job at the pub by the office. I knew she needed friends and I thought working might help her. It didn't turn out that way. In fact, it turned out to be the decision that killed the relationship. She worked nights and ended up sharing drunken kisses with men who'd impressed her, as well as getting into deep friendships with men who wanted her as their girlfriend.

I'd never known a woman who was so militant about fidelity. She'd been the victim of an unfaithful boyfriend in the past, and she read the bible every day, so I never dreamed she betray me – that's why I went all in. But everyone knew me, because I was the YouTube Sensation with the blue haired missus, and when a blue haired woman starts having an affair believe me, everyone notices.

People would look at me with pity. They knew, but they couldn't face telling me. No doubt they were thinking 'Poor bloke, his business is collapsing and his beloved missus is having an affair'. "Concentrate on yourself, mate" they'd say before drunkenly telling me she was a slag. I defended her then, and I thought I always would.

A couple of exes were a godsend and two female friends were there for me throughout, Melanie and Ellie. Both were wonderful listeners but they got sick of me making excuses for her. Gradually the fire was being extinguished under a shower of crap lies though.

She defended her kisses in public by saying her life was boring compared to mine and she was flattered by the interest. And her excuse for having an affair? Well, she said she was numb inside because of the depression, that she wanted the spark back between us and that she just needed someone else to jump start her heart. As I listened to her monumental bullshit, as she constantly fingered the necklace he'd bought her, I thought about all the women in Miami I wished I'd fucked.

To make sense of it all I wrote love letters that she couldn't be bothered to read. As my old mate Gurdo said, it was cruel, as cruel as can be. I looked again at my hollow reflection. It had come to this; I was starting work selling electric door to door, commission only. I was leaving my home not knowing if the woman I loved was dead or alive, but certain I hadn't passed through her brain for days.

I tried to speak but the sound wouldn't come out. Despite being heartbroken something else was scaring me to the pit of my soul. I mouthed words to my pale reflection: "A fucking commission only door to door electric salesman. I used to be someone. I used to be a journalist. I changed the world once, and now I'm nothing. I am nothing".

I closed my eyes and thought 'If Obama could see me now'.

The day I got back into journalism – October 2009

I opened my eyes at 6.30am, ten minutes before the alarm went off. My first thought was 'How can I afford to get to work'? Nicole, who had returned from her weekend soujorn to fuck knows where, was wrapped up in duvets so I couldn't touch her. She hadn't brought any wages back from work and had left me starving all weekend, despite my fronting over £1,500 for the house we lived in. The house was perfect - and art studio for her, a writing room for me and a garden for the dog.

She hadn't even bothered unpacking her stuff. I knew she was using our dream home as a stepping stone, because she'd been about to get evicted from her own flat. She knew I couldn't afford the place on my own, and I didn't technically need an art studio or a garden because I couldn't draw and I knew she'd take the dog with her if she left, but I moved in thinking I'd spend the happiest days of my life under that roof. She'd moved in counting down the days until she could move out.

All my friends had told me not to put my money into the house, on the not unreasonable grounds that they knew she was having an affair. I did too, but I wanted to look in the mirror when she left and see a man who had done everything in his power to hold onto the woman he loved.

The only money in the house was £2 in coppers, and the only food two slices of bread and marmalade. I laughed at the note I'd left her: 'Hey babes, no money for a Daysaver! So borrowed money out of change bag. Didn't want to wake you as you were dead to the world! Ring you later about cheque! Love you!'.

I didn't have enough bus fare to get to work so thought I'd try to jump on the bus with my out of date travel card. The baby worked and I got to work five minutes late and started to write. A few weeks before Gurdip had told me that there were three days of freelancing work available at the Halesowen News. I'd got the gig and chased stories liked my life depended on it. I loved it, loved having power again. I loved being back where I belonged.

I'd only lasted two days as a door to door salesman. It turned out I'd been sent around an estate that already had Scottish Electric, as the woman in the last house I'd knocked had explained to me. I poured my heart out to her, about everything. She made me a cup of tea and when she realised it was commission only told me to give up the job, claim benefits and write a book.

The boss at the Halesowen News liked my style though. He'd been getting more complaints than he'd had for years prior to my arrival, and he kept inviting me back at £85 a day - which, after months of being on the breadline, was like winning the lottery.

At 10am on this particular October day I threatened the Press Officer at West Midlands Police. At 10.10am I demanded that his Dudley Council counterpart get me information about teenage pregnancies, and at 10.30am I phoned George Wimpy's press office and read out inflammatory quotes to scare them into giving me a quote about floods in Halesowen. At 10.50am I scrounged a roll-up off the journo opposite, smoked it and then spotted a half smoked fag in the ash tray, which I finished off too.

At 11am I excused myself to go and get some money from a cheque that should have cleared. I filled the form in and went to the cashier. She took ages and I was nervous. "I cannot authorise this payment, please go to the reception", she said.

My stomach turned as my financial future flashed in front of my eyes. The receptionist disappeared into the back. I was worried he was going to perform a citizen's arrest based on the arrears in the current account, but he came back out and said "There's been a fire in one of our business centres, so your cheque will take a day longer".

At 12.30pm I flirted with an ex-Sandwell councillor who was 65 but sill loved a bit of it. I then conducted a little debate with myself. I had £4.50 with £2 in coppers, and was wondering whether to buy a packet of snouts or save up for a pint. In the event, I bought the fags and a pack of Somerfield cut price ginger nuts, attractively price at 39p. They were my lunch. I plugged my earphones in and listened to Tom Jones 'I'm Never Going To Fall in Love Again' on repeat, following it up with Michael Buble's 'Cry Me A River' and Gordon Lightfoot's 'If You Could Read My Mind'.

At 2.30pm and after more threats to George Wimpy I spotted the boss, Paul Walker, nip out for the fag. I had my own so I followed him. He'd told me he'd make a decision on whether I got a full time job by today. We made small talk. He's from Zimbabwe and after discussing his 20s in Africa we walked back in to the newsroom, at which point he said "You'll get a letter the next few days with the official offer". My spine tingled and my heart missed a beat. "Do you mean I've got the job?" I said. He looked at me and said: "Of course". Relief hit me and I grabbed his hand and shook it too hard. I got back to the desk and the four journalists around me all clapped and gave me the thumbs up.

I knew that Paul believing in me and letting me get back into journalism was massive. I'd thought that getting another job after all the YouTube stuff was going to be nearly impossible, but thanks to him seeing my work day to day he knew I was good enough. I had had an outrageous publicity stunt planned to show the world what Nicole and her new squeeze had done to me, but now I had my dream job there was no way I was going to risk losing it.

Facebook status: **Steve Zacharanda** "The reports of my demise in journalism were greatly exaggerated (had to ask new colleagues how to spell that) – I am a hack again.

The responses started to appear on my Facebook, and I was instantly flooded with happiness. I wanted a pint, I wanted to celebrate, but I had £1.20 and £2 in coins. I decided to try to get back to Brum on my travelcard, and once again it worked. By now I wanted more than a pint though, I wanted a few. I headed to the Crown and Cushion, writing a story on my Blackberry about their new car boot sale on the way. I strode in and read it out to the gaffer before declaring I was now in employment. The world's best landlord gave me a three pint slate. That was perfect. I drank most of it before the pub's resident ink/Viagra salesman got his wad out, and sensing my opportunity I asked if I could borrow £10 from him too. He obliged. I got heroically pissed.

As I walked home I thought of my non-responsive missus. Why didn't she put me out of my misery and end it? She hadn't smiled at me in months, hadn't laughed at one joke, but when he phoned her laughter reverberated around the house. There was no way I was ending it myself though – I didn't want to give her the satisfaction.

Nathan jumped all over me when I got in. He was my little mate. I knew she'd take him too. I wanted her to look in my eyes and tell me the truth. Was she thinking of moving in with someone else after moving in with me? Was she gargling with his spunk? Despite the bravado in my brain I knew I could never win an argument with her, though. She was the kissed, I was the kisser.

She was due back at 3am, but arrived home early to find me half naked and dancing around the living room to Freddie Mercury's 'Living on My Own'. I wanted a hug as it was a special moment - I was back in journalism! She knew what that meant, but she said she couldn't bear for me to hold her. I thought 'Fuck it, let's row!'. I couldn't really argue with her properly back in her flat, as every exchange might have ended with "Get out my house!", despite the fact it was me paying the bills. In this house, the house I paid for by borrowing money from my dad, I'd have my say.

She said she didn't know whether she loved me. I followed her round the house arguing and she said people at her work - at the job I'd got her - thought I was a tramp, that she hated my hairy back, that she shouldn't have to answer questions, she laughed in my face when I dropped love lines. With that, she went to bed.

I went into the garden, pissed everywhere, looked up at the stars and shouted: "Fuck her! I'm a journalist again."

Full Circle – Summer 2012

And that's it. That's the story of me helping Barack Obama. I hope you liked it. It took me three years to write. Sorry it wasn't finished earlier, but well, you know, life just kept on getting in the way.

Nic and Nathan left a couple of weeks after my first day in journalism. I've never seen them since and probably never will. I miss that dog but I'm not bitter, life's too short to poison myself. I hope she's happy and well.

I'm still at the Halesowen News, and still love being a local hard news journalist. I'm better than I was at the Birmingham Mail because I don't take it for granted. I haven't even slept at my desk once.

And as for the Birmingham Mail, well under editor Dave Brookes and head of news Tony Larner the paper is a better read than ever, and I still read it every day, but despite probably fitting in more with the new regime I somehow doubt they would have me back.

This game of mine is dying though, so I've had to branch out. I'm an international travel journalist as well now. I've been to St Louis, Washington, Maryland, Nashville, South Africa, Zambia, India and Ecuador and many other places for free. I've met some amazing people, and amazingly they seem to like me.

Sometimes I sit opposite them in London and pinch myself that I'm speaking on equal terms to such amazing human beings.

Perhaps it's my treasure trove of self-deprecating anecdotes, or perhaps it's because I get the world's best destinations in a selection of papers in the West Midlands, I suppose I'll never know.

I do a bit of PR here and there. Not much, but enough for a few Strongbows along the way, I might even try to bring Goggle-eye back from the dead next year.

Me and Gurdo host The Steve Zacharanda Radio Show every Thursday at 8pm on ScratchRadio.co.uk and after three years on air we still are enjoying every minute of it.

And I am having a documentary made about me – Obama and Me- The Steve Zacharanda Story, hopefully I don't come across as too much of a nob but it will be nice to see it on the telly one day.

My personal life? Well I've a woman who knows me as well as can be and, despite that, still loves me. I'm living in a box room in her mom's house. After all I can't live in my own mom's house but she is on great form and has not disowned me in a while.

I'm still skint. In fact in my mother's words I'm '36-years-old and have nothing'.

Perhaps this book will change everything, or perhaps only a few people will ever read it. But I lived it and finishing the bloody thing is my greatest achievement.

Every time I see my mate Barack Obama on the TV I feel proud that I helped him become the President of the United States. I'm sure he would have made it without me but he changed my life. I'm forever linked to that night in 2008. As is he, because I think getting elected is his greatest achievement. I mean, the poor bloke has gotten enough grief since then.

Still, that's life I suppose. Barack Obama won the White House and the world didn't magically turn into a Utopia, and I ended up back where I started: working for a paper and living day to day. But whatever anyone says, no-one can take away those magical few days in November 2008 when anything seemed possible

And now? Well he needs to win an election and I need to get the money to help him make history. Again.

Acknowledgements

Sam - for putting up with someone as stupid as me and helping us get through this thing called life.

Juliet and Ebony – thank you for letting me share your home.

Gurdip Thandi – no man could ever wish for a better friend, over and over again you help me when I don't deserve it.

John Tipper – for being a great friend, proof reader, editor and drinking partner, I dread to think how much worse this book would have been without him. His massive schlong remains an inspiration.

Anthony Casey – for beating the epic first draft into shape in a way only a top professional proof reader could have.

Jamie Rowland – for so giving me so much encouragement when I needed it the most.

Ben Devise – for giving me a much needed American perspective.

Tom Watson – thanks for being a friend in high places.

Auntie Brenda and Uncle Brian – those blissful weeks writing under a Welsh mountain made me feel like an author.

Ellie Piovesana – thanks for always being my 'do I sound a weirdo' soundboard.

Reiss Parchment – thanks for giving me a captive audience and your insights of a younger generation.

Paul Walker – for my second chance in journalism, I'm scared to think where I'd have ended up without it.

Clare and Brian Beddowes – two beautiful people, who gave me the rather wonderful SteveZacharanda.com.

Lynda Daboh – for being a higher authority, being able to pick a top of the PR food chain brain is something I shall be eternally grateful for.

And for their continued encouragement my Perry Barr crew, Justyn Barnes, Mat Danks, Ed King, Nick McCarthy, Maartje Nevejan, Lee Kenny, Stuart Pickersgill, Danny Kelly, Kevin Moore, Mike Lockley, Steve Dineen, Sam Holliday, Earl Parchment, Steve Wollaston, Marcus Anderson-Hitchen, Tony Larner, Andy Shipley, John Newton, Gary Phelps, Chang Smith, Charlotte Hart, Mum, Graham Woodward, the Departed, Sam Lawton, Natalie Amos, Kym Backer, Kieran Meeke, Carl Cattarell, Lesley Bellew, everyone who has to share an office with me, Kevin McGuire and all those I've forgotten.

And of course all those who have had to listen me talk about this book, if only I'd spent as much time writing it as talking about it....

Printed in Great Britain
by Amazon.co.uk, Ltd.,
Marston Gate.